# UNBOUND

# UNBOUND

How Inequality Constricts Our Economy
and What We Can Do about It

**HEATHER BOUSHEY**

Harvard University Press

*Cambridge, Massachusetts*
*London, England*
2019

Library of Congress Cataloging-in-Publication
Data is available at https://catalog.loc.gov/.

ISBN 9780674919310 (alk. paper)

*In memory of Alan Krueger and David M. Gordon,
who each inspired generations of economists to look
at the evidence and engage with the world*

*And with special thanks to Herb Sandler, who believed
in the power of economic evidence to change
how we think about the economy*

"Stand ye calm and resolute,
Like a forest close and mute,
With folded arms and looks which are
Weapons of unvanquished war.

"And if then the tyrants dare
Let them ride among you there,
Slash, and stab, and maim, and hew,—
What they like, that let them do.

"With folded arms and steady eyes,
And little fear, and less surprise,
Look upon them as they slay
Till their rage has died away.

"Then they will return with shame
To the place from which they came,
And the blood thus shed will speak
In hot blushes on their cheek.

"Rise, like Lions after slumber
In unvanquishable number—
Shake your chains to earth like dew
Which in sleep had fallen on you—
Ye are many—they are few."

—Percy Bysshe Shelley, *The Mask of Anarchy* (1832)

# *Contents*

# Figures and Tables

## Figures

## Tables

# *Preface*

In the postwar decades from the 1940s to the 1970s, the job of economists seemed straightforward: focus on growth, expect the rest to follow, and provide policymakers with the government revenues needed to soften the harshest effects of the market economy. Since then, devising economic policy has become a lot more complicated. Alongside the traditional questions of productivity and growth are now questions of how to address the increasingly uneven distribution of income and wealth in all their complexity. As I'll lay out in the pages that follow, a shift is underway in economics that sheds light on these new concerns, one that must be echoed in how policymakers and the public think about the economy.

Even as economics is changing, much of the thinking on the policy side remains trapped in an old set of ideas which don't fit current economic reality. While an emerging generation of economists—many of them featured in this book—are analyzing more readily available data to discern new patterns that change our understanding of the economy, policymakers have yet to get in sync. Too many policy ideas either ignore inequality or assume that the incentives it creates outweigh the negatives. The repercussions both for individuals and for the economy as a whole are serious. By using empirical data and following where it leads, rather than deferring to theory, today's economists are questioning whether markets work as predicted. This new body of research now needs to be integrated into everyone's understanding of how the economy works, including those in the economic policymaking community.

Case in point: after serving his home state of Kansas in the US Senate for two full terms, Sam Brownback ran for governor in 2010 on what he called a "red state" economic platform. His agenda consisted almost entirely of lowering the costs of doing business. He won. And true to his word, his first act as governor after being inaugurated in Topeka on January 10, 2011, was to establish the Office of the Repealer. The mission of this ominous-sounding body was to "identify laws and regulations that are out of date, unreasonable, and burdensome" on Kansas businesses. Over 2012 and 2013, he signed into law the largest tax cuts in Kansas history. The top state income tax rate fell from 6.45 percent to 4.90 percent, and taxes on business profits from partnerships and limited liability corporations (which passed through to individuals) were eliminated. When his tax cuts became law in 2012, Gov. Brownback predicted great things: "Our new pro-growth tax policy will be like a shot of adrenaline into the heart of the Kansas economy."[1]

The new governor of Kansas made big promises, but simultaneously admitted that putting his plan in place would be "a real live experiment."[2] The hypothesis was that the middle class would be strengthened as lower taxes and lighter regulation encouraged the wealthy to invest more in Kansas businesses, creating new jobs and fueling economic growth. For those in the top 1 percent of incomes—Kansans making more than $400,000 a year—the effect of the tax cuts was to pay about $17,000 less on average. Meanwhile, the bottom 20 percent, making less than $20,000, would actually pay an additional $242 in total taxes, mostly due to the elimination of various tax credits. Brownback told his constituents this new tax plan would ultimately reduce neither government revenues nor government services because it would unleash so much economic growth. These tax cuts would, he said, "pave the way to the creation of tens of thousands of new jobs . . . and help make our state the best place in America to start and grow a small business."[3]

Once the evidence began coming in, it was clear that Gov. Brownback's experiment was failing to deliver on his promises. Instead of reviving the American Dream, he presided over a continuing trend of lackluster income gains for Kansas's working families alongside rising gains at the very top of the income ladder. Menzie Chinn, a professor of public affairs and economics at the University of Wisconsin–Madison, found that after the enactment of the tax cuts, economic growth in Kansas fell well below its pre-Brownback rate. Indeed, by the spring of 2017, job growth in Kansas was lower than in most neighboring states—and not even half the national average. The tax changes also did little to spur business formation. For example, after they were enacted in 2012, the creation of new pass-through businesses—whose profits were no longer taxed at business rates but at their owners' individual tax rates—exceeded its 2011 level for two years, but then dipped *lower* than it had been before. To pay for these ineffective tax cuts, Kansas made cuts to government services in education, pensions, and infrastructure, with the state's general fund spending per resident falling 5.5 percent from 2012 to 2016.[4]

This is only one of many examples of politicians claiming their policy agendas would restore the American Dream, and not delivering on that promise. Five years after Gov. Brownback enacted his historic tax cuts, his own party turned on his ideas. The Republican-dominated state legislature saw the experiment for what it was: a failure. In the summer of 2017, opponents gathered a veto-proof majority and rolled back the tax cuts against his will. Yet this prominent example of a failed program of deregulation plus tax cuts for the wealthy did not put an end to similar experiments. On the heels of the Kansas failure, President Donald Trump in 2017 signed a tax bill that expands the federal deficit by $1.9 trillion over ten years and gives a massive, permanent tax cut to corporations, alongside temporary tax cuts to individuals—mostly benefiting those at the top of the income spectrum. And, like Brownback, Trump is focusing his energy on eliminating regulations.[5]

Today, it is more than evident that this mistaken approach to intervening in the economy has not delivered for the American people. Simple "supply-side" thinking by politicians such as Gov. Brownback (and President Ronald Reagan before him and Trump today) reflects a very flawed understanding of how the economy works and is disconnected from the current empirical evidence. We'll see in the course of this book how applications of this interpretation of public policy, in Brownback's Kansas and in many other ways across the nation, have been economic and social disasters. Indeed, supply-side policies have created perfect conditions for income and wealth inequality to grow and thrive, crimping economic mobility to the detriment of us all. We must reject this pseudoscience.

There is a consensus emerging out of the combination of lived experience and scholarly research examining what drives economic growth and stability. This body of work shows that, when we enact policies that have the effect of undertaxing top income earners, or allowing them to ignore the rules, what we get is not shared prosperity but greater economic inequality. To believe that pure market mechanics will produce socially beneficial outcomes is to take the theoretical logic of Adam Smith's "invisible hand" too far. We need to recognize how economic power translates into political and social power, and reject old theories that treat the economy as a system governed by natural laws separate from society's.

The idea that the economy is embedded in society was put forth three-quarters of a century ago by political economist Karl Polanyi. He argued that the idea of free markets is a utopian myth, since all the freedoms that enable markets to function are secured by a state. In 1944, he critiqued classical economists' faulty belief that the economy has natural laws separate from society's institutions and politics. As he put it, "economic society was founded on the grim realities of Nature" and thus "was subjected to laws which were *not* human laws."[6] With today's rise in economic inequality and growing sense that the market is not delivering as promised, his praise for the subsequent "discovery of society" is being revisited. A key insight of Polanyi's analysis relevant to today's economy is that the market cannot be stripped of power relations. The market, like politics more generally, is always contested. This stands in opposition to the idea, especially as it is narrowly interpreted, that market dynamics obey their own laws, separate from the workings of society more generally. New data and evidence on how inequality affects the economy via second-order effects on politics and society underscore Polanyi's conclusion.[7]

The way forward starts by asking the critical economic question of our time: How can we grow our economy more equitably and sustainably in the twenty-first century? The following pages offer answers. Drawing on interviews with top scholars steeped in the latest empirical evidence, this book presents strategies for delivering strong, stable, and broad-based growth. My purpose is to make sense of the emerging thinking in economics for those who seek to understand these ideas but who are not embedded in the economics community—and especially for those who seek to take action based on the conclusions these ideas lead us toward.

This book builds on the work of my organization, the Washington

Center for Equitable Growth. When I took up the challenge six years ago of launching this research and policy center, I hoped we could inject evidence-backed ideas about how inequality affects the economy into debates over economic policy. At the time, income inequality in the United States had reached levels last seen during the Roaring Twenties, yet many policies and ideas to create more opportunities for children and their parents were dismissed as "bad for the economy" by Washington policymakers. Building and leading Equitable Growth was a once-in-a-lifetime opportunity to bring important ideas and polices to the fore.

For centuries, economists and their ideas have provided the frameworks that policymakers use in deciding what actions to take. To support exploration of these ideas and ensure that new research is relevant, accessible, and informative to the policymaking process, Equitable Growth is building a stronger bridge between academics and policymakers. We seek to ensure that the policymaking community sees the changes going on within economics—and knows how to make use of these new ideas. To that end, we promote rigorous research on the relationship between economic inequality and economic growth through a competitive grants program that elevates both established and new academic voices from economics as well as other fields, by commissioning papers, and by hosting conferences and convenings. Determined not to leave the policy-relevant research we support sitting on the shelf, we deploy our communications and outreach capacity strategically to educate policymakers on matters of economic competitiveness and mobility.

Over the past six years, our startup has grown into an organization of nearly forty staff members dedicated to promoting strong, stable, and broad-based growth by advancing evidence-backed ideas and policies. Our steering committee includes Nobel laureate Bob Solow, John Bates Clark Medal winner Emmanuel Saez, and former Federal Reserve Board chair Janet Yellen, and our Research Advisory Board consists of more than two dozen scholars working at the cutting edge of economics. Since making our first academic grants in 2014, we have funded more than 180 scholars nationwide, giving away nearly $5 million in the pursuit of knowledge regarding whether and how inequality affects economic growth and stability. This book summarizes what I have learned from this work, and offers one way to make sense of the emerging findings and what they mean for economics and policymaking.

My colleagues and I are guided by a hope that more of economic policy will be grounded in evidence of how economies can be made to work for the many, not just the few. This book knits together what has become clear as we've pored over the latest research and worked with the best scholars in the world. It attempts to tell a story that brings this body of work together. The past six years have been an incredibly exciting time to be deeply engaged in economics—as perhaps eras of fundamental change always are. I hope you will find the debates equally energizing.

# UNBOUND

# Introduction

All happy families are alike; each unhappy family
is unhappy in its own way.

—Leo Tolstoy

I N MARCH 2009, in the darkest days of the economic crisis, the US
economy was losing nearly twenty-six thousand jobs each day. Home
prices had plummeted over the prior three years as the credit-fueled boom
of the prior decade fizzled, destroying the value of what for most families
was their most valuable asset. The burst of the housing bubble left millions
unable to pay their mortgages. As overleveraged homeowners curtailed their
spending, the effects pushed the US economy to the brink of disaster and
reverberated around the world. Long-standing Wall Street institutions at
the pinnacle of the financial market disappeared overnight—along with tril-
lions of dollars of wealth. The global economy was headed, it appeared,
into cataclysmic meltdown.

By the time the crisis reached its end, 8.7 million jobs were gone and
$12 trillion in household net worth had disappeared. Cities and states,
shocked by tax revenue shortfalls, cut back education, healthcare, and other
critical spending, laying off tens of thousands of teachers, nurses, fire and
police department workers, and other public-sector employees. The immediate pain was intense. More enduring is the fact that millions of Americans will never make up for that lost wealth and missed income. The trend
toward greater economic inequality continues its seemingly inexorable
march, and the share of the US population whose jobs, family incomes, and

1

net assets put them in the middle class remains below the high of the previous century. The middle class remains mired in debt.[1]

One group has emerged as strong as ever. Those at the top of the income and wealth ladders have not only fully recovered, but are even better
off than before. In stark contrast to the experience of the bottom 90 percent,
the wealthiest 1 percent of families almost completely regained what they
lost during the crisis by 2012. That year, their inflation-adjusted average
wealth (not including any funds hidden in overseas accounts) was $13.8
million—just 3.5 percent below the 2007 peak.[2]

Experts had thought this kind of economic crisis couldn't happen in
the twenty-first century. Nobel laureate Robert E. Lucas Jr., for example,
made the case in 2003 that the "central problem of depression prevention
has been solved."[3] The United States had lived through the Great Depression of the 1930s, and we believed we had learned the lessons of an
economic catastrophe that left "one-third of a nation ill-housed, ill-clad,
ill-nourished."[4] That crisis had also begun with the bursting of an asset
bubble—stocks, in that case—that brought about mass unemployment
and the widespread destruction of wealth. Yet, as the first signs of that
crisis emerged, policymakers dithered. President Herbert Hoover thought
the depression could not be "cured by legislative action or executive pro-
nouncement" and so failed to act as the economy plunged into a downward spiral.[5]

That the crisis of the Great Depression was eventually resolved owed
much to a set of powerful new economic ideas and a revolutionary effort
to collect data to track economic activity, implemented during the presi-
dency of Franklin D. Roosevelt. The importance of John Maynard Keynes,
who published *The General Theory of Employment, Interest, and Money*
in 1936, is well known. His ideas on how to spur aggregate demand continue to serve as a key plank in fiscal and monetary policymaking. What is
less well known is the work, at the same time, by a group of people determined to provide government with better informational tools to measure
and analyze economic problems. As the Great Depression unfolded, economists knew they needed a way to translate the suffering they saw all around
them into numbers that would accurately reflect the problem and, with luck,
illuminate the path forward. They embarked on an ambitious plan to
capture complex and vital economic data and, in 1947, the US government published its first set of national income accounts. These provided

Congress and the president with the first comprehensive snapshot of economic activity. By the admission of Simon Kuznets, the man who did more than any other to pull it together, the data fell short of revealing the country's overall well-being. But it was a major advance.

From the perspective of 2019, it's easy to underappreciate how transformative it was to have data tracking the economy. For the first time in human history, policymakers could design interventions based on a growing body of reliable economic evidence. The systems put in place over the course of the 1940s allow economists and policymakers to gauge unemployment and family incomes and assess how families are faring. For example, we can know today that everyday people's consumption comprises about 70 percent of our economy—and that any crisis that rocks that 70 percent threatens to take down the whole economy.

Equipped with Kuznets's data and Keynes's ideas, economists believed that they had the tools to solve the problem of how to avert crises. Coming out of the Great Depression, economists developed frameworks and methods that were seen as effective and, for the most important purposes, sufficient. Their work was deemed so vital that economists were given their own agency within the Executive Office of the President of the United States—the Council of Economic Advisers. No other social scientists were elevated in this way. There is no Council of Anthropologists or Committee of Sociologists. Over the course of the 1950s and 1960s, economists churned out textbooks codifying and refining the data-informed insights that generations of students would learn and commit to memory. All seemed to be going well.

The policymaking community coalesced around using Gross Domestic Product as the most important metric to track economic progress. This measure of the sum total of all the goods and services produced within a nation's borders was an important part of the economists' data revolution. While not built to measure well-being—it's an aggregate measure of income, not people's welfare—it quickly became policymakers' shorthand for the state of the nation's economy. In December 1960, when a group of nations came together in Paris to launch the Organisation for Economic Co-operation and Development, they named economic growth as its defining goal and adopted GDP as a key indicator of nations' economic development. The prevailing economic doctrine was summed up in a 1963 speech by President John F. Kennedy, when he used the expression "a rising tide lifts all the boats." The belief that when the economy grows everyone benefits would inform economic policymaking for decades to come.[6]

The following decades validated this approach: the US economy experienced solid growth in GDP and the vast majority of Americans benefited. Between 1963 and 1979, US national income grew by an average of 1.7 percent per year and most people saw their incomes rise commensurately. Indeed, this growth lifted the boats of the poorest the most. These trends led economists and the policymakers who relied on their advice to the conclusion that a growing economy and good jobs naturally go hand in hand. The policymaking community began to believe that its job was to keep growth in output strong and steady. The rest would follow. "The rest" is what economists call *distribution*—that is, how the benefits of economic output are shared—and what everyone else calls living standards.

Policymakers believed there might need to be some policy interventions—such as Social Security for the aged and disabled, and unemployment insurance—to ensure that people not able to participate in the market weren't left behind. Certainly there would also be continued need for a set of legal institutions to enforce contracts. But, once those were in place, and as long as policymakers focused on strong, stable growth, the market would take care of the rest—or so the thinking went. For all these reasons and more, economics was hailed as the Queen of the Social Sciences.[7]

Until it wasn't.

The economic crisis of a decade ago didn't come out of nowhere. It had been brewing for decades. By the time the crisis hit in 2007, it was readily apparent that living standards were failing to improve for the majority of people even as great wealth was being created for those at the very top. The institutions that had supported broad-based economic gains—such as labor unions and the government agencies charged with ensuring world-class education, robust infrastructure, and prudent regulation of markets—had been crumbling for many years.

This process began in the late 1970s, when the US economy experienced a slowdown in growth and productivity. But this was only the first hint of a far larger problem. Until the end of the 1970s, everyone's living standards grew in line with overall output growth. Then, things changed. Between 1980 and 2016, the bottom 90 percent of income earners—that's nine out of ten adults in the United States—experienced income growth that was slower than the national average, regardless of whether we measure this income before or after accounting for taxes and government transfers such as supplemental nutrition assistance and other family income supports. Since 1980, workers at the fortieth percentile of the income distribution—which today includes many home care workers, bank tellers, and preschool and kindergarten teachers—have seen their incomes grow by just 0.3 percent per year, from about $26,400 to $29,800 in 2016, in inflation-adjusted dollars.[8]

At the other end of the income ladder, over the same period, the richest have seen their incomes rise sky-high. Someone in the top 0.1 percent, say a banking executive, would have seen his post-tax income almost quadruple since 1980—meaning that with one year's salary, the banker can easily afford to add a holiday home in the Hamptons to his collection of luxury properties and yachts. As Gene Sperling, an economic adviser to presidents Bill Clinton and Barack Obama, said, "the rising tide will lift some boats, but others will run aground."[9]

Even as most people failed to share the gains produced, the economics profession was not yet questioning conventional wisdom or coming to terms with how income inequality affects the economy. Up until the crisis, they—and the policymaking community that relies on their advice—continued to believe that, even though the economy was no longer delivering shared growth, no fundamental rethinking of the advice given to policymakers was required. How the gains of growth were distributed was important, but not of overriding concern. Economist and former government official Brad DeLong once told me that, "when we entered the White House in 1992," the winning faction of economists believed that what was most urgent and doable was "to stabilize America's public finances and strike a deal with [Federal Reserve Chairman Alan] Greenspan to keep interest rates low, so as to enable a high-investment, high-productivity, high-wage-growth recovery."[10] Indeed, the research agenda throughout the 1990s and into the early 2000s focused on why people weren't seeing income gains—not what that trend meant for the economy more generally. Was it technological change? Globalization? A lack of skills? The debate occurred within the general confines of the framework laid out decades before.

Even that framework, moreover, had narrowed in some ways. The influence of Keynes and his ideas about the vital role of the government in the economy had waned. Ideas that rested on faith in the market—sometimes described as neoliberal—became more influential, fueled in part by capitalism's Cold War triumphs. Within this intellectual context, economists didn't see that inequality could have larger—and quite significant—implications. The Great Recession of 2007 to 2009 thus came as a shock to the profession. Economists since have had to grapple with how their models of the economy, to put it mildly, underperformed. We are now learning that the framework within which we have been thinking about how to prevent economic crises and generally improve living standards is broken.

## Transforming Our Understanding of Economic Growth and Inequality

This book is about a transformation underway in economics that is thoroughly upending the conventional wisdom about how our nation can deliver strong, stable, and broadly-shared economic growth. It describes how economists across the profession are using new tools, such as pioneering empirical techniques and making use of big data, to describe what is actually happening in our economy.

I've spent the past decade asking whether high and rising inequality is not only an outcome but in fact a force preventing us from having the kind of economy that delivers for the many, not just the few. I've built an organization—the Washington Center for Equitable Growth—dedicated to advancing research on these questions and have had the privilege to work with and learn from researchers across the country and around the world using innovative approaches to find answers to the many permutations of this basic question. In the pages that follow, I'll showcase what we can learn from the cutting-edge research exploring different kinds of economic inequality—in income and wealth, across firms, by gender and race, and across geographic communities and regions—and how they affect economic growth.

A few themes emerge, some well understood and some less so. In the pages that follow, I'll describe the extensive and impressive new tools economists are using to improve understanding of the implications of inequality for how our economy works. Put together, the evidence shows that inequality doesn't just offend our sense of justice and it isn't merely a nuisance. When the models and theory are so at odds with the available evidence, we need to open our minds to the possibility that a fundamental change is in play.

As University of California–Berkeley economist Emmanuel Saez recently remarked, "When the theory is contradicted by the evidence, you have to go with the evidence."[11]

In economic thinking today, change is afoot. We see a rising generation of scholars, informed by new data and sources of empirical evidence, coming to conclusions that upend the conventional wisdom. Real-world observations are undermining the claim that markets left to their own devices reliably deliver socially beneficial outcomes. These analyses are challenging long-held assumptions about how the economy works and the extent to which those workings can be understood in isolation from the larger dynamics of the rest of society. All this is paving the way for a major shift.

The new framework starts from the understanding—grounded in the evidence—of the ways that inequality obstructs, subverts, and distorts economic growth. While Adam Smith's famous invisible hand pushes the economy toward broadly beneficial outcomes, economic inequality acts as a bind, thwarting the idealized market processes as it transforms into social and political power. A rising tide can't lift all boats when some can't even get launched and others, pushed off course and deprived of navigation tools, founder on the rocks. Inequality constricts economic growth.

This framework exposes dynamics more complex than the conventional economic wisdom of the past can explain. That's the purpose of this book. While it is tempting to embrace the simple tale that a rising tide lifts all boats, we need a more nuanced account. We need to make sense of a large body of evidence, much of which has focused not directly on the question of how inequality affects economic growth but rather on how inequality affects mechanisms that in turn drive investment and productivity. The reasons that economic benefits are not flowing to families may be disparate, but there are many common themes—which, once fully traced, can reveal new patterns to guide better economic thinking and policymaking.

The idea that trends in inequality bear on the workings of economies is fast becoming the consensus view. In 2014, Thomas Piketty's *Capital in the Twenty-First Century* hit bestseller charts worldwide. A profound exposé and critique of inequality, the book touched a nerve, selling more than two million copies in more than forty languages and winning the author what journalists called "rock star" status. Piketty is, of course, a special case. How many economists become international celebrities? But

Piketty is not alone in charting a new course forward for economics. In the pages that follow, I'll show how he's part of a *paradigm shift*, to use Thomas Kuhn's famous term, that has economists increasingly recognizing inequality as an important feature of how our economy works, with implications that reverberate across our political institutions and processes and throughout society more generally. Kuhn, a philosopher of science who studied how scientific revolutions happen, argued in 1962 that in any given era and scientific field, knowledge is accrued and ideas developed within a prevailing paradigm—that is, a set of basic assumptions and respected practices shared by the scholars working to advance that field. According to Kuhn, scientific knowledge isn't accessible as absolute truth; it develops only through the consensus of scholars in a particular field, whose work is occasionally upended by scientific discoveries that challenge existing frameworks and force the paradigm to shift. Groundbreaking, data-driven discoveries are causing just such a revolution in economics today.[12]

Emblematic of this is the work being done by one of the world's most important organizations dedicated to economic policy: the International Monetary Fund. Economists there have conducted a series of research studies showing the link between higher inequality levels and more frequent economic downturns. They find that when growth takes place in societies with high inequality, the economic gains are more likely to be destroyed by the more severe recessions and depressions that follow—and the economic pain is all too often compounded for those at the lower end of the income spectrum.[13]

Indeed, a number of scholars arguing that economists must take inequality more seriously have backgrounds in the economic issues facing developing countries, where inequality has tended to be higher than in the developed world. Prominent among them are the Massachusetts Institute of Technology's Simon Johnson and Daron Acemoglu, Columbia University's Joseph Stiglitz, and the University of Chicago's Raghuram Rajan and James Robinson. Each has explored how high inequality affects macroeconomic and institutional outcomes. Their work also challenges the presumption that economic and political instability is something that nations naturally outgrow as they develop; to the contrary, it may be par for the course in the advanced political economies of the world.[14]

One thing that is clear from the emerging evidence is that economic inequality reinforces differences in political and social power, and these in turn affect market outcomes. This directly contradicts the postwar conventional wisdom, based on a narrow interpretation of ideas handed down from Adam Smith, that the workings of a market economy can be isolated from those of surrounding political and social institutions—that is, that economies operate by natural laws that transcend institutional settings. It also marks a contrast with much of what economists have claimed over the past half-century, as they've spent untold hours documenting how social and political institutions and practices impede the natural functions of the market. The new evidence tells a very different story about the influence of political and social institutions. While they may have been ignored by standard economic models, these institutions created the potential for markets to deliver broadly shared economic growth from the 1940s through the late 1970s—and have allowed them to create rising economic inequality and instability since then.

I don't want to leave the impression that there's been nothing in economic thinking between Adam Smith and Thomas Piketty. All along the way, groups of scholars both within and outside of economics have attempted to come up with a more realistic portrait of the economy and how it functions. This has often entailed looking deeply at institutions. Karl Marx sat in the British Library and pored over all the factory reports; Thorstein Veblen did deep studies of the emerging consumer society; John Commons wrote about social policy at the state level in Wisconsin—and the list goes on. But, especially since the Cold War, these ideas have been outside the center of the mainstream.

Case in point: In the early 1990s, David Card and Alan Krueger developed empirical methods that showed that when policymakers in New Jersey raised the minimum wage, employment in fast food restaurants did not decline relative to neighboring states. Their research was not only groundbreaking and had real-world implications, it directly contradicted a basic tenet of economics—that when a price rises, demand falls—bringing to the fore profoundly unsettling theoretical questions. Card won one of the most prestigious awards in economics—the John Bates Clark Medal—in 1995, the same year that this research was published as a book. Yet, he recalls pushback and hostility from the profession, grounded in the bias of a set of theoretical ideas handed down for generations. In his words, "my belief was that this was purposefully to try and defend the [American Economic Association] from criticism that we were a bunch of left-wing nuts."[15] Indeed, when Krueger passed away in March 2019, his obituary in the *Washington Post* quoted an observation by University of Chicago economist and Nobel laureate James J. Heckman in 1999: "They don't root their findings in existing theory and research. That is where I really deviate from these people. Each day you can wake up with a brand new world, not plugged into the previous literature."[16] Decades later, Card and Krueger are being celebrated as the leading edge of scholars whose research and methods have fundamentally changed the profession.

Card and Krueger's research is just the tip of the proverbial iceberg. From across the profession, evidence continues to mount that we must change our understanding of how the economy works. It's becoming clear that we need to adopt a new framework, one that starts from the premise that unequal access to resources translates into political and social institutions able to obstruct, subvert, and distort the processes that should produce strong and stable improvements in economic productivity and output. Economics must now confront the real-world economy with models that take into account the complexities of economic inequality. There is an urgency to this shift as many economists and other social scientists have pointed out the limited usefulness of prevailing macroeconomic models, and blamed their flaws and omissions for the fact that, even as a grave economic crisis was looming in the mid-2000s, economists lacked the foresight to discern it. Nobel laureate Paul Krugman, now at the City University of New York, summed up the problem, explaining to readers of the *New York Times Magazine* that "economists, as a group, mistook beauty, clad in impressive-looking mathematics, for truth."[17]

## The Evolution of Smith's Invisible Hand into Natural Laws of the Economy

Scientific paradigms are grounded in the prevailing consensus about what the evidence shows. The prevailing one—based on the idea that the economy has natural laws—stems from ideas laid down centuries ago by Adam Smith. Smith, living and working in Glasgow, Scotland, in the mid- to late-eighteenth century, had a front-row seat to the Industrial Revolution. Factories were being built as wealth that had been tied up in entailed estates, handed down from eldest son to eldest son, was freed up and invested in nascent industries. People were moving to towns and cities—forced, in many cases, off land their ancestors had plowed for centuries. The old feudal order was unraveling. Smith's imagination was sparked especially by the scientific discoveries and inventions that were raising living standards and allowing vast fortunes to be built. How was this new wealth being created? Would industrialization benefit everyone or only the rich? In *An Inquiry into the Nature and Causes of the Wealth of Nations*, he laid out the dynamics of the modern economy rising up during his lifetime as he saw them.[18]

Smith's metaphor of the invisible hand remains influential today. At the core of Smith's theory is an honest assessment of people's desire for wealth. "An augmentation of fortune," he wrote, "is the means by which the greater part of men propose and wish to better their condition."[19] His innovation was to show how individuals' pursuits of profits yield overall social benefits because their self-interest motivates production that would otherwise not happen. Smith put it this way: "It is not from the benevolence of the butcher, the brewer, or the baker that we expect our dinner, but from their regard to their own interest."[20] This pithy example packs a punch. In this one sentence, Smith made a compelling case for why, in a market economy, economic growth and well-being for all flows from the incentives of personal gain. When people have the liberty to engage in the economy and pursue their own financial gains as they make the most of their skills and talents, this benefits the whole society, not just those individuals.

For their own selfish reasons, Smith's craftsmen make, sell, and profit from their work. As a butcher, brewer, or baker grows richer, others are inspired to find opportunities to generate the same kinds of profits in the marketplace. Take the brewer. Eager to make an income, he invests his capital in a brewery, hires workers, and sets a price for his beer. Whatever profit he turns is his reward for taking on some risk and working hard. The townsfolk gain the pleasure of drinking the beer.

Note that if there were only one brewer in town, he might be able to charge extremely high prices and take home a lot of profits. This might create or exacerbate inequality between the brewer and townsfolk. Eventually, it might lead to economic and political instability. Recognizing this, Smith specifies the other key element of a successful market economy: competition among sellers. In the competitive market economy he describes, there is free entry and exit of people and capital and no single actor has power over the others. In such an economy, other wealth-seeking people are able to see how much money the brewer makes and can spot the opportunity to build their own brewery (assuming they can access the capital to do so) and lure customers away from their rival by selling their beer at a lower price. Both brewers will profit less than the original one did before, and inequality will be capped. In the words of one economic historian, Robert Heil-broner: "It was Smith's great achievement to show how the mechanism of *competition* would bring about a state of economic provisioning as dependable as any provided by state command, and a great deal more flexible and dynamic."[21] This notion of competition is not the same as the so-called perfect competition theory of today's economics textbooks; Smith made use of a more commonsense understanding of what happens when sellers are allowed to compete for profits. This, in a nutshell, is Smith's invisible hand.[22]

It would be difficult to overstate the revolutionary nature of Smith's ideas. By celebrating the positive public outcomes of self-interest—constrained by market competition—he turned the third deadly sin, greed, from vice to virtue. This was a sharp departure from the prevailing Christian ideology of the day. Smith argued in *The Theory of Moral Sentiments* that the Deity instills in human nature certain passions, including a passion for wealth accumulation that exceeds purely rational considerations, which invisibly motivate people to act in ways that advance the interests of society "without intending it, without knowing it."[23] Eager for the products of the butcher, brewer, and baker, we "address ourselves, not to their humanity but to their self-love, and never talk to them of our own necessities but of their advantages."[24] It turns out that, as the character Gordon Gekko puts it in Oliver Stone's 1987 film *Wall Street*, "Greed, for lack of a better word, is good."[25] In Smith's free market, the selfish pursuit of wealth is socially beneficial.

It's also difficult to overstate the appeal of Smith's ideas. The bare-bones story is beautifully simple and intellectually satisfying, connecting individual liberty to collective progress in one complete, logical system. Smith developed a theory of how allowing markets to work freely delivers broad-based improvements in living standards, so that economic growth and distribution go together.

In the two centuries since the publication of *The Wealth of Nations*, economists have formalized Smith's ideas of the natural laws of the economy into mathematical models. Starting with the actions of individuals, they developed a set of theorems showing that market forces left alone to operate would generate outcomes that were in some sense economically optimal and generally seen as fundamentally fair. The notion that the market had its own rules that were both logically consistent and socially beneficial came to be treated as scientific fact. In the late 1800s, American economist John Bates Clark, whose name is attached to one of the highest honors in economics today, gave the economics profession the "marginal productivity theory of distribution." It predicts that, in a competitive economy, individuals' wages will be proportional to their productivity. As a result, Clark wrote in 1891, "what a social class gets is, under natural law, what it contributes to the general output of industry."[26]

In the 1950s, economists Kenneth Arrow and Gérard Debreu provided the math to support Adam Smith's idea that there is a general equilibrium corresponding to an optimal allocation of resources. In an ideal world, their equations showed, when the butchers, brewers, and bakers all produce and sell in competitive markets, social welfare increases for them and for the consumers they sell to. In a set of mathematical proofs now known as the two fundamental theorems of welfare economics, they established that a perfectly competitive market would arrive at a point where no further improvement could be made to any person's outcome without leaving some other person worse off. At that point it would reach its "Pareto efficiency," named after the nineteenth-century Italian economist Vilfredo Pareto, who pioneered the study of income distribution in an economy. They also found that, under some conditions, any Pareto-efficient allocation of economic resources can be supported by a competitive equilibrium with transfers to those who are worse off. The Pareto efficiency principle implies that the market can deliver optimal outcomes (assuming we agree with the mathematician's definition of *optimal*) and that we should judge the best outcome to be the one that achieves an overall maximum, so that no individual's outcome could be improved without making someone else worse off by a greater degree. Extending this theorem to the scenario where economic equilibrium incorporates transfers to those who are worse off, the implication is that the best way for governments to reduce economic inequality is to provide one-time, lump-sum transfers, after which the market can work its magic.[27]

Around the same time, economist Robert Solow at the Massachusetts Institute of Technology and Australian economist Trevor Swan separately published growth models showing that, for any economy, there is a path along which growth can proceed at a stable rate with capital and labor each benefiting proportionally. While other economists argued that the economy's path was inherently unstable and would require government interventions to sustain growth and avoid crises, the Solow-Swan model showed that the economy could, on its own, grow indefinitely with the factors of production—both labor and capital—seeing earnings proportional to their contributions. When the economy is in its steady state, capital accumulation leads to a constant ratio of capital to output.[28]

To be sure, every economics student is taught that these lessons have their limits. The proofs behind these ideas are based on a set of stringent assumptions that are understood to be an abstraction of the real world. Indeed, students who go on to study economics in graduate school spend years developing tools to address these limitations; much of the research in economics today is about what happens when the assumptions are relaxed, and whole subfields of the profession are focused on these imperfections. Even with these caveats, however, the mid-century data aligned with the theory that inequality did not interfere with outcomes that (ultimately) benefited the nation overall. Economists seemed to have settled a core tension. The market was ruled by a set of natural laws that were both self-regulating and (generally) socially beneficial.

Smith revealed a kind of order in a chaotic new world. Ever since, economists have advanced the idea that there are natural laws governing the economy that push it toward socially beneficial outcomes—and seen it as their job to uncover those laws. His ideas became the launching pad for generations of scholars seeking to reveal the natural laws and universal truths driving the economy. Along the way, Smith's understanding of the economy was reduced to a set of simplistic ideas—stripped of nuance and social and historical context—that he, and many classical economists, wouldn't recognize. Economists began to see their responsibility as explaining and protecting the market rather than the people of the society. As these ideas infiltrated politics, policymakers likewise began to see government not as the protector of people and society but as a source of impediments to the market's natural functioning. The conventional wisdom became that the way to realize broad prosperity gains was for policymakers to promote the productivity and growth that would lift all boats, not to focus on the mechanisms of distribution itself in fostering economic gains more generally.[29]

The work of two economists in particular—one focused on data, one on policy—was central to the conventional wisdom of the mid- to late-twentieth century about how policymakers should think about inequality and economic growth. The first was Simon Kuznets. In his 1955 presidential address at the American Economic Association, he presented what would become known as the "Kuznets Curve"—his novel hypothesis that, as economies become more developed, inequality shrinks. Kuznets, whose work in general was instrumental in creating data to measure economic output, had been working with US tax return records. He used trend data from the United States, the United Kingdom, and Germany, and compared their income distributions in the postwar period to those of India, Ceylon (now Sri Lanka), and Puerto Rico. The paper begins by walking readers through the data issues that complicated the research, but ultimately posits that economic development happens along a predictable path. As a nation begins to industrialize and workers move from agriculture into manufacturing, income distribution becomes more unequal because manufacturing output does more to enrich owners of capital. Then, as the nation advances toward high-value-added manufacturing and services and more of the population begins to participate in higher-productivity industries, that trend toward greater inequality reverses. Kuznets readily admitted that his paper was "perhaps 5 per cent empirical information and 95 per cent speculation, some of it possibly tainted by wishful thinking."[30] But his work did much to create optimism that the US economy would generate growth for all as it became more productive.

The second key economist was Arthur Okun, who gave policymakers a way to think about the economy and those left behind. Okun served in President Lyndon B. Johnson's administration as chair of the Council of Economic Advisers in the mid-1960s. He addressed what he named as a fundamental challenge for policymakers: deciding how to improve the lot of those at the bottom of the income ladder with the least disruption to the optimal conditions for economic efficiency. In a short, widely-cited book published in 1975, when he was a scholar at the Brookings Institution, Okun put it this way: "To the extent that the system succeeds, it generates an efficient economy. But that pursuit of efficiency necessarily creates inequalities. And hence society faces a tradeoff between equality and efficiency."[31] When policymakers tax the rich to provide benefits for the poor, redistributive programs have "an unsolved technological problem: the money must be carried from the rich to the poor in a leaky bucket," such that the total amount of money in productive use is reduced after redistribution.[32]

For decades, Kuznets and Okun have influenced how policymakers think about the relationship between economic growth and the well-being of America's middle class. Policymakers absorbed two basic lessons from the research into how the economy works. The first had to do with economic inequality's role as an incentive. It was accepted that earning more is the reward for innovation, talent, and hard work, and that greater wealth is the reward for investing in ways that lead to greater productivity and growth. This first lesson taught them that, while they might need to address the circumstances of the very unfortunate, the market in general would deliver fair enough outcomes. The second lesson was that, in so-called *perfectly* competitive markets, the share of the gains from growth distributed to a given actor is generally commensurate with the value created by that actor's input to generating the growth. These two ideas point to the conclusion that, as long as the market economy functions as modeled, the beneficial aspects of inequality will be enhanced, the negatives contained, and the distributions (mostly) determined by economic contributions.

At the three-quarters mark of the twentieth century, the data indicated that these ideas were valid. After that point, not so much.

## A Rising Tide No Longer Lifts All—or Even Most—Boats

By the end of the twentieth century, a fundamental shift was underway in the practical workings of the US economy. Growth began to slow and, at the same time, the gains from overall growth accrued to a narrower slice of the population than they had in the preceding three decades. The results were sharp rises in income and wealth inequality and a decline in economic mobility. A new generation of economists has since made use of freshly available data and more powerful computing capabilities to develop an updated understanding of how the economy works. Their research asks whether and how rising income inequality and wealth inequality affect outcomes such as economic mobility, and how the effects shift over time as political and social circumstances change. Let's go through these trends one by one.

## Rising income inequality

In the early 2000s, economists Emmanuel Saez at the University of California–Berkeley and Thomas Piketty at the Paris School of Economics, along with many coauthors, began to document income trends. They focused on earners at the very top of the distribution, building on work Piketty had done using French tax data. Their first joint academic publication was the now-famous 2003 article in the *Quarterly Journal of Economics* where they looked at US income tax data and showed that incomes were rising for the top 1 percent of earners but not for the rest—a finding that Piketty described as the "vertiginous growth of income of the top 1 percent since the 1970s and 1980s."[33]

While the use of income tax records to track trends in economic inequality was not unprecedented—Kuznets relied on them, too, when he laid out his famous curve showing declines in inequality as economies developed—Piketty, Saez, and their coauthors were the first in many decades to use this data source. In the decades between, economists studying incomes had turned instead to survey data, which had become more accurate and easier to access. The advent of personal computers, in particular, allowed researchers to crunch data conveniently in their offices that in the past would have required a special computing center. Surveys also offer the advantages of covering members of a population who don't file taxes, and being able to capture demographic characteristics and income sources not included in the tax data. Yet, these new, more in-depth surveys also have their downsides. They don't cover the years prior to World War II and, to preserve confidentiality of those with very high incomes, they are "top-coded" (all incomes higher than a certain threshold are overwritten with the income cap), making it impossible to track the incomes of very rich households. Using public-use files and aggregate tabulations of the tax data allowed Piketty and Saez to trace incomes back to 1913 and examine the trends for the very rich.[34]

Since this groundbreaking study, they, along with Gabriel Zucman at the University of California–Berkeley, have matched the income tax return data to national income accounts data to devise a way to consistently measure how growth in national income is distributed in the United States. They find that, ironically, the publication of Okun's agenda-setting book coincided with both the delivery of the fullest promise of the American Dream in the US economy and the nadir of overall income inequality. Writing in 1975, Okun correctly noted that "the relative distribution of family income has changed very little in the past generation."[35] (See Figure I.1a.) Since the 1980s, however, overall growth has been slower—keeping an annual pace of 1.3 percent versus 1.7 percent in the decades before—and those at the top of the income ladder have experienced far greater gains than those in the bottom 90 percent. Between 1980 and 2016, those in the top 1 percent saw their incomes after taxes and transfers rise by more than 180 percent, and those in the top 0.001 percent saw their incomes grow by more than 600 percent, while those in the bottom half saw only a 25 percent rise. To be very clear, they show that it truly is only those at the very top that have seen disproportionate gains.[36] (See Figure I.1b.)

The unequal distribution of income exhibits inequalities by gender and race, as well. Those who occupy the highest rungs on the income ladder are much more likely to be male and white, which means that women and people of color are less likely to wield the economic and political power that higher incomes confer. Piketty, Saez, and Zucman show that women, even though they make up nearly half the labor force, comprise just under a third of the top 10 percent of income earners. It gets more unequal the further up you go. Only about 16 percent of the top 1 percent are women, and only about 11 percent of the top 0.1 percent are women. Disparities by race are also large. The US Census Bureau reports that about 30 percent of white households earn $100,000 or more—about double the 16 percent of black households. Meanwhile, about 20 percent of black households make less than $15,000, compared to about 10 percent of white households.[37]

In the latter decades of the twentieth century, economists who were seeing higher inequality in earnings and incomes sought to incorporate these trends into existing understandings of how the economy works—the natural laws laid out in the decades before. Three explanations were proposed by scholars. The first claimed there was skill-biased technical change; its pro-

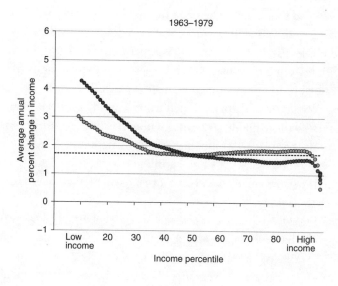

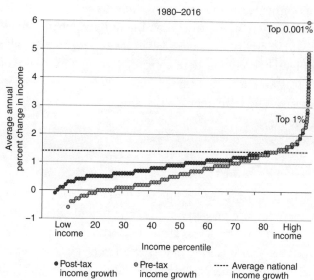

Figure I.1    a. Average growth is used to represent most Americans' experience Average annual income growth for earners in each percentile of the US population, 1963–1979.

b. Only the top 10 percent have seen above-average income growth Average annual income growth for earners in each percentile of the US population, 1980–2016.

*Source:* Author's analysis of Thomas Piketty, Emmanuel Saez, and Gabriel Zucman, "Distributional National Accounts: Methods and Estimates for the United States," *Quarterly Journal of Economics* 133, no. 2 (May 2018): Appendix tables II: distributional series, available at http://gabriel-zucman.eu/usdina/.

ponents argued that a higher demand for highly skilled workers raised their wages relative to less skilled workers. The second claimed that globalization had put less-skilled workers into competition with labor forces all over the world, lowering their wages. While these two explanations focused on why there were rising incomes for those with college degrees relative to other workers, a third theory pointed to the rapidly escalating incomes of "superstars"—those highly successful senior executives at the top of public corporations, big private companies, and private equity and venture capital firms who, like rock stars and sports phenoms, found they could turn incremental performance advantages into exponential compensation gains relative to their peers.[38]

None of these explanations for rising income inequality, however, could account for what Piketty, Saez, and their coauthors were documenting in the United States and around the world. By the early 2000s, rising income inequality—especially at the very top—had become so striking that attempts to cast it as consistent with natural laws of the economy that would eventually benefit society more generally rang hollow. Further, while each of these three productivity-related explanations should apply to all countries at a similar level of economic development, the extent of the rise of incomes at the top was unique to the United States. This raised another question for economists: Why were trends in the United States so much starker than in other countries?

### Rising wealth inequality

Income is the *flow* of money, while wealth is the *stock* of accumulating assets—money, but also property, stocks, bonds, and other kinds of capital. The distribution of wealth across US households follows the same U-shaped curve as income—but it is even more severely unequal. Recent research by Saez and Zucman documents that in the 1920s, the share of wealth owned by the top 1 percent of households by wealth reached 51 percent. As with the share of income owned by the top 1 percent, this fell during the middle of the twentieth century, hitting a low of 23 percent in 1978. Since then, however, wealth gains at the top have grown even faster than income; those in the top 1 percent now control 42 percent of all wealth in the US economy, and the top 0.1 percent control more than 22 percent—three times as much as the late 1970s. To put this into raw numbers, there are 160,000

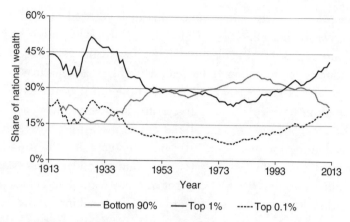

Figure I.2    Wealth is increasingly concentrated at the top
Shares of total wealth in the United States, 1913–2012

*Source:* Emmanuel Saez, and Gabriel Zucman. "Wealth Inequality in the United States since 1913: Evidence from Capitalized Income Tax Data." *Quarterly Journal of Economics* 131, no. 2 (May 2016): 519–78. DOI: 10.1093/qje/qjw004.

families in the United States who held more than $20 million in 2012, the most recent year available, and their average wealth was $72 million. This group's share of wealth was equal to that of the bottom 90 percent of Americans.[39] (See Figure I.2.)

What's more, this massive wealth gap is almost certainly much larger than the data shows. Economists don't have access to wealth data comparable to what's available on incomes because the United States does not tax net worth. Instead they have to rely on self-reported survey data. And even if tax-return data were available on wealth, there would still be a problem: much of the wealth of those at the very top is hidden and difficult to track. Zucman has extensively researched the use of tax havens by corporations and the ultra-rich to shield their profits and wealth from taxation. He estimates that $8.7 trillion in wealth, or 11.5 percent of world gross domestic product, is held in offshore accounts. Of the total value of offshore wealth, he estimates that 80 percent is owned by the top one-tenth of a percent.[40]

The gaps by gender and race are even larger in terms of wealth than they are in income. Columbia University economists Lena Edlund and Wojciech Kopczuk find that, from the late 1960s to 2000, the share of women in the top 0.1 percent and top 0.01 percent of wealth-holders in the United States has decreased from around half to approximately one-third, in no small part because of the declining role of inherited wealth. Duke University's William Darity and Ohio State University's Darrick Hamilton find that, among those in the top 1 percent of the nation's wealth distribution, white families make up more than 96 percent, while black families make up less than 2 percent. To get a granular picture of the racial wealth gap, Darity and Hamilton have conducted surveys in a number of cities across the United States, finding large racial and ethnic disparities in wealth even after accounting for the groups' varying average ages, education levels, and marital status. In Los Angeles, they find that black and Mexican households collectively hold 1 percent of what white households do. In Boston, they looked at the wealth of households making up the twenty-fifth percentile of various groups. For Puerto Ricans, that wealth level was zero. For Dominicans, it was negative $20,000. Only among whites do Boston households in the twenty-fifth percentile have positive net worth.[41]

### Less economic mobility

This brings us to the next major trend: the decline in absolute upward mobility in the United States. Harvard University economist Raj Chetty and his coauthors David Grusky, Maximilian Hell, Nathaniel Hendren, Robert Manduca, and Jimmy Narang looked across generations and found that when people born in 1940 were in their prime work-age years, more than nine out of ten—92 percent—had incomes higher than their parents at the same age. But when those born in 1980—the Reagan-era children—hit their thirties, only half of them had incomes higher than their parents at the same age. Those born in the middle of the income spectrum in 1980 have experienced the largest decline in the share of children out-earning their parents. That's a remarkable decline in Americans' upward mobility in a very short time frame.[42] (See Figure I.3.)

This team of scholars goes on to show that had income inequality not increased, this would have closed 71 percent of the decline in absolute mobility; had growth not slowed, the gap would have closed by 29 percent. The upshot: the idea that inequality is contained according to the natural laws of the economy isn't consistent with what's happening in the US economy. There is economic growth, but this is not leading to upward mobility; most of the gains are being reaped by those at the very top of the

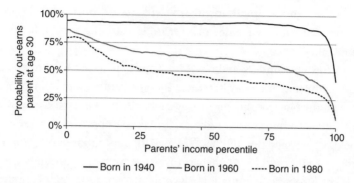

Figure I.3   Recent generations are less likely to earn more than their parents
Percent of US children in each cohort with incomes that are greater than their parents

*Source:* Raj Chetty, David Grusky, Maximilian Hell, Nathaniel Hendren, Robert Manduca, Jimmy Narang, "The Fading American Dream: Trends in Absolute Income Mobility Since 1940" *Science* 356 (6336): 398–406, 2017.

income ladder. Raj Chetty put it this way in a 2018 talk at the Brookings Institution:

> Two-thirds of what's going on is that the way in which GDP growth has been distributed is very different today than it was in the past. In the past, we had much more equal growth across the income distribution. Today . . . much of the growth goes to people at the very top of the income distribution. As a result, fewer kids across the income distribution—in the middle class and at the bottom—end up doing better than their parents did.[43]

In short, for people to be able to move up (and down) the income ladder, the gap between the incomes of those at the top and bottom must narrow.[44]

These groundbreaking, data-rich analyses are causing many to question long-standing ideas in economic theory. Recall that this is how Thomas Kuhn said that scientific fields advance: major shifts occur when researchers bring forth new evidence that doesn't comport with the theories at hand. Thomas Piketty, in *Capital in the Twenty-First Century* and much of the other work he's done with coauthors over the past two decades, observes that income inequality is an economic trend in and of itself—and one that appears to be increasing without constraint, to the detriment of both economy and society. He argues that, as long as the rate of growth is below the rate of return to capital, inequality will rise unconstrained by market forces, providing a new framework for understanding the implications of high inequality.[45]

Key to this new understanding of economics is seeing how trends in income, wealth, and mobility interact. Income and wealth reinforce each other: from the one side, higher incomes can be saved into stocks of wealth; from the other, having substantial wealth makes it possible to invest in ways that yield higher incomes, and lacking wealth cuts children off from many advantages that could boost their future earning power and upward mobility. Piketty focuses on this interplay, describing how high incomes are saved and solidify into stocks of wealth, which then continue to reproduce themselves. This happens both because higher rates of return can typically be achieved from investments requiring greater capital outlays and because highly concentrated capital translates into high inheritances. Chetty and his colleagues focus our attention on how inequality limits opportunity for those not already at the top. Getting ahead in life often requires some investment of capital—whether an entrepreneur is starting up a new business, a student aims for a college degree, or a family must weather a medical emergency—yet increasingly, people of average means find such goals out of reach.

## The Path to Equitable Growth

Understanding how economic inequality affects economic growth and stability is now an urgent research objective. Smith's pared-down account of the butcher, brewer, and baker doesn't capture how private, self-interested pursuits add up to—or undermine—broad-based improvements in living standards in today's economy. Today's coders, chefs, and caregivers have to find their way in an economy marked by high and growing economic inequality—and today's economists are increasingly seeing the need for a shift in their thinking about what inequality means. As Nobel laureate Robert Solow said in 2013, "I really do think that this question of equitable growth is certainly one of the, if not *the* central economic issue of our time."[46]

Changes in the real world are leading economists to work through what new data and evidence mean. As philosopher of science Ian Hackling put it in the foreword to the fiftieth anniversary edition of Kuhn's book, "All is well until the methods legitimated by the paradigm cannot cope with a cluster of anomalies; crisis results and persists until a new achievement redirects research and serves as a new paradigm. That is a paradigm shift."[47] This appears to be happening in economic thinking right now—and needs to happen in policymaking circles, too.

The foundations of our theories as to how economies deliver income and wealth gains were laid during an era of economic transformation when new technologies were profoundly changing what was produced and how. Smith observed and wrote as the old order was disintegrating around him. The feudal system was fading as upstart industrialists were creating massive wealth, disrupting the established elite. Yet his expectations of the ascendant economic system may have been too tempered. It was still a far-fetched idea that the *nouveau riche* of his era would come to be as entrenched as the feudal aristocracy that had been in place for centuries.

We, too, are living in an era of rapid technological, economic, and social change. In factories across the country—and the world—robots are replacing humans. As automation progressed over the twentieth century, fewer workers were needed in manufacturing and more in services. In the 1970s, roughly every fourth worker in the United States was employed in manufacturing, compared to only about one in twelve in 2018. Now, while job growth is fastest in services, these jobs are also being rapidly automated—in fast-food restaurants, warehousing, tax preparation, even legal services. We'll soon have driverless trucks dotting the highways and byways and flying drones delivering goods that may never touch a human hand—already, there's a robot delivering takeout dinners to folks in my neighborhood. Over the past two decades, the caring professions have been expanding rapidly, creating jobs for home health aides, childcare workers, pre-K teachers, and nursing assistants—in part because these jobs are difficult to turn over to robots. But this is little consolation for workers in many other sectors of the US economy.[48]

As the Industrial Revolution did, today's economic transformation is creating great wealth and a new cohort of economic elites, while consigning many others to slow or no economic gains. Many of today's newly minted billionaires made their money in technology-related endeavors. Looking at the top ten in the 2017 *Forbes* 400, five made their money by advancing new technology in innovative ways. Bill Gates (#1) made billions inventing the personal computer operating system at Microsoft. Jeff Bezos (#2) created the e-commerce giant Amazon.com. Mark Zuckerberg (#4) created Facebook. Larry Ellison (#5) founded commercial software giant Oracle, and Larry Page (#9) and Sergey Brin (#10) launched the Google search engine now housed within Alphabet. While these men have acquired phenomenal wealth, America's middle class struggles to keep up with the cost of living.[49]

We need to revisit old ideas with a fresh perspective, grounded in what we're learning from the latest empirical research. The place to start is to redefine the goal and measure what matters. What does a successful economy look like? How can we measure economic progress that benefits everyday families? We can see in the data that the one-metric approach, focusing solely on GDP growth, is insufficient. We must stop using aggregate economic growth as our single most important metric. Instead, we must disaggregate growth, always being mindful of who gains and who loses when output rises.

Then, we must focus on breaking inequality's grip on our economy. We can start with the most straightforward work of removing the *obstructions* it creates. For too many, economic fates are determined by who their parents are and in what neighborhood they live; high inequality and the ability of those at the top to hoard opportunity leaves them with no path upward. As a result, too many people and their families are blocked from fully contributing to the economy and our society. At the top of our priority list should be policies to ensure all boats are launched with the proper tools, for example, ensuring universal access to high-quality childcare and preschool, funding public schools better, and prioritizing infrastructure investments that improve public health.

Yet, we will not be able to clear the obstructions unless we also fight the *subversions* that come with inequality. A true resolve to limit the ability of those with economic power to subvert fair processes and manipulate economic growth in their favor would translate to a long list of policy recommendations, from reining in monopoly power to raising government revenues and boosting the collective bargaining power of workers. Without addressing the social and political ramifications of economic inequity, we cannot deliver strong, stable, and broadly-shared improvements in living standards. We must recognize that no entity other than government has the ability to act on behalf of the public interest and create a bulwark against the economically powerful.[50]

Meanwhile, as we counter inequality's obstructions and subversions, we must also fight the *distortions* it causes to macroeconomic processes that would otherwise yield positive social outcomes. Here, too, economists have many ideas for using the power of our democratic government institutions to make sure that economic incentives push the economy toward the most socially useful purposes. Examples include policies to provide jobs with good pay and working conditions for all who need them, and to discourage certain uses of capital such as investments in financial products that don't fund productive activity, or in credit products that contribute to instability.

To conquer today's high inequality, we must enact policy changes that do much more than tinker around the edges. We may need to revisit fundamental constitutional questions—as the rounds of reforms during the Progressive and New Deal eras did in the twentieth century. As economists increasingly engage with political scientists and constitutional law scholars, it's very likely that the years to come will see more constitutional battles over economic issues, particularly as they relate to inequality. More than a Council of Economic Advisers, our nation's leaders will find themselves in need of a Council of Political Economy Advisers.

■ ■ ■

How inequality affects economic growth and stability is a big, far-reaching question, and there are hundreds—probably thousands—of research studies addressing multitudes of issues relevant to it. It would be impossible for me to summarize them all. Instead, the subsequent chapters focus on just a handful of economists whose research is emblematic of the cutting-edge scholarship on inequality and the new paradigm. Each chapter begins by introducing someone's central ideas and explains why their work is both groundbreaking and shifts our understanding of how to promote economic growth that is strong, stable, and broadly shared. It then explores the wider ramifications of their research and ideas for how to repair the damage caused by high and rising economic inequality.

Before we begin, two caveats. First, this book's focus is on evidence from the United States and from research conducted after the turn of the century. Think of it as a case study. Examining how high inequality affects the functioning of our economy in various respects will reveal where empirical reality bumps up most against conventional wisdom, and suggest where economic policy interventions could be most fruitful in general. Second, this book does not address the potential impacts of climate change, even though that existential planetary crisis is the context in which all of the twenty-first century's social and economic policies will be formulated. It is my conviction, however, that just as the problems of inequality and climate change intersect, there are solutions that can address both realms. Reducing economic inequality and improving our environmental stewardship are not competing priorities, but can—and must—go hand in hand.

# I

# HOW INEQUALITY OBSTRUCTS

Who are the twenty-first century equivalents of Adam Smith's butcher, brewer, and baker? Can we test the relevance of his invisible hand in an economy now populated by coders, chefs, and caregivers? Embedded in this question is another one, of whether all of us get to pursue careers that suit our particular skills and talents. I enjoy spending days working with spreadsheets, so economics is a good match for me. But I'm not very good at growing things in my garden, so if the only path available to me had been the life of a farmer, I'm not sure I would be thriving.

Workers finding their right fit is the foundation for economic growth not only because it allows them to do what they like but also because it allows the economy to gain most from their efforts. One of the great things about a market economy is the greater access it affords to opportunity. Whereas feudalism—like most other ways of organizing an economy—features strictly defined classes of people playing assigned roles, our economy invites people to try their hands at whatever roles they choose. This creates enormous incentives for people to find realms of work where they can be most successful, to commit to improving their skills, and to work hard. But success also hinges on the rewards one can gain through merit and hard work; the system crumbles when people are obstructed from pursuing or earning those rewards.

Today, income inequality—like inequality rooted in racial, gender, or geographical discrimination—translates to unequal access to skill acquisition and to the rewards that talent and hard work should earn. Standard economic theory tells us that market competition will drive out any firms—and people—who favor one group over another for reasons other than productivity. No economically irrational obstruction can be sustained. On this principle, companies harboring men who sexually harass the women they work with, or refusing to hire black people, should be less successful than those hiring and rewarding employees based on their merits. Markets can and will deliver the most optimal outcomes if we just let them work. Allow professionals to compete, and the most talented and hard-working among them will be rewarded.

Yet the logic of this theory fails to map to a real world in which economic inequality creates all kinds of obstructions in the marketplace and across the broader economy. Imagine a woman who has an idea for a game-changing technology. Will she have the opportunity to realize that dream, or will she face discrimination? Is someone bound to recognize her talent, skills, and passion and hire her? What are her chances of accessing capital to launch a startup company? How will her ingenuity be rewarded in the market? Sadly, it increasingly depends on where she and her family started out on the wealth and income ladder.

■ ■ ■

There is growing evidence that economic inequality hinders productivity and growth by blocking the flows of people, ideas, and new capital. The research paints a picture of those at the top of the economic ladder hoarding the best economic opportunities, ensuring that their good luck solidifies into ongoing privilege by putting up barriers to upward mobility for others. Economists and policymakers—and increasingly, everyday consumers—are learning that, as Adam Smith's invisible hand attempts to push the economy to "advance the interest of the society," high inequality powerfully blocks it.

The next two chapters describe this body of research. Chapter 1 starts at the beginning, with the work of economist Janet Currie at Princeton University. It focuses on how children's economic circumstances when they are very young— even still in the womb—have lasting implications for them, their families, and the economy. Children's development is affected by the health and nutrition of their parents, the levels of stress they face, and the access they have to resources. Thanks to work by Currie and many others, we now see the links between factors such as children's varying birth weights and their different levels of school performance, job-holding, and earnings as adults relative to others with similar skill sets. We have a better understanding of the dynamics—which play out in complex ways across race, gender, and geography—that bar people from gaining the skills they need to realize their full economic potential and block new ideas from being brought to market. We have greater awareness of how inequality drags down national productivity by making our workforce less capable than it could be, and our economy less innovative.

Further evidence shows that, even when children have access to skills, inequality obstructs their contributing to the economy to the best of their abilities, and the obstructions hinder productivity and growth. Chapter 2 highlights research led by Raj Chetty into a surprising area where people's talents don't prove more important than their parents' income. Starting with a database of decades of patent applications, Chetty and his colleagues added data from the applicants' childhoods: their parents' incomes and grade-school test scores. The correlations point to a disturbing conclusion: the richer the family, the more likely the child will be to gain a patent. More broadly, Chetty comments that, "kids from lower-income backgrounds are no longer experiencing the same prospects of moving up in the income distribution and getting those pay raises that people at the bottom were getting in the past."[1] If a child who shows aptitude early on cannot make it up the ladder, then there's something broken in the way our markets work. Inequality has blocked the process.

Americans are routinely taught that opportunity follows merit—that, with a little talent and a lot of hard work, anyone can learn how to make delicious fried chicken and waffles and launch a restaurant chain, or create the next great app downloaded by millions. Yet research shows that your chances of being able to put your talent and skills to best use are affected by who you are and how wealthy your parents are. Economists can easily show that opening up professions to a diverse array of workers improves innovation and productivity, and therefore growth. Yet this truth doesn't translate into markets where rewards necessarily reflect merit. This disconnect is a direct result of the obstructions caused by inequality, and it threatens economic growth and stability.

# 1

# Learning and Human Capital

I N 2012 AND 2013, when Kansas Governor Sam Brownback enacted a key part of what he called his "red state" economic platform—the largest tax cuts in state history—he said the move would create unprecedented prosperity and state government surpluses. Instead, massive budget shortfalls led school districts across Kansas to cut programming and, in some cases, shorten the length of the school year. In a December 2017 op-ed, Dayna Miller, president of the Kansas Association of School Boards, laid out the numbers: "Since 2009, total funding per pupil has fallen more than $700 million behind inflation through 2017. Between 2010 and 2017, average teacher salaries when adjusted for inflation decreased nearly 8 percent. Kansans are investing a lower percentage of personal income in K–12 education than they have for more than twenty-five years." The cutbacks were larger in low-income neighborhoods.[1]

About eight hundred miles to the northeast, a community hit by a budget crisis of another kind was dealing with its own dire consequences. In February 2015, the Environmental Protection Agency reported that the water in Flint, Michigan, had toxic levels of lead. Flint had fallen far from its heyday in 1978, when eighty thousand people were employed building cars there, mostly for General Motors. Over the ensuing decades, the auto company cut its workforce to eight thousand, and Flint's population fell dramatically. The predominantly black population saw their incomes fall far below the national average. By 2011, the city had a $25 million budget deficit and the state had taken control of Flint's finances. In a cost-cutting move in April 2014, the state-appointed mayor ended Flint's fifty-year history of contracting with Detroit for its water supply. While a new pipeline to Lake Huron was being constructed, the city pumped in water from the Flint River. Almost immediately, citizens reported that the water smelled foul. Tests showed it had high levels of fecal matter and *E-coli* bacteria. It would take nearly a year for the state to tell people that the water was poisoning them and their families with lead.[2]

Flint and Kansas are particularly vivid examples of how economic inequality obstructs opportunity. In Flint, parents know this disaster will affect their children's futures. There is no safe level of lead exposure, and its effects are particularly pernicious for young children; ingestion leads to developmental problems, affecting the brain and nervous system. Flint's parents also know they had no way of avoiding this toxic exposure without help. No smell or color indicates when water contains lead, so there's no way to detect contamination without testing. Flint's people know that their community lacked the political power that could have prevented this tragedy.[3]

In both places, state leaders had decided to cut back on public expenditures in favor of tax cuts and, in both cases, the outcomes were worse for low-income and communities of color. Governor Rick Snyder of Michigan, like Brownback, argued that economic growth would follow if those with money were not overly burdened by taxes and regulations. Also like Brownback, he chose cutting tax rates over ensuring access for the people in his state to resources they needed to be, and become, the kinds of workers who could drive future improvements in economic productivity. Investing in children—through educational funding or through ensuring a safe water supply—isn't only a family concern. These investments have effects on the US economy's future productivity and growth because they affect human development. The two Republican governors were fixated on creating financial incentives to boost investment in businesses. Meanwhile, many economists were arguing that the best investments a nation could make to promote economic growth were early childhood interventions to protect health and ensure access to high-quality education through post-secondary school.[4]

Janet Currie, an economist at Princeton University, is among the most-cited economists in the world. Her research has reshaped how we think about human capital—that is, people's economically-relevant skills and training—and she is highly respected for her groundbreaking empirical investigations into how policy affects low-income children. And Currie hasn't just been a researcher. She's been a leader. In 2015, she was awarded the Carolyn Shaw Bell award for her mentorship of the next generation of women economists.[5]

Currie was trained as a labor economist and began her career focusing on unions and collective bargaining, but she became increasingly interested in understanding what goes into human capital. Up until she earned her degree and took her first appointment at the University of California–Los Angeles, she told me, "people had thought about human capital in kind of a limited way, captured by things like: How many years of education did you have? Did you go to high school? Did you go to college?" Through those years, economists focused a lot on formal schooling and workplace training, fitting these indicators into what economists call the "Mincer earnings equation"—after Columbia University economist Jacob Mincer, who first developed this empirical technique in the 1950s and 1960s. It's a workhorse equation that remains among the most used in all of economics.[6]

Over recent decades, in no small part due to Currie's scholarship, economists have focused on compiling data and analyses that trace the implications of early-life experiences for adult economic outcomes—factors established long before the educational attainment and experience that informs the Mincer equations. The most important papers on these implications have been written since the late 1990s and mark a sharp break with the past in terms of how economists think about the role economic inequality plays in what kinds of skills people have. A highly influential 1999 study that Currie wrote with Rosemary Hyson at the US Bureau of Labor Statistics marked a key moment. It found that children's health at birth correlates with health issues far into adulthood. They tracked seventeen thousand children born in the United Kingdom during one week in 1958 and compiled data on them through adulthood. They found that children born healthier were more likely to pass their high school exams—their English and Math Ordinary Levels—and more likely to have a job by age thirty-three.[7]

This study stands out because Currie and Hyson were among the first economists to show that what happens in a mother's womb interacts with other forms of economic inequality to have long-lasting economic effects. They used cutting-edge data and empirical techniques to account for all kinds of differences known by economists to affect employment outcomes— such as a child's family circumstances, family income, and race—and demonstrated causality from low birth weight to adult employment experiences. Causality is notoriously difficult to prove, but Currie and Hyson succeeded in showing it.

This research is emblematic of the rigorous work now being done in many quarters to explain varying employment and earnings outcomes that is both changing economics and the discipline's policy recommendations. It's long been accepted within economics and policymaking circles that providing universal access to primary, secondary, and even higher education is important to keeping our nation's workforce among the most productive in the world. Harvard University's Claudia Goldin and Lawrence Katz summarize findings to date about how education spurs innovation and higher productivity in *The Race Between Education and Technology*. Strong evidence also suggests that the United States' early investment in widespread education was the key factor propelling the US economy throughout the twentieth century. Currie and her colleagues find that we need to look further back in people's lives than previously understood. If we can determine that inequality blocks opportunity very early—and admit that there's nothing an infant or toddler can do to overcome it—then we have our proof that society must step up its support for them.[8]

To be sure, the purpose of child-rearing is not solely to produce the best future workers. Yet, if we care about the future of our economy, we as citizens need to close the large and growing gaps in resources available to young children and their parents, and remove the obstructions created by socioeconomic inequality. This is especially imperative because skill gaps found among even the youngest children can persist across lifetimes. Investments in young children pay off in higher productivity and growth for decades to come.

## The Opportunity of a Lifetime

One of Currie's contributions is a series of comprehensive reviews of the growing literature about long-term effects of early childhood experiences, laying out what's known and where questions remain. In 2011, she and Columbia University economist Douglas Almond published a 171-page summary of the available research on early childhood learning and how it affects adult outcomes. Summing it up, they conclude that "child and family characteristics measured at school entry do as much to explain future outcomes as factors that labor economists have more traditionally focused on, such as years of education."[9] This literature review highlights how the "credibility revolution" in economics has changed the profession's conclusions. Despite its newness, Currie and Almond argue that the evidence on the importance of early childhood is compelling because researchers have by now conducted so many studies showing causality running from certain childhood experiences to particular adult outcomes. The research could be done in a rigorous way only because of the emergence of new data and methods.[10]

A particularly strong example is an early paper Currie wrote with Duke University economist Duncan Thomas, reporting that children's test scores at age seven can explain 4 percent to 5 percent of the variation in employment at age thirty-three. They also found that, all else being equal, among thirty-three-year-old men in their study, those whose reading scores at age seven had been in the bottom quartile had lower wages by 20 percent than the men whose scores had been in the top quartile. For women, the difference in wages was 26 percent. The study made clear that economists had been focusing too much on people's later education and not enough on the early years.[11]

Many of the studies Currie and Almond review are of the type economists consider the gold standard of research: controlled experiments. In a controlled experiment, the researcher starts with a population of similar people and intervenes by giving one group of them the "treatment"—whether that be a new drug in medical research or, here, access to a high-quality preschool program. The remaining subjects make up the "control group" that does not receive the treatment. Researchers then measure outcomes for both groups, having already established relevant baseline information about subjects before they experienced the treatment. Assigning otherwise similar children to treatment groups and control groups means that researchers can be confident that any statistically significant differences in outcomes can be attributed to the treatment, rather than some other factor.

More than a half-century ago, a study was conducted at a preschool in Ypsilanti, Michigan—the High/Scope Perry Preschool Study—that would turn out to be one of the most famous controlled experiments. Researchers studied a group of 123 children from low-income, African American families who were considered to be at high risk of school failure. At ages three and four, about half of the children were randomly assigned to a high-quality preschool program, while the rest did not attend preschool. Researchers have tracked the outcomes for this population since. Around the turn of the century, when the subjects turned forty years old, those who

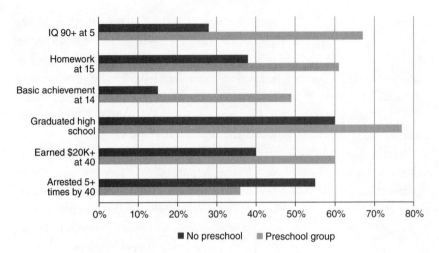

Figure 1.1    Early childhood education has important lifetime outcomes
Major findings of the High/Scope Perry Preschool Study.

*Source:* Lawrence J. Schweinhart, Jeanne Montie, Zongping Xiang, W. Steven Barnett, Clive R. Belfield, and Milagros Nores, "The High/Scope Perry Preschool Study Through Age 40: Summary, Conclusions, and Frequently Asked Questions." High/Scope Press, 2005.

had attended preschool were found to rate higher on a variety of success measures. Greater percentages of them had completed high school, attended college, had stable housing arrangements, and invested in savings accounts. On average, they accrued higher earnings, had significantly fewer arrests, and had better relationships with their families.[12] (See Figure 1.1.)

A few other such experiments have yielded similarly incontrovertible evidence that participation in high-quality preschool programs improve people's lifelong outcomes. This kind of research cannot be done in the same way today, however, precisely because social scientists are now more attuned to how dramatically preschool can affect subjects' later lives. Just as medical scientists today would not conduct a controlled experiment on the effects of levels of lead in children's drinking water, it would be unconscionable to stage an experiment that deliberately denied to some toddlers a factor that researchers now know to be vital to their development. Fortunately, scholars have developed more ethical ways to gather the data needed to show causality, including through so-called natural experiments.[13]

The effects of early-childhood programs weren't immediately obvious to researchers. During the 1970s and 1980s, a series of studies—including analyses of the Perry Preschool data—found that while these kinds of interventions appeared to have immediate positive effects in boosting skills, these advantages faded over the course of children's elementary and secondary schooling. Newer and more detailed research, however, showed that while the effects may fade for a while, they show up again later in life. Currie was a key player in this academic debate. Along with Duncan Thomas and Eliana Garcés, a former deputy chief economist of the European Commission, she reexamined early findings from a study of the Head Start program in the United States, which had shown the positive effects on reading and math test scores fading over time. This was a natural experiment because many children had been eligible for the program in the 1960s, but not all of them were enrolled. Currie and her coauthors compared the adult experience of people who had participated in Head Start to people who had been eligible for the program but did not participate. The Head Start participants, they found, had higher rates of high school graduation and college attendance, earned more on entering the job market, and were less likely to have been charged with a crime.[14]

While much of this research on early childhood interventions focuses on poor children, there are also indications that universally-available programs do good. In Oklahoma, for example, Tulsa's universal pre-kindergarten program has been shown to have significant, positive effects on students' academic outcomes and well-being through middle school. A long-term study of the program by Georgetown University professors William Gormley and Deborah Phillips and Sara Anderson at West Virginia University reports that, eight years after pre-kindergarten, participating children performed better on standardized math tests and were more likely by six percentage points to be enrolled in an honors class.[15]

Studies like these have made researchers curious about just what happens in the preschool years. Is it that children learn basic things—such as the alphabet—that lay the foundation to acquire skills like reading and writing earlier? Or is it more important that preschool teaches them how to sit still and focus, so that they enter elementary school better able to learn in general? Or is it both kinds of skills? To explore this, University of Chicago economist James Heckman introduced the concept of "non-cognitive skills" into econometric modeling and the measurement of human capital. These skills include behavioral habits, social strengths, and emotional tendencies such as a child's perseverance or ability to get along with others.

According to Heckman, non-cognitive skills develop early in life and, besides being important on their own, support later acquisition of the skills economists more traditionally study. A child who can delay gratification, for example, or who displays grit and tenacity, is better equipped to learn and acquire other, measurable skills, even if that advantage doesn't show up yet in school testing. While the term is uncommon in other disciplines, economists use it to distinguish between skills that can and cannot be measured by standard cognitive assessments.[16]

Currie takes issue with this framing, arguing that it's not a useful way to think about the question of human capital, especially because it isn't clear what exactly is covered by the term *non-cognitive skills*. "Do you mean somebody's mental health?" she asks. "Do you mean something that's constant over time, like a personality trait?" She knows that "what people have in mind when they say cognitive is something like an IQ test." But her point is that those tests have always been confounded by other variables: "if I was to give you an IQ test when you were really hungry and tired, you would get a different mark on it than if I gave it to you when you had just eaten well and were well rested and were in a good mood. So, there is a distinction there, but it shouldn't be as rigid as people like to draw it." Given what we know about human development, Currie generally believes that distinguishing between cognitive and non-cognitive skills isn't "very meaningful."[17]

In her view, a better question to ask is: How far back in a person's life can researchers go as they attempt to link measurable adult outcomes to identifiable differences in the childhood experiences of otherwise similar people? Currie points to David J. Barker's "fetal origins hypothesis"—the idea that adult health outcomes have their origins in experiences in utero—which triggered an explosion of research in his field of epidemiology. As she says, "It's a sea-change in the science, as well. So, things like understanding epigenetics as well as genetics—I would say that's all in the last twenty years that we've understood that."[18] Barker was a physician as well as a clinical epidemiologist, and was one of the first scientists to challenge the prevailing wisdom that many disorders were primarily the result of bad genetics and bad lifestyles. One of his most compelling and commonly cited studies was a 1993 *Lancet* article describing how undernutrition during gestation increases likelihood of disease in adult life—and emphasizing the role of maternal nutrition in determining fetal health. He and his coauthors discovered that a child's birth weight is not just an indicator of infant health but also a key predictor of future health; in particular, relationships were shown between birth weights and increased rates of cardiovascular disease and diabetes in later life. Currie and Almond would later write about an important implication of this fetal origins hypothesis for human capital development: if the objective is to help children throughout their lives, then policies that focus on pregnant women (and more generally, women of child-bearing age) may be more effective than current policies that direct most resources to the sick.[19]

Six years after publishing their first literature review—a short time for academic research—Currie and Almond, along with University of Sydney economics professor Valentina Duque, again surveyed the latest research on early childhood learning. They found a multitude of new studies by economists confirming and extending the early findings highlighted in their first review. One study exemplifies the work being done; it finds that a 10 percent increase in birth weight increases a child's probability of graduating high school by a little less than 1 percent, their earnings by about 1 percent, and their height by three quarters of a centimeter by age eighteen. Currie, Almond, and Duque find the body of research so compelling that they open with a declaration: "That prenatal events can have life-long consequences is now well established."[20]

This is not to say that people's life paths are set before they're even born. Later interventions can and do matter and, even for the very young, policy can and does make a difference. "I think it is hard to talk about prenatal influences or fetal influences without sounding deterministic, but it isn't actually deterministic at all," Currie told me. "And one way that you can see that is that the same shock will typically have a much greater effect on a poor person than on a richer person. What that tells you is that there is something that can be done about it—and the richer parents are doing it, whatever it is. So, if you could find that and put it in a bottle or put it in a program, then you would be able to mitigate the effects of these early-childhood insults."[21]

As of now, the United States ranks twentieth out of thirty-one member nations of the Organization of Economic Co-operation and Development in the share of infants and toddlers in formal childcare, and ranks twenty-ninth in terms of children enrolled in preschool. Now that we know more about whether and how inequality affects children's access to resources early in life, we need to be asking how policy could improve outcomes across the income spectrum.[22]

## Income and Wealth Inequality Obstructs Children from Having Access to Resources

As researchers document how important it is for children, parents, and parents-to-be to have access to resources, the economic trends have been discouraging. In recent decades, economic inequality in the United States—in income, in wealth, and across neighborhoods—has risen markedly. In many homes and neighborhoods, there's not enough food to eat or books to read or afterschool programs to attend. In others there's a bevy of food options, books and quiet places to study, heat in winter and ways to cool off in the summer, access to prenatal care, high-quality teachers, and extra-curricular lessons and activities. These economic circumstances affect children's development in everything from their health and ability to focus at school to their educational opportunities—and these, in turn, affect their economic outcomes as adults.

At some level, this is all about money. A comprehensive literature survey by London School of Economics researchers Kerris Cooper and Kitty Stewart looked at thirty-four relevant research studies from 1988 to 2012 and drew this conclusion: "Poorer children have worse cognitive, social-behavioral and health outcomes in part *because they are poorer,* not just because low income is correlated with other household and parental characteristics."[23] Case in point: University of California–Irvine's Greg J. Duncan, New York University's Pamela A. Morris, and Columbia University's Chris Rodrigues find that a $1,000 increase in annual income among parents increases young children's achievement by 5 to 6 percent of a standard deviation. Their results, they write, "suggest that family income has a policy-relevant, positive impact on the eventual school achievement of preschool children."[24]

Policy can address inequality and improve children's outcomes by simply giving low-income families money. Economists Gordon B. Dahl of the University of California–San Diego and Lance Lochner at University of Western Ontario use an innovative method to study the impact of income changes on children's development outcomes focusing on a population of low-income families with at least one person in the workforce. They looked at changes in the amount of money families could receive from the Earned

Income Tax Credit (EITC), a federal tax credit to working low-income families. They find that a $1,000 increase in the EITC has a causal effect on children's performance in school, at least in the short run, raising combined math and reading test scores by 6 percent of a standard deviation. University of British Columbia economist Kevin Milligan and INSEAD professor Mark Stabile look at expansions in the Canadian child-benefit program and find the same positive effects of extra income on children's test scores there.[25]

Policymakers can also give families access to resources—such as high-quality public schools, pre-kindergarten programs, libraries, parks, safe neighborhoods, and safe drinking water—that close the gaps created by economic inequality. In a recent paper, economists Hilary Hoynes at University of California–Berkeley and Diane Whitmore Schanzenbach at Northwestern University looked at the research on whether children's varying access to safety net programs—nutrition, cash payments, and health care—affects adult outcomes. They found compelling evidence that safety net programs have lasting effects on the lives of poor children. "We've started to accumulate a body of evidence," Hoynes recently told me, "that all points to the fact that providing more assistance when children are young seems to lead to important improvements in where they end up in adulthood." This gives them the confidence "to say something—while it's still a young and emerging literature—about the potential benefits of protection in the long run."[26]

Other research by Hoynes and Schanzenbach, with Almond, found that children whose mothers had access to the Supplemental Nutrition Assistance Program (formerly food stamps) when they were in utero were born healthier. This study linked the receipt of this nutrition benefit by a child's family to the child's later outcomes in terms of health and economic well-being as an adult. Adults whose families had received the benefit were significantly less likely to have "metabolic syndrome"—that is, a combination of obesity, high blood pressure, and diabetes. They were more likely, by 18 percentage points, to graduate from high school. They were also less likely to receive the benefit as an adult. The early investment in their well-being seemingly led to economic outcomes that meant fewer of them needed such supports later on. These add up to economywide implications.[27]

The time parents spend with their child during a child's earliest years is also critical and the evidence indicates that this may be just as important as monetary expenditures. Using detailed information on the time children spend in activities with both parents, economists Daniela Del Boca at the

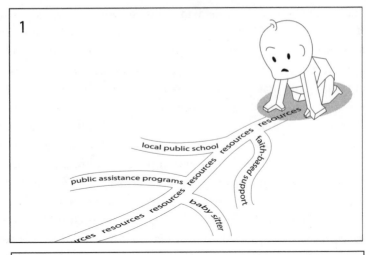

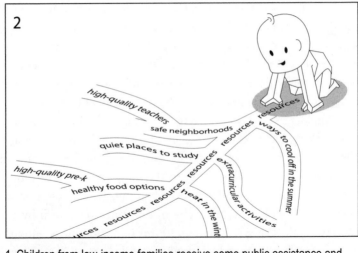

1. Children from low-income families receive some public assistance and community support but... 2. children from wealthy families have more resources available to them.

University of Turin, Christopher Flinn at New York University, and Matthew Wiswall at Arizona State University find that both mothers' and fathers' time is critical to a child's development. They focus not just on family income but on what money means for a family. They conclude that while monetary expenditures on children affect their cognitive development, this impact is modest compared to other factors. This is consistent with research by University of Wisconsin–Madison professor Lawrence M. Berger, Brown University president Christina Paxson, and Columbia University professor Jane Waldfogel. They examined data from the Fragile Families and Child Wellbeing Study, which tracks a cohort of five thousand children in several large US cities born between 1998 and 2000. While parental income has an effect on children's outcomes, they found that what is important is what that income buys and what this means for a child's home environment.[28]

Parents with higher incomes and more advanced education seek to make the most of their time with their children by investing in parenting techniques to boost their children's skills development. Child development expert Ariel Kalil at the University of Chicago's Harris School of Public Policy shows that, over the past few decades, big differences have emerged in how rich and poor parents interact with their children. While some environmental characteristics have improved for low-income families, particularly with regard to literacy, rich families have pulled ahead in terms of their children's school-readiness activities. High-income parents, for example, read to their children more than low-income parents do, and engage their children in cultural activities, such as visiting zoos and museums, at a higher rate than low-income parents. University of California–San Diego economists Garey Ramey and Valerie Ramey argue that the increased time college-educated parents spend caring for children is due to the heightened competition around college admissions. In what they call the "rug rat race," they see parents driven to do ever more to help their children get into better-ranked colleges.[29]

To be sure, one aspect of economic inequality is that most parents do not have access to the work-life scheduling policies and support they need to address conflicts between work and caring for young children. Among the world's most advanced economies, the United States stands alone in not providing paid family leave to all parents nationwide, and neither does it ensure that parents have family-friendly schedules that allow them time to care. Its lack of such supports disproportionally harms lower-income families.[30]

Money can buy a family solutions that reduce stress. There is evidence that the greater stresses associated with lower incomes lead to worse outcomes that stay with the children of over-stressed parents over time. The psychology literature shows that economic hardship is associated with parental emotional distress and conflict, as well as harsh parenting and behavioral problems for children. Economists have applied this knowledge to economic questions. Ann Huff Stevens at the University of California–Irvine and Jessamyn Schaller at the University of Arizona find that when a parent loses a job, this increases the chances that a child is held back a grade by 15 percent. University of California–Berkeley professor Rucker C. Johnson and his colleagues look at the stress of inflexible workplaces. They find that children of working mothers exhibit fewer behavioral problems when their mothers experience job stability, relative to children whose mothers' work arrangements are unstable.[31]

There is also evidence that economic stress blocks parents' access to the services they need for their children to be healthy. The Great Recession led families to sharply curtail spending as the collapse of the housing bubble led to both high unemployment and declines in home values—for homeowners, usually the family's most important asset. Currie asked what the lifelong implications might be for children in such economically stressed families. In places with more home foreclosures, she found increased numbers of urgent and unscheduled hospital and emergency room visits. According to her research with Erdal Tekin at American University, much of the increase in urgent care was due to cutbacks people made on other kinds of doctor visits, such as preventive care or care for chronic conditions. Currie and Tekin showed this wasn't just a consequence of unemployment; urgent-care visits increased at the beginning of the crisis, as home values began plummeting but long before unemployment rose.[32]

One often overlooked aspect of parents' financial resources is how they determine the neighborhoods in which families live. In the United States, inequality across neighborhoods explains a great deal of the variation in children's access to high-quality education and public services. As Raj Chetty's Equality of Opportunity project shows, children who grow up in communities with less income inequality, less residential segregation, better primary schools, and greater family stability are more likely to be upwardly mobile. In a paper with Harvard economist Nathaniel Hendren, Chetty shows that neighborhoods have causal effects on children's outcomes—or, to put it another way, some neighborhoods obstruct children's ability to be upwardly mobile. A child who moves from a low-mobility to a high-mobility neighborhood is more likely to earn higher income as an adult, all else equal, and the younger that child is when her family moves, the larger the effect.[33] (See Figure 1.2.)

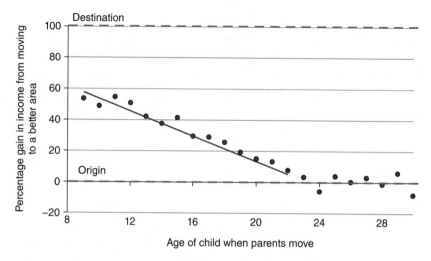

**Figure 1.2** Moving to a different US neighborhood as a child affects income in adulthood

Source: Raj Chetty and Nathaniel Hendren, "The Impacts of Neighborhoods on Intergenerational Mobility: Executive Summary," April 2015.

A particular feature of low-income neighborhoods is that they are more likely to have higher levels of air pollution and other pollutants. "Whether it's air pollution or factory emissions or living near a busy highway or water pollution," Currie says, "almost anything that I've looked at, more disadvantaged women are more likely to be exposed to it."[34] Currie and University of Zurich economist Hannes Schwandt document that when pregnant women are exposed to high levels of pollution, their children have a higher-than-average chance of having low birth weights. Thus, a child's neighborhood can have a detrimental effect on her well-being that carries into adulthood. For this study, the catastrophic September 11, 2001, terrorist attack on New York City created the conditions for a natural experiment: data could be compiled on pregnant women who were exposed to the air pollution caused by the collapse of the twin towers. Compared with their older siblings, children born in the aftermath of the attack were more likely to be born early, to be in the neonatal intensive care unit, and to have low birth weight.[35]

More generally, Currie and her colleagues find that exposure to pollution could explain up to six percent of the gap in birth weights between infants of white, college-educated mothers and infants of black mothers who didn't finish high school. This is especially high because black families and low-income families are more likely to live in communities near highways and traffic congestion, and less likely to have sufficient insulation in their homes. Compared to children of white, college-educated mothers, children born to less-educated mothers and mothers of color are simply more likely to be exposed to pollution in utero.[36]

## Educational Inequality Blocks Opportunity at All Levels

The message of Currie's work is that, if we want to remove the obstructions to children's development that inequality causes, we need to focus on families with the youngest children—even families as they plan to have children—and particularly, families of color. The findings of this revolutionary research are reshaping our understanding of how education investments affect people's lives as they grow up. While we've long known that education matters for future economic outcomes, this new body of scholarship sheds light on how and where policy can have the largest positive effects.

The United States became an economic powerhouse in no small part because it was first to use tax revenues to provide free, universal primary education—ensuring that not only wealthy children but all children had access to skills. In the late nineteenth and early twentieth centuries, the United States trailed only Norway, the Netherlands, Sweden, Canada, and Switzerland in average years of education for those fifteen years and older; by the mid-twentieth century, the United States led the world in secondary school enrollment and graduation rates, and trailed only Switzerland in literacy and numeracy. In economist Claudia Goldin's words: "The rate of increase was nothing short of spectacular and the levels attained were unequaled by any other country until much later in the century."[37] Yet, today's high inequality is creating serious obstructions to maintaining this lead.[38]

Comparing different neighborhoods, one of the most important outcomes of inequality in family incomes is the varying quality of public schools. In the United States, roughly 45 percent of funding for public schools comes from local sources—mostly from property taxes—which means that higher-income neighborhoods typically have better-funded schools. For a long time, the economic research was mixed on whether these large gaps in public school financing mattered to children's outcomes. The past few years have brought important research using newly available, long-term data. Now able to examine whether the amount of money a school has affects educational outcomes, researchers are discovering how some lifelong outcomes are rooted in economic inequality, and where children grow up.[39]

Schanzenbach, with University of California–Berkeley economists Jesse Rothstein and Julien Lafortune, have examined what these differences in financing mean for children's outcomes. They studied student achievement across high-income and low-income school districts by making use of a natural experiment. In more than twenty-five states over the course of the 1990s, court orders and legislative reforms led to sharp, immediate, and sustained increases in spending in low-income school districts. This allowed the researchers to compare high-income and low-income districts within a state before and after the change in policy, using test score data from the National Assessment of Educational Progress. They found that financial reforms led to a slow but steady rise in test scores of students in low-income school districts. Their results indicate that addressing school financing could be one of the most important tools available to policymakers to improve student outcomes. As Schanzenbach notes, "there are just not that many tools at policymakers' disposal at a large scale to be able to move student achievement."[40]

In a related study looking at the effects of school financing reforms, economists C. Kirabo Jackson at Northwestern University, Rucker C. Johnson at the University of California–Berkeley, and Claudia Persico at the University of Wisconsin–Madison examine the long-term economic outcomes for children. They find that a 10 percent increase in per-pupil spending each year across twelve years of public school leads to 0.3 more completed years of education, 7.3 percent higher wages, and a 3.7 percentage-point decrease in the annual incidence of adult poverty. They also find that the effects are much more pronounced for children from low-income families.[41] (See Figures 1.3a and 1.3b.)

The effects of economic inequality on children's educational attainment don't end with secondary school; inequality in parental income also affects children's college attendance. University of Michigan economists Martha

## Effect of school spending changes on high school graduation

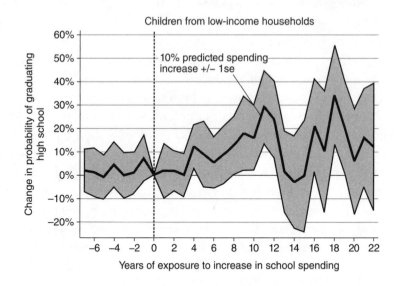

Children from low-income households

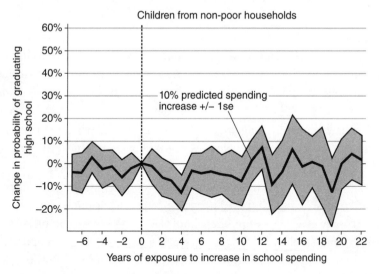

Children from non-poor households

## Effect of school spending changes on adult poverty

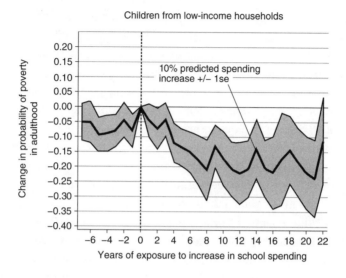

Children from low-income households

10% predicted spending
increase +/– 1se

Years of exposure to increase in school spending

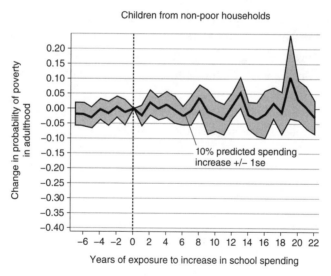

Children from non-poor households

10% predicted spending
increase +/– 1se

Years of exposure to increase in school spending

Figure 1.3   School spending levels matter for adult poverty
Note: Estimates for a predicted 10 percent increase in school spending. Shaded
area depicts +/– 1 standard error.

*Source:* C. Kirabo Jackson, Rucker C. Johnson, and Claudia Persico, "The Effects of School Spending on Educational and Economic Outcomes: Evidence from School Finance Reforms," Working Paper (National Bureau of Economic Research, January 2015).

Bailey and Susan Dynarski have documented that the fraction of children attending college has risen markedly among children of high-income families, but far less among children of low- and moderate-income families. Further, the most selective colleges tend to draw students from the very top of the income distribution. In their recent study, Chetty and Hendren estimate what percent of students in colleges across the United States come from the top 1 percent of families by income. They also calculate how well colleges do at moving lower-income students up the income ladder. Their findings are striking: Ivy League colleges enroll more students from the top 1 percent than from the entire bottom half of the income distribution. While some top-end colleges enroll sizable numbers of low-income students, state universities tend to do better at delivering upward economic mobility.[42]

Inequality's effects on children attending college may also be about the social and cultural capital held by higher-income families. Caroline Hoxby of Stanford University and Christopher Avery of Harvard's Kennedy School wondered how much of the college education gap could be attributed to adults in low-income children's lives being unfamiliar with the college application process. They looked specifically at low-income students whose achievements would likely mean that selective colleges would not only admit them but provide financial aid generous enough to make attendance affordable—perhaps even more affordable than attending a less selective school. The majority of these high achievers did not even apply to selective schools. The authors surmise that many students were simply uninformed about their college options given their qualifications. For others, social and cultural concerns held them back from applying to selective colleges despite knowing they were qualified. In a similar vein, a research team led by the University of Michigan's Susan Dynarski recently found that a group of low-income students who were encouraged to apply and promised free college tuition submitted more than double the number of applications of a group of students who were not contacted. More than a quarter of the additional students who applied would otherwise not have attended college at all.[43]

Getting into college, of course, isn't enough. A student also needs to graduate. There is growing evidence that economic inequality not only plays an important role, but that, increasingly, college students from less-privileged, low-income backgrounds are less likely than others to finish their degrees. Bailey and Dynarski compare two cohorts—one of people born around 1960 and the other of people born around 1980—and find that gaps

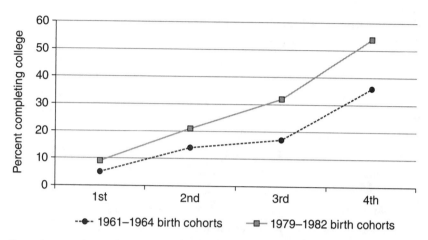

Figure 1.4   College completion gaps persist and grow
Share of students completing college in the United States by income quartile and year of birth.

*Source:* Martha Bailey and Susan Dynarski, "Gains and Gaps: Changing Inequality in US College Entry and Completion," National Bureau of Economic Research, 2012.

in college completion have not only persisted but grown. In the top quartile, college completion rates increased from 36 percent to 54 percent, while completion rates for the bottom quartile increased minimally, from 5 percent to 9 percent. Inequality in both college entry and completion between the top and bottom is greater compared to two decades ago, even among students with the same measured cognitive skills.[44] (See Figure 1.4.)

Inequality in access to higher education has been magnified in recent years as for-profit colleges have focused their recruitment strategies on lower-income students. For-profit colleges, which grew rapidly in number and size from the 1970s until they received greater scrutiny under the Obama administration, are run by private, profit-seeking businesses and rely on their students' federal financial aid for the vast majority of their revenues. Tressie McMillan Cottom, a sociologist at Virginia Commonwealth University, has both worked in the for-profit college industry and studied it. According to her, for-profit schools prey upon disadvantaged demographic groups and their hopes that higher education is a ticket to a better life and fulfillment of the American Dream. These colleges use highly aggressive sales tactics targeted at low-income people, but they don't deliver on their educational and career promises. On average, they are 30 percent to 40 percent more expensive and have four-year degree completion rates 12 percent to 19 percent lower than their not-for-profit peers. Students who graduate from for-profit colleges are also more likely to suffer bouts of unemployment six years after graduation than those who graduated from not-for-profit schools.[45]

To be sure, schools are not the only factor explaining differences in upward mobility and labor market outcomes across places. "The educational system plays only a small role in explaining differences between high- and low-opportunity areas," Rothstein argues. "Labor market institutions—such as minimum wages, the ability to form and join unions, the career structures of local industries, and other determinants of earnings inequality—are likely to play much larger roles and are also likely to be more powerful levers with which to promote equality of opportunity."[46]

## Loosening Inequality's Grip on Our Economy by Investing in Children

Economic inequality in a variety of manifestations creates obstructions in children's ability to have access to the opportunities they need to be successful later in life. From the womb to early adulthood, a child's position on the income ladder determines her access to resources and education, with effects that can affect adult employment and earnings. The common view in America has long been that inequality is not worrisome as long as there is ample economic opportunity. To the extent that Horatio Alger's classic stories still applied—that people could by their own efforts rise from rags to middle-class stability—the American Dream remained alive and well. Indeed, it provided the incentive to work hard. But the body of research profiled in this chapter makes clear that, if Alger's characters were created today, they would need to start their determined climb upward from the womb, or at least from toddlerhood—which certainly isn't reasonable.

The evidence today points to the conclusion that there is no generational "reboot" putting everyone at an equal starting position. We must implement new policy to make that a reality. By showing that investments in early childhood are a cost-effective way to improve children's outcomes as adults, the research presented here underscores the folly of Gov. Brownback's education cuts and the tragedy of Flint's water crisis. The studies are so rigorous and, by now, so numerous that this conclusion is beyond reasonable debate. Fortunately, they are generating a broad consensus that investments in education—especially early childhood education—are in the national interest. The US Chamber of Commerce has weighed in, as have former Federal Reserve Chair Ben Bernanke and many others. Even so, there is too little action.[47]

Today, we need a national commitment not only to ensure equal access to primary and secondary school, but to end unequal access to early childhood education and care. We will need a range of policies working synergistically. Currie put it this way: "I'm not sure that you can even identify policies that only affect one aspect [of human capital] and not affect other aspects. By their nature, there's going to be a lot of spillover and overlap in the effects of policy."[48] To this end, the federal government should establish a standing working group to coordinate efforts across government to ensure that all children have access to adequate resources. They should start by considering how environmental factors—from lead in the water to smog to climate change—harm the next generation and exacerbate inequality, and implement ways to ensure that all children have access to a healthy environment.

To ensure that all children—rich and poor alike—have access to the resources they need to thrive, policymakers must focus their attention on a number of areas simultaneously. First, the United States should embark on a plan to ensure that every child has access to safe, affordable, and enriching early childhood education. This should be set up in a way that recognizes that most parents now hold jobs outside the home; in other words, these programs must address not only children's educational needs, but also parents' childcare needs while they are at work. There are plenty of models to choose from. In Washington, DC, all children are entitled to two years of free, full-day preschool across the city's public schools and some private programs, and this program currently serves nine out of ten of the city's four-year-olds and seven out of ten of its three-year-olds. As well as improving outcomes for children, the program, rolled out in 2009, has increased mothers' labor force participation rate by about ten percentage points. Many other states and local governments offer variations of preschool programs, but access to high-quality preschool should not vary based on a family's zip code.[49]

The benefits to families and the economy are substantial. Currie has found that universal pre-kindergarten and quality childcare helps all children, but helps those from disadvantaged backgrounds the most. It both improves later earnings and reduces the likelihood that a child will grow up to live in poverty or commit a crime. Economist Robert Lynch at Washington College and former Washington Center for Equitable Growth research analyst Kavya Vaghul estimate that if a public, voluntary, high-quality, universal pre-kindergarten program were made available to all three- and four-year-olds across the United States, it would address significant social and health problems and more than pay for itself over time. It would take just eight years for the total annual benefits of such a program to exceed the costs, and within thirty-five years, the surplus would total $81.6 billion—more than double the costs.[50]

Early childhood education must be paired with a sensible policy on childcare. In the United States, there is too little quality care available and where it is available, it's too expensive—especially for the youngest children. Policies to both improve quality and ensure affordability need to be fully integrated into the early childhood education agenda. Louisiana, for example, offers tax credits to low-income families who enroll their children in high-quality childcare programs, and to businesses with childcare expenses. A tax credit program, however, doesn't help parents with up-front costs or ensure that childcare workers receive good pay and benefits—which is necessary to ensure high-quality care. The primary source of federal funding for childcare subsidies for low-income working families is the Child Care Development Fund, but this reaches only about one in six eligible children—and the eligibility thresholds mean that many who could use it are ineligible. Ideas for improving access to childcare include expanding subsidies to ensure that no family pays more than a reasonable share of its income—perhaps seven percent. This would improve the wages of childcare workers, and in doing so boost quality. We must also expand current programs that we know are effective, like Head Start, so as to reach more children.[51]

Early childhood education will take families only so far. All parents need access to workplace policies that allow them time to care for their children. Six states have put in place statewide paid-family-leave programs (and soon the District of Columbia will join them), which ensure that any parent, not just one at a high income level, can spend time with a new baby or a seriously ill child and have income support. Families also need new rules governing work hours. In the United States, we have a federal limit on overwork for some workers, but no rules requiring schedules to be family-friendly or mandating paid time off to care for loved ones. In 2014, San Francisco enacted the Retail Workers Bill of Rights to limit the ability of employers to set unpredictable and last-minute schedules. Soon thereafter, in 2015, eighteen states and municipalities introduced similar work-hour legislation.[52]

One thing is clear: where a child lives affects what resources they have access to, from clean water to good schools. When policymakers increase elementary and secondary school spending broadly, with larger increases in low-income districts, the absolute and relative achievement of students in low-income districts rises. This evidence counters claims that school spending increases are spent inefficiently. The research also shows that the average low-income student does not live in a particularly low-income district, meaning that increases in funding aren't enough—we need policies designed to tackle achievement gaps within districts between high- and low-income (and white and black) students.[53]

There is evidence that removing obstructions to educational opportunity will improve children's skills and future macroeconomic outcomes. According to the internationally conducted Program for International Student Assessment test, as of 2015 the United States is ranked thirty-first out of the thirty-five OECD countries in mathematics, twentieth in reading, and nineteenth in science. Lynch finds that if the United States could bring test scores for US high school students up to the average of other developed economies, this would generate a cumulative increase in US gross domestic product of an estimated $2.5 trillion by 2050—more than 12 percent of US GDP in 2017.[54]

Time and time again, we see that having a more productive and more innovative workforce comes from providing widespread access to education and training. This is one conclusion that economists are in general agreement upon—and have been for a long time. Economists have recognized the importance of human capital at least since the 1960s, when Nobel laureate Gary Becker published *Human Capital*. In it, he laid out how investments in people—through education, training, and care—are as important to the economy as physical capital. What we know now is that, to ensure every child has opportunity, we must focus on addressing inequality's gaps down to the youngest ages. These findings underscore how we need both policies that are universal—giving every child the opportunity for an education—and policies that are targeted toward those at the bottom of the socioeconomic ladder. This is especially important given our nation's stark divides by race.[55]

# 2

# Skills, Talent, and Innovation

I N THE FALL OF 2017, #MeToo lit up the internet. Women—and some men—shared their gut-wrenching stories of sexual harassment and assault in the workplace. The catalyst for the national conversation was the allegation that famed film producer Harvey Weinstein had sexually assaulted and harassed women who had reason to fear his power over their Hollywood careers. According to a number of women, Weinstein had been using his industry clout to compel actresses to succumb to his lechery, rewarding those who did and punishing those who did not. As well as being morally repugnant, behavior like this is economic discrimination; people were punished in the marketplace for non-economic reasons. Actress Ashley Judd filed a lawsuit against Weinstein saying that he "torpedoed" her career after she refused his advances. For example, Weinstein told director Peter Jackson that he'd had "a bad experience" working with her. This, her suit alleges, prevented her being cast in the Oscar-winning trilogy *The Lord of the Rings*.[1]

The #MeToo moment provides a dramatic reminder that the market doesn't always reward talent, skills, and hard work. If the market for actresses worked in practice the way it does in introductory economics textbooks, then Weinstein would have been driven out long ago by competitors whose casting decisions were based solely on assessments of whose talent shone brightest onscreen. This should have been the case especially because Weinstein's behavior was an open secret. During the 2013 Oscar ceremony, host Seth MacFarlane followed his introduction of the nominees for best supporting actress with a joke: "Congratulations, you five ladies no longer have to pretend to be attracted to Harvey Weinstein." The Hollywood-insider audience responded with uncomfortable laughter.[2] Yet the market neither corrected Weinstein's behavior nor punished his production company, Miramax. Instead, it took the pressure of social media—and the bravery of many willing to speak up—to end his reign of terror.

The #MeToo movement is not, of course, only about the film industry. Across the economy, workers in all kinds of jobs have to deal with on-the-job harassment. And that's only one kind of discrimination rearing its ugly head in the United States. These kinds of obstructions have large economic costs. If firms are profit-seeking enterprises, they should simply want the most productive workers; if investors wish for higher returns, they should be searching for the most innovative people to invest in. For these reasons, Nobel laureate Kenneth Arrow went so far as to say that, with the erosion of legal structures that promote discrimination, exclusion along the lines of race and gender would disappear. Yet that hasn't happened. The market on its own hasn't eradicated discrimination, even though it is economically irrational. Indeed, a few years before #MeToo, the famous investor Warren Buffett reflected on how economically dumb it is to discriminate against women: "we had all this marvelous progress in the time we became a country until today. It's incredible what's happened. And for over half of that period, we wasted half our talent."[3]

Empirical evidence supports Buffett's view. One study by researchers at the University of Chicago's Booth School of Business and Stanford University shows that the entrance of women and people of color into a wider array of jobs, after the passage of the Civil Rights Act, was responsible for much of the economic growth the United States saw in the latter half of the twentieth century. They found that as historically marginalized groups were able to enter professions in which they could thrive, there was an improved allocation of talent across the economy, accounting for roughly one-quarter of the growth in output per person over the half-century they studied. Similarly, in a speech at Brown University in May 2017, then Federal Reserve Chair Janet Yellen estimated that more female participation in the workforce accounted for about a half percentage point of economic growth every year between 1948 and 1990 in the United States (years over which the share of women in the workplace grew sharply).[4]

These findings are consistent with Adam Smith's economic story that the profit motive and competition push economic actors toward productive ends. But, for his invisible hand to deliver win-win outcomes, incentives must encourage activities that are economically beneficial—such as brewing a better-tasting beer by inventing a better brewing vat—and people, ideas, and capital cannot be blocked from opportunities to participate fully in the marketplace. Workers must be able to get jobs that will make the most of their skills and interests and allow them to contribute most to the productivity of the nation. What happened at Miramax—and in so many other workplaces across the country—signals that this doesn't always happen.

Whether talent and skill are fully rewarded in the market or whether economic inequality of one variety or several (based on gender, race and ethnicity, education, consumption, income, or wealth) gives some people or institutions the power to block Smith's invisible hand is an empirical question—one that has been explored by Raj Chetty, a founding member of the steering committee of my own organization, the Washington Center for Equitable Growth. When I asked for his thoughts on the links between economic inequality and economic growth and stability, he was eager to share his research. New analysis based on better data "provides some of the first sharp microeconomic evidence on issues related to inequality and growth," he told me. I could hear the excitement in his voice as he went on to say, "I think we'll be able to make a rigorous case that inequality and lack of mobility clearly dampens innovation and ultimately growth." The set of data he shared that day showed that, in a group of people with similar aptitudes, those who grew up in higher-income families are more likely to hold patents.[5]

This was especially intriguing to hear because economists have long argued about what leads people to come up with innovative ideas for building a better mousetrap—or genetically engineering a better mouse, or programming a more compelling mouse emoji. What's different now is that economists such as Chetty and his colleagues have access to more data and better methods to evaluate whether and how inequality obstructs economic opportunity and, with it, talent, productivity, and economic growth. What we're learning is that the standard economic model's hypothesis—the math which, in an earlier era of economics, John Bates Clark used to show that, in a competitive economy, people's wages are proportional to their productivity—may not represent what actually happens. Where children grow up, the color of their skin, their gender, and who their parents are all have profound effects on what kinds of economic rewards come their way.

Chetty's data and analyses on patents—like the proliferation of stories tagged #MeToo—pose serious challenges to the idea that the economy reliably rewards the talented and skilled. If all it took were financial incentives to connect talent to opportunity, then family income should not have a significant effect on whether a child grows up to be an inventor. If the market for labor worked as advertised, then sexual harassment in the workplace would be stamped out. The extent to which someone is rich or poor, experiences discrimination, or grows up in an opportunity-rich or opportunity-poor neighborhood definitely affects future economic outcomes. That's precisely how economic inequality blocks the processes that lead to productivity gains, which ultimately drive long-term growth—and why unblocking requires more than relying on the market alone to deliver solutions.

## Obstructing Potential Innovators

In "Who Becomes an Inventor in America?," Chetty and economists Alexander M. Bell, Xavier Jaravel, Neviana Petkova, and John Van Reenen provide evidence that income inequality obstructs the process of becoming an innovator—and thus, constrains innovation itself. Chetty and his colleagues looked at a child's aptitude for becoming an innovator and asked whether he goes on to become an inventive adult, measured by whether he is ever granted a patent for a new idea. To do this, they matched the names of everyone who applied for a patent in the United States between 1996 and 2014 to their parents' federal tax return data when they were children, and to the applicants' own incomes later in life. From this, they created the early drafts of the figures Chetty shared with me. They showed that someone from a family in the top 1 percent of income earners was ten times more likely to hold a patent than someone whose family was not rich.[6] (See Figure 2.1)

Figure 2.1 tells us only that parental income matters; it tells us nothing about why. Does income inequality block talented children from becoming innovators? What if rich parents are simply more likely to have innovative offspring? Econometrics can illuminate what's really going on, and Chetty and his team have the skills and talent to do the analyses. In 2013, at age thirty-three, Chetty was awarded the John Bates Clark Medal, an honor

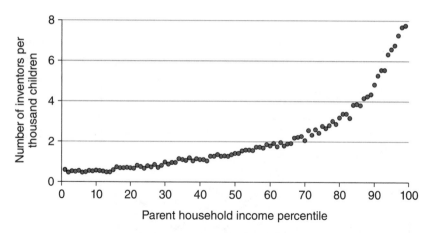

Figure 2.1   Patent rates vary with parents' incomes
Note: US citizens in the 1980–1984 birth cohorts. Parent income is mean household income from 1996–2000.

*Source:* Alexander M. Bell, Raj Chetty, Xavier Jaravel, Neviana Petkova, and John Van Reenen, "Who Becomes an Inventor in America? The Importance of Exposure to Innovation," National Bureau of Economic Research, November 2017. DOI: 10.3386/w24062.

bestowed by the American Economic Association every year to an outstanding American economist under age forty. At the time, the committee said that he had "established himself in a few short years as arguably the best applied microeconomist of his generation."[7]

For this paper, Chetty assembled a superstar research team, built a data set from a variety of original sources, and then used cutting-edge methods to show causality, not just correlation, on an economically and socially important question. He and his colleagues found a measure of children's aptitude for innovation—test scores across grades three through eight for over two million children who attended New York City public schools. Adding these scores to their data set on incomes and patents, they found that children who scored high on their third-grade math exams were more likely to grow up to be innovators, confirming the commonsense notion that children who show an aptitude for math are more likely to invent things as adults. They also found, however, that income played an important role. Among children who scored high on their third-grade math exams, those from families in the top 20 percent of the income spectrum were four times likelier to hold a patent as an adult than those who came from families in the bottom 80 percent. Inequality indeed obstructs.[8]

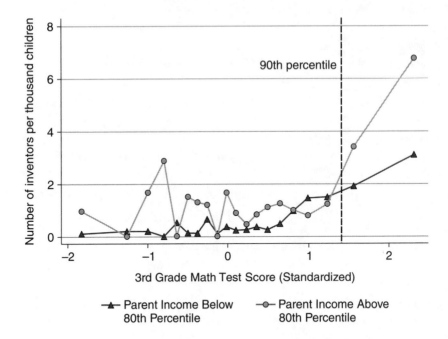

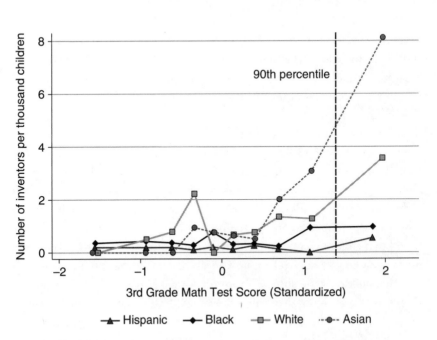

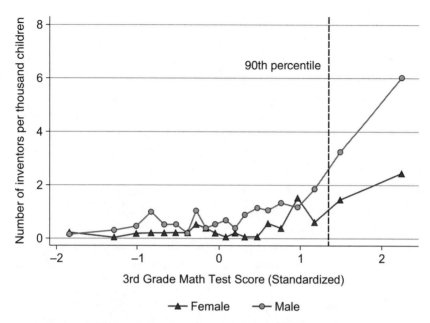

**Figure 2.2**  Patent rates vary with third-grade math test scores
a. By parental income
b. By race and ethnicity
c. By gender

*Source:* Alexander M. Be, Raj Chetty, Xavier Jaravel, Neviana Petkova, and John Van Reenen, "Who Becomes an Inventor in America? The Importance of Exposure to Innovation," National Bureau of Economic Research, November 2017.

The research team also found that the obstructions aren't only about income, they are also about a child's race and gender. Among adults who had scored high on their third-grade math tests, whites were roughly three times more likely to hold a patent than blacks—and eight times more likely than Hispanics. For blacks, there remains a gap even once the researchers account for family income—among the high-scorers, whites are almost twice as likely to become inventors after adjusting for income differences—and the gap between Hispanics and whites stays the same. There are similar gaps by gender: among those in the 1980 cohort of children who had the highest scores, men were about four times more likely than women to be inventors.[9] (See Figure 2.2.)

Based on their findings, Chetty and his colleagues decry the number of "lost Einsteins" in the United States—the smart kids who aren't lucky enough to have been born into rich families and never get to make the most of their talent, skills, and hard work. (Einstein himself worked in Switzerland's patent office and, in addition to developing his groundbreaking theories of physics, held nineteen patents, giving society his new ideas to improve refrigeration, camera technology, and even a blouse.) Chetty and his coauthors argue that there are many children who could grow up to deliver valuable ideas to the world, if only they had the same opportunities as richer children. They say the economic effects are shockingly high: "if women, minorities, and children from lower-income families were to invent at the same rate as white men from high-income (top-quintile) families, the total number of inventors in the economy would quadruple."[10]

Somewhere along the line, children from lower-income backgrounds are thwarted as they try to make their way in the US economy. They experience discrimination in the form of unequal power relations and the fact that hiring and capital investment decisions are persistently dominated by certain groups of people—many of them unwilling to open opportunities to people against whom they are biased. Given that those at the top of firms are disproportionately non-Hispanic white, male, and straight, workplace inequality often looks like discrimination based on race and ethnicity, gender, or sexual orientation. Similarly, those with power in the workplace—be they owners of auto repair franchises or heads of Wall Street investment banks—often hail from particular socioeconomic and educational backgrounds and carry implicit socioeconomic biases with them into their firms. Recent research has done much to expose the implicit biases that all of us carry—biases that infect decision-making and cause unfairly disparate outcomes. Even so, many have a hard time accepting that discrimination exists.

Discrimination is hard to measure. Economists typically start from the premise that discrimination is the gap in pay or other aspects of employment—hiring or promotion rates, for example—that's left unexplained once all the productivity-related factors have been accounted for. Chetty's research is compelling because he and his colleagues looked at multiple aspects of people's backgrounds—some of which should reasonably affect the work they go on to do and some of which should not—and then tease out the difference in outcomes attributable to each. While the study cannot tell us exactly where, it proves that discrimination does enter the picture somewhere along the path from childhood to becoming an innovator.

To be sure, this way of uncovering discrimination makes two big assumptions about merit: that it can be identified in data, and that it should and does get rewarded in the market. Basing policy on the idea that those with more talent—for example, with higher scores on third-grade tests—are more valuable to society because we hope for more inventors might well have unintended consequences. It's easy to imagine a new class structure emerging, with some people thinking they deserve all they have and looking down on others, alongside another class of people raised to think of themselves as losers. Linking market value too tightly to merit also runs the risk of devaluing those people who choose to work in the public interest even though doing so does not maximize their earnings. When talented and skilled people opt to, for example, run homeless shelters or become teachers, they certainly do not become less important to our society.[11]

These are important issues and add to the concerns about trends in the markets for labor and entrepreneurship and what they mean for our society. If evidence shows that talent and skill are obstructed from being rewarded in the market, this means we need to do more to understand how economic inequality translates into social and political power. Chetty continues to look into the details of why so many children with the potential to become inventors don't wind up developing and applying their talents. Is it usually because they don't have money for college? Or is it something else? At what point in their lives would interventions do most to improve opportunity in the US economy and society?

## Obstructions in the Market for Entrepreneurs

It's difficult to name the one biggest thing blocking would-be inventors from opportunities to participate in the marketplace, but Chetty told me that he and his team have a hunch: "our leading hypothesis, and there's evidence to support this, is that this is about differences in environmental exposure to innovation."[12] While Janet Currie and her colleagues have been showing how inequality blocks opportunities at the beginnings of children's lives, Chetty is more focused on the point when children begin to gain awareness of career options. Others have suggested that policymakers focus their attention on different life phases. At a Brookings Institution event to discuss Chetty's research, Anthony Jack of the Harvard School of Education said "we need to focus on when people are most developmentally malleable"—

that is, early in life. Yet, there are other views—Reshma Saujani, founder and CEO of Girls Who Code, insisted "it's never too late to invest in people."[13]

Let's start with the perspective that emphasizes what happens once a child has grown up and is considering a career possibility—perhaps to be an entrepreneur. There's evidence that women who want to become entrepreneurs experience a harder time tapping into funding sources. The Diana Project, founded in 1999 by a group of scholars to track the success of women-owned businesses, found that many female entrepreneurs had the required skills and experience to lead ventures with high growth potential—yet they were "consistently left out of the networks of growth capital finance and appeared to lack the contacts needed to break through."[14] According to *TechCrunch*, which covers startups, only about 8 percent of partners at top venture capital firms are women. If women aren't in the rooms where investment decisions are being made, this may affect their access to seed capital.[15]

Looking at the data, it's hard not to conclude that venture capitalists prefer financing startup projects pitched by men. According to *Fortune*, in 2016, 80 percent of companies that received venture capital funding were founded by men, and 15 percent had founding teams made up of men and women. Only 5 percent were purely female-founded. That translated to venture capital investments of $58.2 billion in companies with all-male founders versus $1.46 billion in companies launched by women.[16]

Scholars are documenting that bias may be driving these outcomes. At Harvard Business School, Paul A. Gompers and doctoral student Sophie Q. Wang find it makes a difference if senior partners in venture capital firms have daughters. Whether a senior partner has a daughter is a random variable that should not affect firm performance—but this doesn't mean it can't affect the behavior of people in firms. The research shows that firms with senior partners with daughters have a "significant and economically meaningful increase in the proportion of females hired" and that this, in turn, has a causal, positive effect on business performance. Gompers and Wang also find that firms with women achieve on average higher deal and fund performance—yet another piece of evidence that discrimination is economically irrational.[17]

The data also indicates that, when people of color want to start a business, they face more obstacles to accessing capital. According to a 2010

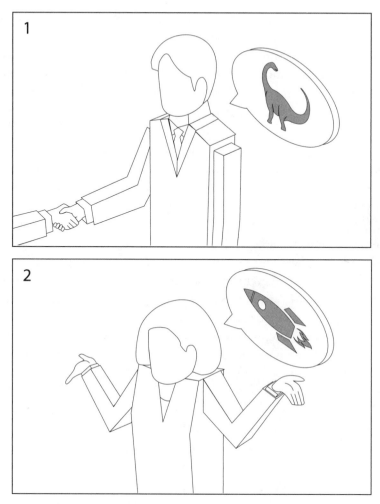

1. Companies with male founders have little trouble getting venture capital investments but... 2. just 5 percent of companies that receive venture capital are female founded.

study commissioned by the Minority Business Development Agency, there are "large disparities in access to financial capital." The agency pulled together data from the US Census Bureau's Survey of Minority-Owned Business Enterprises and the Survey of Business Owners and found that minority-owned businesses pay higher interest rates on loans, are more likely to be denied credit, and are less likely to apply for loans due to concerns that their applications will be denied. What's more, minority-owned firms "have less than half the average amount of recent equity investments and loans than non-minority firms."[18]

A 2013 report commissioned by the US Small Business Administration found that entrepreneurs of color are more likely to finance their companies out of their own wealth and, again, that part of what makes them less likely to apply for external financing is their expectation of being turned down. The fear is justified, this study found, because people of color are more likely to be denied loans than whites, even after controlling for various factors, such as credit scores, college degrees, and professional certificates. Considering the enormous wealth gaps between people of color and whites laid out in the Introduction, this creates a large disadvantage for people of color going into business.[19]

Overall, whether entrepreneurs have access to wealth appears to determine whether they will ever start a new company. Global Economics Group economist David Evans and New York University economist Boyan Jovanovic found a positive relationship between wealth and the probability of becoming an entrepreneur. Further, World Bank economist Camilo Mondragón-Vélez shows that budding entrepreneurs below the top of the wealth distribution face capital constraints at the early stages of starting a business. Probably not coincidentally, there's been a long-term decline in the share of firms that are startups: since the late 1970s, the number of startups relative to the population of all firms has trended downwards from about 160 startups per 1,000 firms down to about 80. The growing wealth gap in the United States over the past four decades could well be a key impediment to innovation. This brings us back to the other recent economic reality in the United States—the lack of a generational reboot.[20]

Even so, not all the evidence points to obstacles. Economists Lisa Cook and Chaleampong Kongcharoen at Michigan State University pulled together data on the gender and race of US patent holders and found that those women and people of color who do hold patents are almost as likely as men and whites are to commercialize their ideas into new products and services. Their data spans three decades and shows that between 2001 and 2008, women and black inventors commercialized 79 percent and 77 percent of their inventions, respectively, compared to 80 percent for all US inventors. This encouraging news may indicate that addressing problems earlier in the pipeline can have a real-world effect, encouraging more women and people of color to join the ranks of innovators.[21]

## Obstructions in the Workplace

If the US economy worked as advertised, everyone would be able to find the economic roles that best suited their talents and skills. There is strong evidence—even within the most innovative professions—that those with economic power often block this process and prevent people from accessing the jobs and opportunities that could spur greater productivity and growth. Harvey Weinstein's alleged actions to keep talented actresses—and actors, directors, and others who called him on his behavior—from working is only one of many examples of such bias in action. Even for inventors, the uncertain struggle to get a job can determine whether they get to pursue their vision, since seven in ten are not entrepreneurs on their own but work at a fairly large firm.[22]

Of course, some biases are trickier to root out. Society's biases make possessing a specific trait that ought to be unrelated to merit genuinely relevant, or at least seem to be genuinely relevant. For example, 30 percent of male CEOs of the biggest US companies are at least six foot, two inches tall, compared to 4 percent of the American male population. Leaders are supposed to be commanding, and many people perceive tall people as more commanding, all else being equal. So companies disproportionately "select tall" in their search for strong leaders. Author Malcolm Gladwell calls this bias the "Warren Harding Error," after the twenty-ninth US president. Historians say he was elected because he had the looks for the part, not because he had the chops. When we mistake charisma for capabilities, we can overlook people who are actually best suited for the job.[23]

One novel piece of evidence documenting this kind of discrimination in the labor market was published in 2000 by economist Claudia Goldin of Harvard and Cecilia Rouse, now dean at the Woodrow Wilson School at Princeton. Prior to 1980, in every one of the five top orchestras in the United States—Boston, Chicago, Cleveland, New York City, and Philadelphia— women made up fewer than one in eight members. Since then, many reputable orchestras in the United States have since switched to blind auditioning for new musicians, meaning that audition committees and music directors are unaware of the musicians' physical attributes, at least in preliminary rounds. If the market always rewarded merit, the number of women in orchestras should not have risen after blind auditioning was introduced, since what a person looks like shouldn't affect the assessment of their musicianship or the audience's enjoyment of it. But it did. Goldin and Rouse found that orchestras using blind auditions hired more female musicians. This means that, for decades, audiences didn't get to hear the best musicians because of the biases of orchestral hiring committees.[24]

Many studies since have used other methods to expose bias. In some cases, researchers send out resumes that are identical except in some respect that cues the reader to believe something about the job applicant's demographic traits. Then they see how the variation affects invitations to interview. In others, researchers give survey respondents information about job or promotion applicants and ask them how they would rate them as candidates. Across many variations on these kinds of studies, researchers find that varying the information about a candidate's race, gender, or some other characteristic subject to bias causes that candidate to be rated lower on average.

Here is just one of many examples. A recent study focused on whether job applicants with black-sounding names were less likely to be called in for job interviews. The researchers, Marianne Bertrand at the University of Chicago and Sendhil Mullainathan at MIT, replied to actual help-wanted ads in Boston and Chicago for sales, administrative support, and customer service jobs by sending in fictitious resumes—some with "black-sounding" names, others with "white-sounding" ones. The applications submitted under black-sounding names received 50 percent fewer invitations to interview than those with white names, and this gap was consistent across job types, industries, and employers. Measured by the response rate, a white-sounding name provided an advantage equivalent to eight additional years of experience.[25]

The research evidence resonates with the news stories we read seemingly every day. Take the stories now coming to light about widespread harassment and discrimination in Silicon Valley's most profitable startups and in the online gaming world. The early-stage venture capital firm Binary Capital imploded following reports that one of its partners, Justin Caldbeck, had sexually harassed six women. Dave McClure, who founded the incubator 500 Startups, resigned after the *New York Times* reported he sexually harassed a woman applying for a job; the ride-hailing company Uber fired twenty employees—including its founder—after an internal investigation discovered rampant sexual harassment at the company. The list goes on.[26]

These are all data points that add up to an undeniable reality. A recent project entitled "Elephant in the Valley" surveyed more than two hundred women, all of whom had worked in Silicon Valley for over a decade. The survey uncovered a dizzying—and disgusting—amount of gender and sexual discrimination. Women reported a variety of experiences that seemed more akin to television's *Mad Men* era of blatant sexism than what we like to think is normal today. Nearly half reported being asked to order the food or take the notes at meetings, or perform other housekeeping tasks that were not requested of their male peers. As for sexual harassment, 60 percent had been on the receiving end of unwanted sexual advances—two-thirds of which from their supervisors!—and 90 percent had witnessed sexist behavior in the workplace.[27]

The fact that complaints about technology sector working conditions are increasingly being aired publicly could mean progress for those currently excluded from one of our nation's highest-profile and most cutting-edge professions. Certainly there's lots of evidence that obstructing people from doing jobs for which they've trained or have the aptitude isn't economically rational. There is also evidence that companies that embrace diversity see higher productivity and, thus, stronger economic outcomes. According to Vivian Hunt, Dennis Layton, and Sara Prince at the global consultancy McKinsey and Company, the most diverse companies in terms of race and ethnicity are 35 percent more likely to see above-average financial returns, while the companies most inclusive in terms of gender are 15 percent more likely to experience above-average returns. Those in the bottom quartile for gender, racial, and ethnic diversity are less likely to achieve above-average financial returns. Innovation thrives on diversity.[28]

## Obstructions in Particular Places

Raj Chetty's family immigrated to the United States from New Delhi, India, when he was nine years old. As he tells it, he always knew he was lucky. His parents believed that if he, his brother, and his sister grew up in the United States they would have great opportunities. His parents were skilled professionals, each being "the one" in their family given the gift of higher education. In a conversation with George Mason University economist Tyler Cowen, Chetty reflected: "I see through the generations the impact that that has had, not just on their outcomes—my mom's a physician, my dad's a statistician and an economist—but on the subsequent generation with myself and my cousins. The opportunities I've had were dramatically shaped by those decisions many generations ago."[29]

Chetty grew up mostly in Milwaukee and the data he and Hendren have compiled shows that Milwaukee County is the kind of place that limits opportunity; out of the hundred largest counties in the United States, it has the ninth worst rate of upward mobility. To make their comparisons, the researchers use the US Department of Agriculture's delineation of "commuting zones," which divide the entire country into geographical areas clustered around metropolitan areas. Their analysis shows that up to 80 percent in the variation of children's outcomes can be explained by where they are raised; children who grow up in commuting zones with higher incomes have higher incomes as adults, all else being equal.[30]

Chetty's parents didn't need such well-constructed studies to see that geography mattered. They sought to overcome neighborhood effects by sending him to an "outstanding" private college prep school: the University School of Milwaukee. Chetty took a crosstown bus to get to his school, and the neighborhoods he rode through didn't compare favorably to the acres and acres of pristine grounds surrounding its campus. In his words, "you could feel the degree of segregation. . . . seeing those disparities made me wonder how much of where I will end up in life happens to be because of having the opportunity to go to *this* school as opposed to going to some other school within that city."[31]

Chetty's study on inventors showed that exposure to a community of scientists and innovators was an important factor in some children's success pursuing ideas that led to patents. Specific places—and the people living there—nurture innovation. Children from low-income families are far less likely to be exposed to role models and opportunities that allow them to see their full range of options, especially if they live in low-income neighborhoods. Chetty and his coauthors estimate that "if girls were as exposed to female inventors as boys are to male inventors in their childhood [commuting zones], the current gender gap in innovation would shrink by half." Perhaps unsurprisingly, they also found that individuals were likely to pursue patents in areas of research connected to the place they grew up. People who grew up in Minneapolis tended to pursue ideas related to medical devices, while those who grew up in Boston or Silicon Valley pursued ideas connected to information technology. Other research confirms that if a parent works in a particular industry, a child is more likely to start a firm in that industry.[32]

Tatyana Avilova at Columbia University and Claudia Goldin at Harvard have been working to remedy this place- and gender-based inequality within the field of economics itself. In 2015, they launched the Undergraduate Women in Economics Challenge as a randomized control trial to evaluate whether better career information, mentoring, and encouragement, along with more relevant instructional content, could encourage more women to enter economics. They randomly selected twenty schools to adopt the treatment, and identified more than thirty control schools. While their trial is still in the field, they reported early findings at the American Economic Association annual meetings in January 2018. Consistent with Chetty's conclusions, they are finding that mentorship matters: exposing women to female economists and to economics more generally increases women's likelihood of pursing the field.[33]

Place matters in another way, as well. There is evidence that communities that welcome families such as the Chettys see greater economic gains. In one study, economists Ufuk Akcigit and John Grigsby at the University of Chicago and Tom Nicholas at Harvard Business School show that, historically, places with more immigration also register more innovation. Areas that experienced more immigration over the period from 1880 to 1940, such as New York and Illinois, saw more patenting and higher growth from 1940 to 2000. This suggests that places that are more open to immigrants see higher rate of patents—and the economic growth that follows. Over the earlier time period, in the top ten most inventive states, about one in five inventors were foreign born, compared to fewer than one in fifty in the least inventive states. In another study, this same group of scholars found faster long-term growth, higher population density, lower slave ownership (pre–Civil War), more developed financial markets, and higher social mobility in the more inventive regions.[34]

There's a long history in the United States of some places having less economic opportunity than others. Many historians and contemporary thinkers believe that slavery created a climate where white elites sought to limit both low-income white workers and black slaves from accessing education—and obviously, slavery prevented millions of black people from making the most of their innate talents. This was an argument made by Abraham Lincoln—the only US president to date to be a patent-holder, by the way, having invented a "manner of buoying vessels." In a speech in 1858 at the Wisconsin Agricultural Society, Lincoln made the case that universal education would foster "economic creativity," and that the South's way of using enslaved people—and workers more generally—worked against innovation and growth. Lincoln said that Southerners saw workers as "a blind horse upon a treadmill" and educated workers as "not only useless, but pernicious and dangerous. In fact, it is, in some sort, deemed a misfortune that laborers should have heads at all. Those same heads are regarded as explosive materials, only to be safely kept in damp places, as far as possible from that peculiar sort of fire which ignites them."[35]

There is evidence that this affected the economy—and not in a good way for the South. In the decades just before the Civil War, the North was a wellspring of innovation. Northern states far outpaced Southern ones in securing new patents; they even outpaced Great Britain. By 1860, just before its secession, the South accounted for just 5 percent of all US patents, although it was home to 30 percent of the nation's population. The same geographic trend holds for schooling: most counties in the North had a higher share of children attending school, ranging from 60 percent to 90 percent, while across the South, only a handful of counties had school attendance of more than 50 percent of free children—and, of course, enslaved children were denied an education by law in many southern states.[36]

What economists are finding is that, while the market dictates outcomes, those outcomes are also very much affected by the institutions the economy is embedded in. Based on their research, Chetty and Hendren document the five most important factors about a place that affect children's chances of doing better than their parents. They show that a child who wanted to move up in the world would do well to ask his parents to raise him in a community that is less segregated by race and income; has a strong middle class and less income inequality; has better schools with higher funding levels, smaller classes, and better test scores; has fewer single-parent families; and has more social capital—as measured by indices of the strength of social networks and relationships as well as engagement in community organizations. It's too bad, of course, that children don't get to tell their parents where to raise them.[37]

## A New Understanding of the Markets for Labor and Entrepreneurship

If people are blocked from doing jobs they are qualified to do—or from accessing the skills they need to get those jobs—then the markets for people and ideas don't work in reality like they do in the bare-bones textbook model. This means that differences across the income spectrum affect market outcomes—both labor markets and entrepreneurship—in profoundly important ways, and that potential productivity is being left untapped. It also has implications for how economists understand the workings of the labor market.

Economists don't have to look far to find evidence that the labor market doesn't always reward talent and hard work. One of their own favorite haunts, the popular job-hunting website Economics Job Market Rumors, was the focus of a 2017 study by Alice Wu, then an undergraduate at UC-Berkeley. She scraped the site's data and conducted a textual analysis of how economists and economists-to-be talked on the site as they anonymously discussed, debated, and dissected who was hiring and who was applying. The analysis picked out the most common words used by this online community to comment on men and women candidates. Among the top twenty for male candidates were mainly descriptors of their professional focus and strengths, such as *adviser*, *pricing*, and *mathematician*. Among the top twenty for women candidates were *hotter*, *tits*, *anal*, *marrying*, *pregnant*, *gorgeous*, *horny*, and *crush*.[38]

One could dismiss this outrageous vocabulary as the bad behavior of a small group of anonymous trolls, but it needs to be taken more seriously given other evidence from the profession. There are far fewer women in economics than men. As female economists move up the career ladder, they have fewer and fewer female peers. Women make up about 30 percent of assistant professors in economics, but their numbers drop to 23 percent among associate professors and fall to less than 14 percent among full professors. To be clear, it's not that women cannot handle the math. Women account for more than 40 percent of undergraduate math and statistics majors—and have been a large enough share of math majors for long enough to thoroughly reject the argument that economics has a paucity of women because the math is too hard.[39] And it is important to note that gender is not the only problem facing the profession. The percentage of nonwhite undergraduate economics students is about 15 percent, and this number declines considerably as careers advance.

There's growing evidence that the lack of gender diversity is rooted in bias within the profession. As in many academic fields, in economics, people move up the job ladder by getting their research published in top journals. New evidence shows that women have to work harder than men to get their work published. Economist Erin Hengel of the University of Liverpool finds that female economists are held to higher standards than men. Papers by women submitted to academic economics journals take longer than those by men to make it through peer review, by about six months. This slows the women's productivity rates and makes it harder for them to get tenure. Over time, women realize their papers simply have to be better than the men's.[40]

Even accomplishing that might not help much. While still a PhD candidate in economics at Harvard, Heather Sarsons found that women in economics also have to do more work on their own. She gathered data on publications by economists at top US universities over the past forty years and found that, compared to men, women were less likely to get tenure if more of their publications were coauthored. Women are as likely to publish in top journals as men, but over this time frame, women were about 30 percent less likely to get tenure. The evidence suggests that when a woman works on a team and the individual contributions of participants aren't clear, economists discount her contribution. To the extent this is discrimination, it damages productivity within economics.[41] (See Figure 2.3.)

These biases don't only obstruct women's careers, they carry real-world implications for our nation's economic policy agenda. There is growing evidence that social scientists—including economists—bring implicit biases into their framing of research questions and their interpretation of evidence. Marion Fourcade of the University of California–Berkeley, a sociologist who studies economists, finds that their varying policy recommendations depend significantly on where they live and work. US economists tend to be "more favorable to economic ideas based on free trade and market competition" than their British, French, or German peers. Along the same lines, a recent survey of American Economics Association

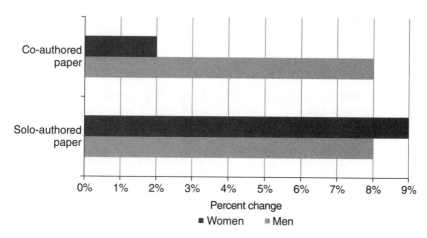

Figure 2.3   Women in economics are held to higher standards
Increase in probability of earning tenure from authoring one additional research paper.

*Source:* Heather Sarsons. "Gender Differences in Recognition for Group Work," Harvard University, November 4, 2017, https://scholar.harvard.edu/files/sarsons/files/full_v6.pdf?m=1509845375.

members finds that male economists are more likely than female economists to prefer market solutions to government intervention, are more skeptical of environmental protection regulations, and are (slightly) less keen on redistribution. And Zubin Jelveh of New York University and Bruce Kogut and Suresh Naidu of Columbia University find that political ideology affects the outcomes of economic research.[42]

Given the failure of even the economists' job market to work as textbooks describe, we need to challenge our assumptions of fairness in the labor market. We need to be especially concerned about high economic inequality. Naidu cautions that if your success in a workplace is contingent on the whims of another, then you don't have economic freedom, even if you are free to move from job to job. He likes to call this the "Don't have to laugh at unfunny jokes of superiors" test. In many fields, the relative productivity of workers is subject to interpretation; whether a research paper is good or bad, or one actress better than another for a specific role, is a more subjective call than which mousetrap is more effective. This means we need to be especially vigilant about identifying and removing blockages caused by inequality.[43]

All of this accumulating evidence leaves economists and policymakers with profoundly unsettling questions about whether we truly understand labor markets. The research outlined in Chapter 1 showed that economists need to look earlier in life than educational attainment to understand human capital; this chapter concludes that we cannot assume that pay—or opportunity—reflects the underlying talent or skills of the individual. All the more disquieting for those who believe labor markets respond purely to supply and demand is that this is not the only contrary evidence.

## Loosening Inequality's Grip on the Labor Market

People and their ideas drive innovation, but inequality means that too many are blocked from finding their best fit. Governor Brownback of Kansas assumed that if financial constraints were lifted—if taxes were cut and regulations eliminated—then this would free up innovation and investment in his state. But that's not enough. Not by a long shot. Indeed, research shows that changes in top tax rates are highly unlikely to affect innovation. Chetty and his coauthors tested whether policymakers could increase innovation by increasing children's exposure to innovators, by expanding access to internship programs to reduce barriers to entry, or by cutting the top tax rates for inventors to increase private returns. Their model predicts that the first policy—increasing exposure—does far more than the other two.[44]

So what should policymakers do? The reality is that the market is not inherently perfect. It is embedded in a society full of institutions that allow inequality to obstruct some people, and these constraints on their contribution to labor markets or ability to become entrepreneurs have widespread economic implications. We need to move beyond blind faith in Smith's invisible hand to ensure that the barriers to opportunity are eliminated. A top-of-mind concern for policymakers, based on the evidence, should be to address the skills and employment pipeline itself, not only the flow of people seeking to move through it. Beronda Montgomery, a biochemist at Michigan State, puts it this way: "Pipeline—great, let's get more people. But it gets in the way. When you have trouble with your pipes at home, you don't try to push more water through, you get a plumber to find out what is the structural defect."[45]

Policymakers should design and fully embrace policies to eliminate discrimination in the labor market. The 1963 Equal Pay Act prohibits sex discrimination, and the 1964 Civil Rights Act prohibits discrimination along the lines of race, color, religion, sex, and national origin. Back when these were passed, the United States was a global leader on equity statutes, but we've since fallen behind. To catch up again, policymakers can start by giving themselves—and the American people—the tools to see the structural problems. This requires collecting firm-specific employment and pay data by gender, race, and ethnicity. If it isn't clear how to do this, there are models we can look to. Quebec, for example, requires that employers audit their pay practices to ensure that compensation within firms is equitable; Iceland imposes fines on firms that take no action to ensure equal pay. In 2016, the US Equal Employment Opportunity Commission announced that, starting March 2018, it would require the collection of summary pay data and hours worked by pay bands and by gender, race, and ethnicity from employers with more than one hundred employees. The Trump administration stopped this action, however, before the policy went into place but soon after—in March 2019—a federal court ordered the EEOC to reinstate the pay data collection requirement. There are still open questions as to how and when employers must report their data.[46]

To address the structural defects, policymakers have a variety of options. There are simple steps, such as implementing blind application processes, and there are more complex steps, such as thinking through how to better match people with skills to good opportunities. One thing is clear: discrimination follows people over time. Imagine that, at your first job, you were paid 5 percent less than similarly qualified colleagues. If, when you applied for your next job, the hiring manager used salary history to decide what salary to offer you, that first shortfall would rob you again. You might never make up the gap. To remedy this, eleven states (including Massachusetts, California, Oregon, Delaware, and New York), nine local jurisdictions (including San Francisco, Pittsburgh, and New Orleans), and the US territory of Puerto Rico have passed measures banning employers from asking about previous wages during the job application process, as of the end of 2018.[47]

To stimulate entrepreneurship, policymakers must expand access to capital, particularly among minority entrepreneurs who have less personal wealth that can be used as seed capital or loan collateral. One example to consider: state-run capital access programs that pool and match contributions from borrowers and lenders to create a reserve fund that lenders can claim against to cover losses on loans. These programs have had a good track record in helping small businesses obtain credit. They got a boost of

$28 million in federal investment under the US Treasury's State Small Business Credit Initiative, part of the 2010 Small Business Jobs Act. Yet only California, Michigan, New York, North Carolina, and Massachusetts, all of which already had similar programs, were able to use the investment successfully to operate the capital access programs at scale.[48] Research also shows that universal access to affordable health insurance can be key in encouraging entrepreneurship. A study on health care reforms in Massachusetts, which predated and were similar to the Affordable Care Act, found that they supported self-employment in the state by expanding access to all types of insurance. The Kansas City Fed researchers found that while the self-employment share of total employment in other Northeastern states and in the United States as a whole continued to drop, the self-employment rate remained flat in Massachusetts after the state health-care law was enacted in 2006.[49]

The private sector has to step up to address these issues. Economist Byron Auguste and his team at Opportunity@Work are seeking to do just that. Their basic premise is that the way firms hire tends to prevent people with the right skills and talent from finding the best fit. Too many people with the skills and potential to be successful are turned away in today's labor market, which drags down productivity and growth. To fix this, Opportunity@Work works on creating pathways to meaningful careers through partnerships with employers, community organizations, and job seekers. They provide ways for employers to find skilled people without overlooking those who "screened out" based on pedigree, not skills.[50]

Given what we know about the importance of early childhood, as well as how place matters, another logical place to start is by ensuring that every child gets a strong start in life. This means addressing gaps in access to early-childhood education, as well as gaps in access to high-quality primary and secondary schools, as outlined in Chapter 1. This will take public resources and investments in public education, which as the next chapter will show, have broad popular support. Unfortunately, the elites who control the political debate tend to prefer giving themselves big tax breaks. Making sure that every community has opportunities for children—whether their parents are rich or poor—is the only way to ensure that inequality doesn't block children from finding their best fit in the economy later on in life.

And, of course, one of the best ways to create opportunity is full employment. In 2018, as the unemployment rate hovered below 4 percent, employers turned to some groups that often have a hard time getting work (which is also what happened during the low unemployment years of the late 1990s). Even though unemployment rates for blacks and Latinos remain higher than for whites, less skilled workers, those with a history of incarceration, and others have been able to find economic opportunities as employers searched for workers.[51]

Policymakers can think of this agenda as one that breaks down the divide between those looking in and those already inside. This is how Chetty describes his own realization of what inequality meant when he was young. As he told Tyler Cowen, when he was about eight or nine, his parents took him to visit the famous seventeenth-century mausoleum the Taj Mahal:

> Seeing the Taj Mahal is a striking experience in its own right because the monument is so majestic. But what struck me was the incredible contrast between the monument itself and what was outside. It was one of the most impoverished areas in India, in Agra. Just seeing that incredible contrast between the tourists and the people who were begging for food . . . left a mark on me. I think back to that experience, wondering why things were so different on the inside versus the outside.[52]

If every policymaker started from this same state of wondering, we'd make progress addressing inequality's obstructions.

# II

# HOW INEQUALITY SUBVERTS

Part I examined the supplies of people, ideas, and capital to the market. Part II turns to the institutions that support a well-functioning market. In the simplistic, bare-bones framework, our coders, chefs, and caregivers don't need the government to embark on collective endeavors. If our coder and her team, for example, need their customers to have broadband, some private investor will spot that gap and jump in to fill it. That market model doesn't allow for a situation where it is the public provision of broadband that creates the market the coder takes advantage of. Yet, in reality, public investments do drive private ones. This makes it all the more worrisome that the United States lags behind other countries in a variety of public investments. The shortfalls show up in areas from the quality of our schools to the coverage of our broadband to the state of our transportation infrastructure.

For the economy to function, the public sector needs to function, and function well. America's early promise was supported by government. In the nineteenth and twentieth centuries, as America grew, we implemented policies that launched many families with a solid set of tools, including the Homestead Act, the estate tax, universal primary and secondary schools and land grant colleges all across the nation, and the GI Bill. Not everyone had access to these policies—the Homestead disproportionately gave land to whites, black veterans were denied access to GI Bill benefits, and black people couldn't attend many land-grant institutions that were segregated—yet they showed that the federal government could embark on big agendas to reduce inequality. These kinds of programs must be more inclusive, but now they aren't even happening; there is emerging new evidence that growing inequality is subverting the public institutions and the policymaking process we need to support our economy. It discourages a focus on the public interest and promotes what economists call "rent seeking"—the efforts of firms to take home larger profits than truly competitive markets would allow.

The ramifications of rent-seeking are widespread. Firms are able to manipulate the functioning of the marketplace because economic inequality gives their owners the financial wherewithal to wield political influence. They can exert pressure on political processes in our country to benefit them above all, they can minimize the taxes on firms, owners of capital, and top-salaried workers, and rewrite laws and regulations in their favor. This is why the increased concentration of economic power in the United States reduces market competition, lowers productivity, and drags down economic growth and stability: it undermines sustained investment in public goods and services such as broadband (for the coder), food safety (for the chef), and laws that ensure competitive wages and benefits (for the caregiver).

Inequality is not just about a few at the top getting a bit more than their fair share. By subverting our economy in various ways, it undermines confidence that institutions of governance can deliver for the majority. There is an argument that the United States is on the cusp of being, or has already become, an oligarchy—a society where economic elites have been able to amass and manipulate their economic and political power, focusing on enriching themselves. As those institutions focus more on protecting those at the top than supporting equitable growth, this erodes the ability of public institutions to do even the most basic functions, stymying economic growth and stability—and our trust in government to act on behalf of working people.[1]

It requires a huge lift for a society to get to the point where government is capable of making sure that monopoly or oligopoly interests don't run amok every night, taking more effective control of our complex twenty-first-century global world. The United States achieved this big lift during the Progressive and New Deal eras in our history, but now we are in danger of unraveling all that's come before. Inequality in wealth and power is thwarting us from taking on collective endeavors that provide the foundation for broad-based growth, while promoting the interests of monopolists and oligopolists over others.

■  ■  ■

The next two chapters focus on how inequality subverts institutions and the market process. Chapter 3 looks at how economic power undermines our democracy and our ability to generate the revenues necessary for broad-based economic growth. It starts with the research of Emmanuel Saez on how to think about structuring the tax system to generate sufficient revenue to make the investments necessary to deliver on the American Dream. Saez and his colleagues show that lower taxes on those at the top of the income ladder do not lead to the kinds of beneficial outcomes some suggest—indeed, the evidence is that when the rich pay less in taxes, this encourages them to act in unproductive ways.

Chapter 4 dives deep into how our economy is increasingly dominated by a few firms. Harvard Business School economist Leemore Dafny has studied what's going in healthcare markets and found evidence that the biggest healthcare companies are increasing their stronghold in the market by merging and then charging higher prices. This in turn leads to higher profits for managers and shareholders and less affordable—and sometimes lower-quality—healthcare for everyone else, alongside lower wages for those working in increasingly monopolized jobs.

What's happening in health care is emblematic of changes across our economy. When a firm has too much power in its product market, it has monopoly power, which means it can raise prices with impunity and stymie competition. Indeed, there is evidence that concentration sits at the core of the problems that inequality poses for the level and stability of economic demand. To make matters worse, there is evidence that dominant economic power is reinforcing itself in the political world, further entrenching those at the top, shutting everyone else out, and subverting the market process.

The implications are clear: To revive our democracy, and with it our investments in public endeavors, we need to rebalance the strength of the voices. It also means we have to think about markets that benefit a few, such as platform firms that dominate major sectors of the US economy today. If we live in a world where those with the loudest voices stand to gain the most then we need to be very thoughtful about ensuring that the rules of the market don't only benefit them, to the detriment of the economy more generally.

# 3

# Public Spending

KANSAS GOVERNOR SAM BROWNBACK'S tax cuts reduced the state's individual income tax by over $800 million annually between fiscal years 2015 and 2017—a drop equal to more than 11 percent of the state's annual total tax revenue. What he called his "red state" experiment meant state policymakers had no choice but to make spending cuts. Most of the options weren't popular. Within the first two years of the tax cuts, the state's funding levels for schools, healthcare, and other public services fell by 8 percent and the state transferred almost $1 billion from its Highway Fund to its General Fund, postponing numerous transportation projects indefinitely. That was only the beginning; more cuts were necessary in later years as tax revenue continued to fall. As a result, in 2015, in a wildly unpopular move, schools across Kansas closed a week to twelve days earlier than usual, affecting the educational progress of children throughout the state and leaving working families scrambling for childcare.[1]

Waves of frustration rippled across Kansas. By 2016, more people in this very Republican state reported being "very dissatisfied" with Republican Gov. Brownback (53 percent) than with Democratic President Obama (43 percent). As Dinah Sykes, a Republican state senator from a suburban district, told the *New York Times*, "Email after email after email I get from constituents says, 'Please, let's stop this experiment.'"[2] In response to the public outcry, the Republican-controlled legislature sought to undo the tax cuts. The governor, however, held fast to his theory that the tax cuts would lead to broad-based economic gains. He twice vetoed legislation to reverse most of them, in February and June of 2017. This did not improve his standing with the public. By the summer of 2017, his 27 percent approval rating made him the second-most unpopular governor in the United States, falling behind only Governor Chris Christie of New Jersey. Ultimately, what happened in Kansas was a failure of Brownback's theory to match reality.[3]

While paying taxes is probably no one's idea of a fun thing to do, people understand that to provide public goods, government needs tax revenue. This leads to two basic questions: How much revenue is necessary? And how can government optimally raise those funds? The first depends on need. Government helps to provide all the things required for the economy to function, from good schools and access to healthcare to transportation infrastructure and the rule of law. At the top of the list are the desperate needs laid out in Chapter 1: our nation must make more public investments in education, especially to provide early-childhood programs and access to high-quality childcare, and it must ensure economic opportunity across the income spectrum, including access to affordable healthcare, nutrition, and safe housing. Also key are public investments to keep essential infrastructure, including our water supply, safe and in working order. To fuel growth, governments need to spend wisely and regulate—not cut and run.

Studying the economic effects of taxation and the tradeoffs involved is generally the domain of public finance economists. In the 1970s and 1980s, a theory emerged in policy circles claiming that cutting taxes would actually increase revenues. In 1974, Arthur Laffer, then at the University of Chicago, met with President Gerald Ford's deputy chief of staff, Dick Cheney. Trying to explain the logic of how a reduction in taxes can spur economic growth to the extent that revenues actually increase, he pulled out a pen and drew a curve on a paper napkin. The "Laffer Curve" on that little napkin started a revolution in policy circles. There was no solid empirical evidence from economics research supporting the claim that cutting taxes would increase revenues would hold true in the US context. Still, conservatives began arguing that we could have it all—lower tax burdens and more of the public goods people want and need—if policymakers cut taxes for the rich. Brownback adhered to this same idea.[4]

Nearly a half a century later, there's still no evidence that lowering taxes on those with the highest incomes leads to the kinds of behavioral responses Laffer suggested. It doesn't require sophisticated econometrics (although this chapter will provide some) to see that Laffer got it wrong; we can simply look at what happened in Kansas and in the United States more generally. Lowering taxes on the rich always means less revenue. Tax cuts don't pay for themselves; instead, the tax-cutting mania we've seen in the United States has left us highly indebted and falling behind in public goods investments relative to the past and to our economic competitors.[5]

The public is clamoring for government to do more and better—and is willing to pay for that—but keeps seeing taxes and services cut. The evidence is growing that taxpayers up and down the income ladder are in favor of paying more for public investments as long as they believe that tax dollars are being put to good use and the tax system is fair. For example, the spring of 2018 witnessed teachers in a number of states walking off the job to protest not only their pay but also cuts to school funding—and garnering widespread public support even in Republican-dominated regions. In another example, surveys at both the state and national level also show that vast majorities of voters are willing to see payroll taxes rise to fund paid leave insurance programs—and in the states that have established such programs over the past decade, there has been no notable backlash from workers or employers after implementation.[6]

Rising economic inequality has subverted our political system and is behind a growing imbalance between what people want and the outcomes of policymakers' decision-making about government revenue and public investment levels. This is confirmed by a large and growing body of political science research showing that growing inequality makes it harder to get anything done in Washington, DC, and in statehouses and town halls around the nation. Worse still, the things that do get done tend to align with the priorities of the wealthy, and don't necessarily support the growth of the whole economy. Increasingly perceiving that the political system can't be trusted to respond to the democratic will, people grow more frustrated: in a recent poll of taxpayers, a majority of taxpayers said it bothered them "a lot" that some corporations and wealthy people don't pay their fair share.[7]

What can we do about all this? We can start by rejecting the long-told story that it would be counterproductive to raise taxes on the wealthy. Indeed, we must do so, both to pay for investments and to improve trust in the fairness of the system. Traditionally, as economists analyze different types of tax systems, they stress the degree to which taxes create disincentives for people to work, save, or invest. Emmanuel Saez suggests that this thinking is too simplistic, and there are other factors to take into account. Saez argues that policymakers need to focus much more on what taxes buy: "you can't judge taxes purely on the tax side. You have to see what you *do* with the taxes and [whether it is] worth spending or not."[8]

The emerging evidence has changed the minds of some of the earliest proponents of the supply-side hypothesis. Bruce Bartlett was on New York Representative Jack Kemp's staff in the 1970s, then served as executive director of the Joint Economic Committee under Iowa Senator Roger Jepsen in the 1980s. He helped lay out the economics behind the Reagan tax cuts of 1981 and 1986. But while he wrote the book (literally) on supply-side economics—publishing *Reaganomics: Supply Side Economics in Action* in 1981—he now argues that the more recent rounds of tax cut fever have gone too far. In September 2017, Democrats on the House Ways and Means Committee held a forum about President Trump's proposal to cut taxes by $1.5 trillion by lowering the top rate from 39.6 percent to 35 percent and reducing the tax on capital income to below that of labor income. "Give me a break," Bartlett said. "How many incentives could that possibly create?"[9]

## What's the Best Way to Bring in Tax Revenue?

Saez is probably best known for his work with Thomas Piketty documenting the dramatic rise in high-end income inequality in the United States since the early 1980s. They showed how the income of the top 1 percent had been growing, while that of bottom 50 percent had not. While that work is certainly important, economists associate Saez more with the field of public finance, in which he is one of the world's preeminent scholars. When he was awarded the John Bates Clark Medal in 2009, the committee emphasized these contributions: "Through a collection of interrelated papers, he has brought the theory of taxation closer to practical policy making, and has helped to lead a resurgence of academic interest in taxation."[10]

A question he has asked in particular is whether the trend toward greater income inequality is a cause or consequence of changes in tax policy. At the time that Saez embarked on his career, the United States and other countries around the world had seen many years of tax reductions for those at the top of the income ladder. Back in 1945, the top US income tax rate was 94 percent; twenty years of tax cuts brought that top rate down to 70 percent by 1965. Then came the Reagan administration's two rounds of tax cuts, which set the top income tax rate at 28 percent in 1988, and also reduced the rate of taxation on capital gains.[11]

Saez starts from the observation that each time taxes were lowered, proponents argued that this would spur sustained growth, which, in turn, would generate additional tax revenue so that there need not be any harmful cuts in services or needed investments. Yet, standard economic theory rejects this simplistic idea—and the data never materializes to support it. The United States case is shown in Figure 3.1—a simple graph showing the top marginal tax rate and economic growth, as measured by gross domestic product—from 1948 to 2018. A quick glance over the past fifty years reveals no strong or simple relationship. If the idea that lower taxes lead to sustained growth is true, then the evidence is extremely elusive.[12]

To the contrary, it's clear that tax cuts for the top haven't paid for themselves. Successive rounds of cutting the top marginal tax rate and capital gains taxes have been followed by higher federal budget deficits. With too little tax revenue to cover the federal spending needs identified by Congress, the federal government has deferred spending cuts and increased its debt

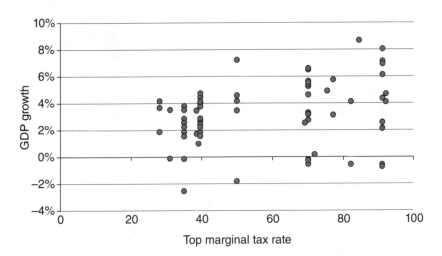

Figure 3.1   There is no obvious relationship between top tax rates and growth rates
Top marginal tax rate and GDP growth rate in the United States, 1948–2017

*Source:* US Internal Revenue Service and US Bureau of Economic Analysis.

load. By 2022, the US federal deficit is projected to hit $1 trillion—4.5 percent of GDP—the largest peacetime revenue gap ever. States, on the other hand, are generally constrained by balanced budget amendments. When their tax cuts don't lead to more revenue, they are quickly forced to cut back on spending.[13]

A question for economics to answer is whether the higher incomes of those at the top are only deserved rewards for the hard work that tax cuts incentivized, or whether something else is going on. There is a large body of economics research on how people respond to changes in tax rates as scholars have tried to discover their effects on levels of work, investing in businesses, saving, tax avoidance, and tax evasion. But all that research hasn't addressed the real rationale behind the repeated calls for tax cuts. "A number of studies have shown large and quick responses of reported incomes along the tax avoidance margin at the top of the distribution," Saez and Nobel laureate Peter Diamond point out, "but no compelling study to date has shown substantial responses along the real economic responses margin among top earners."[14] In other words, the research does not show whether lowering taxes on high-income earners actually boosts economic growth.

In search of answers, Saez, Piketty, and Harvard economist Stefanie Stantcheva model a wider range of responses to lower taxes using data from across OECD nations from 1960 to 2010. Their research takes advantage of the variations in tax policies and economic outcomes as European countries have followed the US model by reducing taxes over time. They conclude that, first, in terms of work effort, the response of those in the top 1 percent to tax rate changes is relatively small; top earners do not appear to work substantially harder (or, in economics parlance, to "vary their labor supply") in response to tax rates. Second, those in the top 1 percent do not tend to use the tax-avoidance tactic of changing the types of income they receive. Examining US income data, the researchers find relatively minimal evidence of this type of behavioral response, though this does not rule out other types of tax avoidance.

What Saez and his colleagues conclude is that the most important reason incomes are rising at the top is that the wealthy can get away with it, not because falling tax rates encourage behavior that leads to higher productivity. Perversely, lower tax rates seem to encourage those at the top of the income ladder to bargain for even higher pay since that extra effort will be more richly rewarded. For this to be true, those at the top would need to have some—or even a high level of—control over their pay, which is consistent with the evidence. About four in ten of those in the top 0.1 percent are executives who tend to sit on interlocking boards of directors, and there is strong confirmation that they vote to increase pay for each other in mutually beneficial ways.[15]

There is no logical reason that being paid more because you can get away with it leads to stronger economic growth or provides more opportunity for those not already at the top to realize the American Dream. Indeed, this manipulation of pay subverts market forces since it focuses the attention of the rich on collecting more for themselves rather than investing their firms' money in other, more productive ends. It turns out that Gov. Brownback isn't wrong: taxes do affect behavior. But his policymaking focused on only one channel through which lower taxes could affect growth. Reality is much more complex.

This reminds us that pay isn't the only motivation for hard work, a point understood by the writers of the AMC television series *Mad Men*, set in the 1960s. The show revolves around highly-paid advertising men living luxurious lifestyles of three-martini lunches, illicit affairs, and gorgeous Manhattan apartments. In one episode, perpetual striver Harry Crane gives a colleague the following advice on the level of pay to ask for: "Do you understand there's no point ever in making over forty thousand when you'll be taxed 69 percent? You're working for them! And God forbid you *really* make it—everything over seventy grand is *81* percent!"[16] Crane urged his colleague to focus on what mattered: the high status of an important job title. It's only fiction, but it resonates with a truth we all know: even if taxes are high, go-getters are wildly ambitious in the workplace (and capable of living perfectly decadent lives).

We are left with a story where the effect of taxes on incentives to invest are just one small piece of the puzzle. Further, there are serious concerns that lower taxes lead to unproductive responses as the rich respond to tax hikes with sophisticated tax-avoidance moves. As Saez told me:

> when you look at taxes on the rich and how the rich respond to taxes, you realize that it's very hard to find good evidence that taxes have a real impact, say, on work, savings, business formation decisions of high-income people. But what you see very clearly is that, when the tax system changes, the rich are really good at finding ways to avoid taxes if there are tax avoidance opportunities in the tax code—that is, loopholes.[17]

For researchers, then, an obvious first step policymakers should take is to close the loopholes. On that front, the Kansas experiment also provides an interesting case study because it created a loophole by eliminating state income taxes on so-called pass-through entities. Recall that these are a form of business organization where income is passed through to the owners and taxed only at the individual owners' level, not at the corporate level. Research by J. M. DeBacker of the University of South Carolina Darla Moore School of Business and colleagues finds that the first effect of Kansas's tax reform was to induce some small business owners to recharacterize their earnings as pass-through income in order to lower their taxes rather than because of other business-related reasons.[18]

The conclusions of Saez and his colleagues add to the accumulating evidence that inequality subverts the way the economy works. In the 1980s, when growing inequality began to show up in the data, economists sought to explain the new trend using productivity-related arguments, starting from the premise that there must be an economic rationale for those at the very top of the income ladder to earn such higher pay. Otherwise, why would firms keep paying them so much? While many of the theories they devised had some explanatory power, none could explain the full extent of rising inequality. As a result, notes Nobel laureate Paul Krugman, thinking gradually changed: "Some—by no means all—economists trying to understand growing inequality have begun to take seriously a hypothesis that would have been considered irredeemably fuzzy-minded not long ago. This view stresses the role of social norms in setting limits to inequality."[19] Since that observation in 2002, scholarship has produced evidence that social norms and bargaining power can drive increasingly unequal compensation—to the extent that a few, already highly-paid managers at the very tops of firms are able to garner, along with the firms' majority shareholders, the majority of the gains from corporate growth due to these firms' organizational structures.[20]

Given the lack of clear correlation between top tax rates and economic growth, Saez, Piketty, and Stantcheva ask why we wouldn't *raise* tax rates at the top rather than continue to cut them. They estimate that, for the top 1 percent of income earners in the United States, a rate as high as 83 percent might be the optimal tax rate—that is, the rate that would deliver to the federal government the revenue it needs without discouraging too much productive activity. To be sure, their proposal is a speculation based on extrapolations from the data. Rather than the last word, it is meant to shake economists—and those who listen to them in making policy—out of the habit of focusing narrowly on how one theory predicts taxes at the top affect private-sector investment. To understand a tax system's contribution to economic growth, we need to take a lot more into account than that.[21]

## The High Price of Low Taxes

Over the past forty years, we've seen the implications of Laffer's misguided theory as the public debate has focused too much on the rate of taxation and how government distorts growth and too little on how public investments in infrastructure and processes that support growth. In 2013, I had lunch with Harvard University economic historian Claudia Goldin in Cambridge, Massachusetts, and asked for her take on what makes the US economy grow. We talked about a mantra often heard in Washington: since economic growth comes from investments that boost productivity, and since the rate of taxation drives investment, lowering the top marginal tax rates should promote long-run economic growth. "Has any historical research shown that?," I asked her. Goldin replied that although high taxes could potentially stifle productivity, "no serious economic historian believes that the marginal tax rate is what drives productivity," she told me. To understand productivity and growth, we have to focus on the government's provision of public goods—things such as universal access to education and healthcare, transportation infrastructure, and the legal system.[22]

Increasing or decreasing public investments in education and other investments in human capital may have even greater consequences in an era of high economic inequality; indeed, ramping up public investments may be the only way to undo the obstructions that inequality creates. A paper Goldin wrote with Harvard University economist Lawrence Katz and University of California–Berkeley economist Brad DeLong makes this argument based on historical analysis. "During the twentieth century, America's investment in education was a principal source of its extraordinary performance," the authors conclude. "Projections indicate, however, that the increase in the educational attainment of the American labor force is slowing. A renewed commitment to invest in education is probably the most important and fruitful step that federal, state, and local officials can take to sustain American economic growth."[23]

The United States has a long history of making big, game-changing public investments. Consider the GI Bill of 1944 and its subsequent enhancements, which have allowed millions of military veterans to receive the benefit of higher education—although whites benefited much more than blacks, limiting the bill's effectiveness. Now, even though the United States remains a very rich nation, our government is not only failing to make these kinds of investments inclusive, we are failing to make them at all. Case in point: after a century of providing high-quality college education free of charge to California residents, the University of California system abandoned its commitment to zero tuition in 1975, after then-Governor Ronald Reagan began significantly cutting funds to the UC and community college systems in 1966. Between 2000 and 2012, state spending per student almost halved from $23,000 to $12,000 per student, and California public funding now covers less than 40 percent of the UC system's budget. The lagging state support also continues as California's population and need for skilled workers grows, threatening the university system's enrollment capacity and education quality.[24]

The lack of public investment follows the long-term decline in revenue, powered in large part by an increasing anti-tax sentiment that spread across the country decades ago—a trend in which racial animosity played a large role. In communities across the country, there was widespread frustration among high-voting, middle-class homeowners as real-estate values soared, property taxes rose, and local governments accumulated revenue, alongside a sense that government programs were benefiting some, not all. In 1978, California Republicans Howard Jarvis and Paul Gann capitalized on homeowner anger to reverse the higher public-spending trend in their state by putting forth Proposition 13, a measure that caps property taxes at a mere 1 percent of value and annual assessment increases at 2 percent. This law, which was approved by two-thirds of Californians and is still in effect today, set off the modern tax revolt across the country, as many states also passed measures to constrain state and local taxes and spending. More recently, during the late 2000s, tax revenue fell due to the Great Recession, which meant, among other things, sharp cuts in funding for public education at all levels.[25]

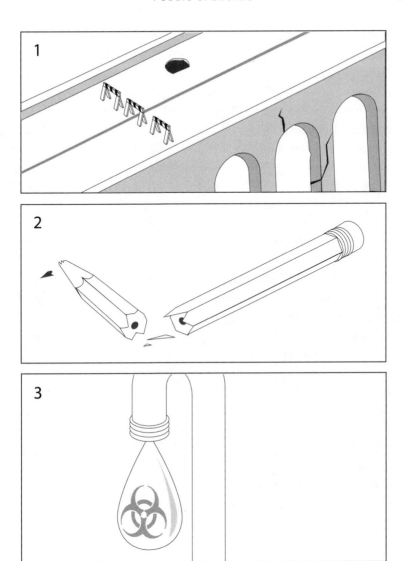

Government investments that make economic growth possible include...
1. transportation infrastructure for shipping and other commerce, 2. education
to train the workers of tomorrow, and 3. investments in public health.

Education is, of course, not the only form of government investment that spurs economic growth. Spending on infrastructure—roads and bridges, public transportation, safe drinking water, sewage systems that don't foul waterways, energy-efficient electricity generation, access to air clear of pollutants—is essential to strong and stable economic growth. A city pumping out lead-laden water to its citizens, as happened in Flint, Michigan, threatens not only the immediate well-being of residents through poisoning, but also future economic growth as lead accumulation affects the health and development of the children who will become our next generation of workers. In a city with a dysfunctional public transit system, the fact that employees are regularly late to work drags down productivity and leads to grumpiness all around—as we learned recently in Washington, DC, when the Metro system experienced major challenges. In other places, infrastructure has failed catastrophically. In Minneapolis, for example, in 2007, an eight-lane bridge packed with evening commuters collapsed into the Mississippi River, killing thirteen people and injuring 145. None of this seems consistent with the United States' standing as one of the richest countries in the world.[26]

The costs to our economy and society of failing to make these investments are both immediate and long-term. The management consultancy McKinsey and Company finds that $150 billion a year would be required between now and 2030 (about $1.8 trillion in total) to meet all the country's infrastructure needs. A 2018 report on America's sixty-year-old Interstate Highway System, prepared by the National Academies of Sciences, Engineering, and Medicine, estimates that federal and state governments would have to more than double their current annual spending of $25 billion to avoid worse traffic congestion, higher maintenance costs, and reduced safety. Interstates account for one percent of public road mileage but a quarter of the country's vehicle miles traveled. Investment in them, however, has been insufficient, and backlogged structural and operational deficiencies have mounted over time; one-third of interstate highway bridges are more than fifty years old, for example, and need to be repaired or replaced. Another area ripe for public investment is broadband infrastructure, which is uneven across the country and inadequate overall. Close to one in four Americans live in low-subscription neighborhoods, where less than 40 percent of residents have access to broadband. To be cut off from the benefits of high-speed internet connectivity is increasingly limiting in our digital economy.[27]

There are other long-term costs, as well. It's now well documented how government investments pave the way for private-sector innovation and growth. Many of the biggest advances in economic productivity, innovation, and technological capacity have been the result of government action. Take the internet—originally a Department of Defense funded project—or the many breakthrough technologies of the space program. University College London economist Mariana Mazzucato notes about Apple, one of the most successful firms the modern world has ever seen in terms of both market capitalization and profitability, that much of its value derives from government investments in fundamental research. Leslie Berlin, in *Troublemakers: Silicon Valley's Coming of Age*, points to Global Positioning System technologies and touchscreen capabilities as immensely valuable discoveries that required such large investments of resources, and offered so little certainty that the research would lead to anything commercially important, that no private sector business pursued them.[28]

Without revenue, however, governments cannot make these investments, a scenario that economists have shown is bad for long- or even short-term growth. The same goes for education. As Saez put it in a recent conversation, "the evidence shows that mass education can *only* be something that's provided by government. There's no example of private institutions able to really provide mass education." He said the same thing about meeting the needs of aging people for retirement resources: "these are almost always provided through the government, or through institutions that are quasi-governmental, that had people essentially save for retirement."[29]

For too long, market fundamentalists—from Reagan to Brownback to Trump—have repeated Laffer's claim that tax cuts will generate so much growth that revenue will not fall. That's a nice theory, but it doesn't hold up in practice. Instead, we must figure out the best way to tax to bring in enough revenue for needed investments—the investments that will support strong, stable, and broadly-shared growth.

### The Public Is Willing to Invest for the Public Good

A century ago, one of the most important investments communities made were in high schools, which quickly spread across the country. According to Goldin, "when the high school movement got under way in the nation, by the 1910s, it exploded in some areas that are even today very sparsely settled. Places like Iowa, Nebraska, Kansas, Oregon, Washington, and California." She argues that success story depended on the ability of local communities to tax wealth: "So what ties all these places together? One thing is that all had relatively high wealth per capita that was taxable. Land in the prairie states was . . . highly taxable wealth and it was extremely fertile, and thus valuable, agricultural land. Plus, education is governed by very small communities, just about throughout America, and small communities responded to the desires of parents and civic leaders."[30] In Goldin's telling, the ability of communities to make investments for the common good hinged on their governments' ability to capture the large economic gains at the very top.

People continue to be willing—and often eager—to pay taxes for investments in their communities. When asked, citizens say they would like to see more investment in public goods, including schools, alongside infrastructure, such as transportation and water and sewage systems. A majority of Americans believe that poorly maintained schools are a threat to our children, and a majority think that all Americans are endangered by the poor quality of our drinking water infrastructure. A Harvard-Harris Poll in 2017 found, more emphatically, that 84 percent of Americans want to see more investment in infrastructure, and 76 percent agree that government should be at least partially responsible for that investment.[31]

Research by Vanessa Williamson, a fellow in the governance studies program at the Brookings Institution, finds that Americans almost universally support spending in their local communities. Infrastructure and education are especially popular across the political spectrum. Where there is opposition to social safety-net spending, it is driven by a misperception that low-income people and immigrants do not pay taxes. Williamson's detailed quantitative and qualitative evidence on Americans' attitudes toward taxation reveals that Americans see paying taxes as an ethical act. She cites survey data from the IRS oversight board showing that Americans from all walks of life believe that contributing to the common good is their "civic duty." They understand that their tax dollars buy things that are important to their families, communities, and the national interest.[32]

This shows up in the voting booth and in people's policy preferences. The rate at which voters approve tax increases at the ballot box has gone from one in five in the late 1970s and early 1980s to over half in the past decade, Williamson reports. In her book, *Read My Lips: Why Americans are Proud to Pay Taxes*, she explains that the anti-tax sentiment presented by much of the media as commonsense thinking is no longer true. In the late 1960s, when tax rates on those at the top were much higher than today, Gallup reported that nearly seven in ten Americans thought the amount of federal tax they had to pay was too high. Now, Gallup finds that fewer than half think so.[33]

People's attitudes about taxes are affected by what their tax dollars buy, and they are most willing to pay taxes—and less likely to avoid them—when they approve of where their money is going. Lab experiments conducted by Harvard Business School professor and psychologist Michael Norton and various colleagues reveal that giving taxpayers any choice about how their money is spent reduces anti-tax sentiments. In one experiment, for example, they found that when taxpayers were able to signal to the government how they would like their taxes spent, they were 15 percent less likely to express willingness to take advantage of a dubious tax loophole when filing their tax returns.[34]

Case in point: over the past fifteen years, six states and the District of Columbia have put in place statewide programs to give workers paid family and medical leave. These have been paid for by new payroll taxes, the highest of which are less than a percent. While businesses actively campaigned against these, people were willing to raise taxes on themselves to cover this new cost. A 2018 survey by the National Partnership for Women and Families found that 84 percent of voters are willing to pay for a national paid leave program through payroll deductions. Asked to respond to specific levels of tax increase, seven in ten were willing to pay at much higher rates than a comprehensive national program would actually cost. Similarly, a 2018 Cato Institute survey of Americans found a majority—54 percent—willing to pay an extra $200 per year in taxes for a federal paid leave program.[35]

The single biggest complaint Americans have about taxation is that they don't believe the rich and corporations pay their fair share. In Williamson's survey, about 80 percent of respondents think the rich pay too little in taxes. The percentage goes even higher when citizens are given facts about how much of their income poor people pay in taxes or how extremely wealthy the rich are. According to research by political scientists Benjamin Page at Northwestern University and Lawrence Jacobs at the University of Minnesota, more than half of Americans think the government should apply "heavy taxes on the rich." One reason people believe we should tax the rich more—above and beyond the need for revenue—is that leaving too much wealth untaxed at the top is perceived to reduce economic mobility. Analyzing taxpayer attitudes internationally, Stantcheva and her colleagues Alberto Alesina and Edoardo Teso find a clear relationship between pessimism around intergenerational mobility and higher support for redistributive tax policies.[36]

People are right to be concerned. It's not just that taxes at the top have been lowered, it's also increasingly well-documented that the wealthy avoid paying the taxes they do owe. Tax noncompliance costs the US government more than $400 billion annually—more than twice what we would need at the federal level to cover the costs of both a paid family and medical leave insurance program and a universal childcare program. New research documents that tax avoidance is much more common—and possible— among the very wealthy. Economist Gabriel Zucman estimates that $8.7 trillion in wealth, or 11.5 percent of world gross domestic product, is held in offshore tax havens, and 80 percent of it is owned by the top one-tenth of one percent of the world's wealthy. Using leaked data and administrative tax and wealth records for Norway, Sweden, and Denmark, Zucman, along with Annette Alstadsæter at the Norwegian University of Life Sciences and Niels Johannesen at the University of Copenhagen, found that those in the top 0.01 percent of the wealth distribution—those who have personal net wealth greater than $45 million—evade about 25 percent of their personal income and wealth taxes. This level is ten times greater than the average of all tax avoidance in these countries' populations.[37]

It gets worse. Experts agree that the tax cuts President Trump signed at the end of 2017 will increase incentives to abuse loopholes; among those who can afford sophisticated tax advice, we can expect tax avoidance to be exacerbated. As soon as the new tax law was passed, lawyers and accountants got to work on ways to interpret vague new rules to the advantage of their wealthy and corporate clients.[38]

Over the past few decades, the very rich have not only come to pay less in taxes but also increasingly campaigned to push rates even lower over the preferences of the majority. In the months leading up to the passage of the Trump tax cuts, corporations and corporate donors were the ones pushing Republicans to get the bill passed, spending millions. Further, the anticorporate advocacy nonprofit Public Citizen reported that there were eleven lobbyists engaging with tax issues for every member of Congress. Yet, most Americans were not in favor of the legislation: in November and December 2017, support for the bill was only 32 percent. The negative polling increased as the legislation was closer to passage it remains unpopular in 2019, a year after implementation.[39]

Strangely, even as they lobby for lower taxes, business leaders agree that we need to make more public investments. In 2015, the Association of Chamber of Commerce Executives, including signatories from cities, towns, and groups in all fifty states, wrote to Congress urging members to shore up the federal Highway Trust Fund and pass a longer-term federal transportation funding bill. In local Chamber elections throughout the United States—such as in Rowlett, Texas, a suburb of Dallas—infrastructure is arguably one of the most cited issues. State chambers of commerce have also been advocating for investments in early childhood education and the US Chamber of Commerce, which represents three million businesses, runs a nationwide initiative with state and local chambers that is committed to high-quality education for children from birth to age five, recognizing its importance to the future competitiveness of the US workforce. Still, this support is tepid compared to the lobbying efforts to reduce their tax burden and seems disingenuous.[40]

## Lack of Investment in Public Goods is a Political Failure

If more government tax revenue is good for more people, their communities, and overall economic growth—and if people are willing to raise taxes to fund needed investments—then why do policymakers keep cutting taxes and lowering investments? To understand this, we turn to the growing political science literature documenting the subversive effects of inequality on democracy, as those with the most money manipulate political processes. The emerging consensus is that politics and policymaking today are increasingly geared to the priorities of the very rich, and not focused on the needs of the nation as a whole—and certainly not on promoting economic growth that is strong, stable, *and* broadly shared. What happened in the debate over tax cuts in 2017 is increasingly the norm rather than the exception. While most Americans were not in favor of the legislation, the support from elites and corporate interests superseded the democratic will.

New evidence shows that elite voices carry more weight than others in determining policy outcomes. Recent research from political scientists Martin Gilens at Princeton University and Benjamin Page at Northwestern University finds that policies supported by the rich are two-and-a-half times more likely to pass into law than those not supported by the rich. In their study—using a unique data set of key variables relating to 1,779 policy issues—policies with low support among the rich became law only about 18 percent of the time, whereas policies with high support among the rich ended up as law about 45 percent of the time. To explain this disparity, they note the decline of the countervailing organizations—such as unions—that might give more influence to other perspectives. Vanderbilt University political scientist Larry Bartels has conducted complementary research showing that when senators vote, they are more likely to align with the rich than the poor. Republicans overwhelmingly respond to the policy preferences of the rich—but so do Democrats, to a lesser degree. And the two parties' senators are similar in their unresponsiveness to low- and middle-income constituents.[41]

The control of outcomes is in no small part because elites increasingly set the agenda. In their groundbreaking book *Winner-Take-All Politics*, political scientists Jacob Hacker at Yale University and Paul Pierson at UC-Berkeley explain how economic inequality affects both the politics of agenda-setting and the relative strengths of the organizations central to making policy changes happen—and show that the rules of the game matter. They present evidence that the rich are more able than the rest of us to get their interests heard in the political process. In an interview with Bill Moyers, Pierson said the data should not surprise anyone: "You just have to look at recent headlines to see a Washington that seems preoccupied with the economic concerns of those at the top and is resistant in many cases to steps that are clearly favored by a majority of the electorate." It may be that being rich means having more opportunities to give politicians a piece of their mind: when political scientists Benjamin Page and Jason Seawright at Northwestern University, and Larry M. Bartels at Vanderbilt University surveyed Chicagoans whose incomes put them in the top 1 percent (respondents had an average net worth of $14 million), 40 percent reported having made contact with their senator at some point, and nearly 50 percent had made at least one contact with a congressional office.[42]

These challenges for our democracy are magnified by the role of economic elites—and their money—in the political process. It's well known that the US political system is awash in money. The US Supreme Court ruled in 2010, on First Amendment grounds, that the government cannot deny the freedom of speech of organizations—including corporations—by restricting their spending on communications.[43] The *New York Times* reports that in 2015, just 158 families and the companies they control gave a total of $176 million toward the 2016 presidential campaigns, accounting for nearly half of all donations at that point.[44] The 2018 midterm election cycle is estimated to have driven $5 billion in total spending, making it the costliest congressional election cycle in US history. More than $24 million of that came from just 388 CEOs of big American companies.[45] All this money affects political outcomes—even if it cannot be proven that a particular donor is buying a particular vote.

Page and Gilens document how money tilts the political playing field. They find that political campaign contributions writ large have a filtering effect on candidates, nudging out candidates on the political left and even in the center, and favoring those on the right. Because being electorally competitive depends on fundraising, politicians spend a lot of time with people who have money, listening to their concerns. It is also easier for wealthy candidates to run for office because they can, at least in part, self-finance their campaigns—discouraging many without resources from even trying.[46]

This is not the way the US democracy is supposed to function. In the postwar period of the twentieth century, at the height of our nation's era of broadly shared economic growth, the interplay of competing but balanced political forces led to policy outcomes reflecting a wider diversity of views. This was the era in which Yale political scientist Robert Dahl did the research for his 1960 classic *Who Governs?* In it, Dahl argues that US democracy is characterized by *inclusive pluralism*, with individuals' competing priorities being represented by active interest groups all competing in a political sphere where no one group dominates. Dahl was writing when overall income inequality in the United States was at its twentieth-century low and the gains of growth were more broadly shared even as, to be sure, people of color and women were worse off in terms of both civil and economic rights. In the society he observed, political power was more widely dispersed across people and institutions—including strong civic institutions. There was more participation in the political process and higher trust in political institutions. Little did he know that the US economy would become vastly more unequal in terms of income and wealth, creating a new political process bearing little resemblance to the dynamics he described.[47]

In the end, one of the most subversive effects of economic inequality may be that it's making the United States virtually ungovernable. Political scientists John Voorheis of the University of Oregon, Nolan McCarty of Princeton University, and Boris Shor of the University of Houston document how the rise in inequality has gone hand in hand with a rise in ideological polarization, posing serious challenges to the policymaking ability of the US constitutional system. The checks and balances between the executive and legislative branches, combined with the need in the Senate to get a 60 percent majority for significant legislation to avoid a filibuster, mean that bipartisanship is necessary to Congressional action, yet political compromise is increasingly rare. This builds on research by McCarty and his coauthors Keith T. Poole of the University of Georgia and Howard Rosenthal of New York University, who were the first to show that economic inequality and political polarization have risen together for the past half-century (Figure 3.2). Indeed, the southern political realignment around racial issues in recent decades has been so polarizing because, in fact, it is driven largely by economics.[48]

Economic inequality simultaneously subverts the institutions that work in the public interest and efforts to engage in collective endeavors. If we want the economy to deliver growth that is strong, stable, and broadly shared, the US government—and state and municipal governments—needs to make more investments to ensure that people with talent are able to acquire skills and access capital. In doing so, we all would reap the benefits of a well-educated labor force and steady stream of entrepreneurial ventures. Our government also needs to make more investments in broadband, transportation, and other public goods. Economic inequality prevents this from happening because the power to make policy increasingly resides with a tiny minority of people who are accruing the most from economic growth and focus their political energy on lowering their own taxes. Important investments that would benefit us all—and the economy overall—are not their priority.

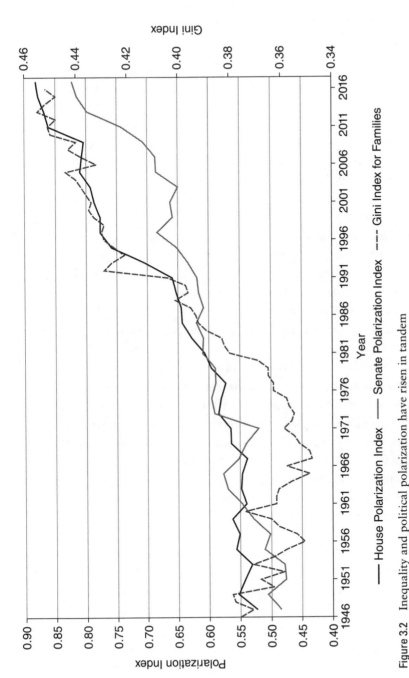

Figure 3.2  Inequality and political polarization have risen in tandem
US House and Senate Polarization and Gini Index, 1947–2016.
Adapted from Nolan M. McCarty, Keith T. Poole, and Howard Rosenthal, "Political Polarization and Income Inequality,"
*SSRN Electronic Journal*, January 2003.

*Source:* Keith T. Poole and Howard Rosenthal, Voteview: Congressional Roll-Call Votes Database; World Bank.

## Releasing Inequality's Grip on Our Democracy

Policymakers must find ways to ensure that our tax system delivers the revenue necessary for public investments. The wealthiest segments of society are clearly far better off than they have been in the past, in part because of political decisions they help to bring about using their money and influence. Reining in top incomes through the tax system would shift incentives away from focusing on ever-higher incomes, and perhaps toward more investments that would improve outcomes for the many, not just the few.

The top marginal income tax rate is now less than half what it was in the mid-twentieth century, and this has allowed individuals at the top to amass wealth and power far beyond what previous generations of wealthy Americans could. Policymakers have lots of room to raise taxes at the top of the income ladder and, indeed, doing so might have economic benefits beyond the extra revenues it would raise. Diamond and Saez note that if the United States had approximately doubled the tax burden on the top 1 percent of income earners in 2007, that "would still leave the after-tax income share of the top percentile more than twice as high as in 1970."[49]

Beyond simply raising income tax rates for the highest earners, policymakers have a variety of other tools at their disposal. Given that the top 1 percent controls about 40 percent of US wealth, policymakers should also come up with more and better ways to tax wealth. There are a number of possible avenues to pursue, as laid out in a recent report for the Washington Center for Equitable Growth by New York University legal scholar David Kamin. First, while the tax system imposes taxes on gains on property, they are often easy to limit or avoid entirely. Policymakers could fix this by changing how we determine capital gains and when we tax them—such as by moving to so-called mark-to-market taxation of investments. Second, policymakers should make it harder for corporations to avoid taxation by shifting income across international borders. They could do this either by moving to a destination-based system or by imposing a minimum tax (higher than the one imposed by the Tax Cuts and Jobs Act of 2017). And, third, an outright wealth tax could be imposed.[50]

Policymakers should also consider pursuing accumulated wealth in more targeted ways. Imagine a new tax specifically imposed on the wealth generated by new technology—not so radical an idea, given that much of it grows out of federally funded primary research at national labs and universities and colleges. And imagine that the proceeds of this tax were distributed as an annual dividend to every American citizen—let's call it the National Technology Revolution Fund. If the concept sounds familiar, that's because it is akin to what Alaska decided to do after oil was discovered on its North Slope in 1969, realizing that the state's natural resources were its people's collective inheritance. In 1976, it changed its constitution to create the Alaska Permanent Fund, and has since collected at least 25 percent of all oil and mineral royalties, invested them in a balanced portfolio of domestic and international equities, bonds, and real estate, and distributed an equal annual dividend to every man, woman, and child with established residency and a stated intention to stay in Alaska.[51]

Another path would be to increase the role of *corrective taxes* in the tax system. Commonly referred to as "sin taxes," these are designed to discourage activities that are not illegal but are known to be harmful to people and which incur public costs. As such, they can increase living standards while also raising revenue. The single most important corrective tax the United States could enact is a federal carbon tax. It should be set based on the best estimates of the economic harm resulting from carbon emissions—what economists call the "social cost of carbon." The available evidence suggests that a tax of roughly $40 per ton would be appropriate. This tax would deliver gains at home and to the rest of the world by reducing the accumulation of greenhouse gases and the associated environmental harms.[52]

Taking these steps will require working through democratic processes. This, however, is not easy when there's little counterweight to Big Money. Civic institutions, especially unions, that once served as voices for everyday wage-earning workers have suffered a long decline. Unions were traditionally the most vocal and ardent advocates for the middle class, but now only one out of every fifteen private-sector workers belongs to a union. This is a sharp drop from the early 1950s, when a third of private-sector workers did—and among private sector employees, in fact, is a smaller share than when workers were first guaranteed the right to organize and bargain collectively without fear of retaliation from employers under the National Labor Relations Act in 1935. Public-sector employees, who now make up about half of all union members, are also seeing their unions' power diminished. In the June 2018 Supreme Court case *Janus v. American Federation of*

*State, County, and Municipal Employees*, the plaintiff prevailed as the court ruled it unconstitutional for unions to compel employees who are not members, but who stand to benefit from a union's collective bargaining activities, to pay agency fees (also known as fair share fees—in Janus's case, amounting to $600 per year). Unions instantly lost the fees of nonmembers and it is not hard to predict that they will also lose members as a result of the ruling. Now that the option exists to free-ride on collective bargaining efforts, some public employees will choose not to pay the dues that also cover the lobbying and campaign contributions that are core to unions' political influence.[53]

There are many new ideas for how to revitalize the labor movement, some of which look outside the traditional realm of unions. In a recent report for the Roosevelt Institute, political scientist Todd Tucker named seven ways policymakers could strengthen worker bargaining power: launch a global agreement modeled on the Paris Climate Accord that explicitly targets higher unionization rates; privilege firms that cooperate well with unions; make labor law enforcement more favorable toward labor; extend union contracts to non-union workers; structurally incorporate unions into the policymaking process; allow unions to manage public benefits; and make union membership the default status for workers. While putting in place the whole package would certainly address the power imbalances in our economy, implementing any one of these could improve workers' ability to bargain with employers over pay and working conditions.[54]

Putting up a serious fight against growing inequality will also require shoring up our democracy. Powerful and wealthy interests are able to subvert our government and election systems against the public will at every level. We need to give the majority back its voice. Gerrymandering, for example, allows politicians to redraw maps to choose their voters, making them immune to the popular will. In the 2018 general election in Wisconsin, Democratic candidates for the state assembly received 54 percent of all votes cast. But because Republicans drew the maps to give themselves an insurmountable advantage, Republicans won 63 percent of assembly seats. This is a form of election rigging that can be fought with ballot measures. Michigan, Colorado, Missouri, Utah, Florida, and Maryland all approved reforms to increase popular accountability and fair representation in their political systems in 2018, often over the fierce opposition of groups representing wealthy special interests. Missouri's ethics and redistricting overhaul was vehemently opposed by the state's powerful business lobby, even after it was approved by 62 percent of voters, underscoring the need for a counter-balance to their money and influence.[55]

Another tactic is to encourage small-donor matching systems, where the government multiplies the donations small contributors make. This kind of system—already in effect in localities such as New York City, Maryland's Montgomery County, Berkeley, California, and Portland, Oregon—makes it easier for candidates with large grassroots support to compete with ones bankrolled by a handful of large donors, and pushes all candidates to interact more with regular folks, amplifying their voices. Publicly financing elections not only gives candidates who aren't billionaires a chance at running for office, but also allows aspiring lawmakers to spend less time asking for donations from the wealthy. We can look to Seattle for another example of public financing: the city began an experiment in 2017 to fight big money in politics by increasing the clout of small money. Half a million Seattle residents received $100 in "democracy vouchers" to donate to the local political candidate of their choice. The vouchers significantly raised the number of Seattle residents participating in the campaign-finance system, and initial analysis suggests the program diversified the pool of donors, though not to the extent that it fully represented the electorate. Given the results of these smaller-scale programs, public financing deserves to be added to the national agenda.[56]

Big money influence is the key reason that the failed ideas underlying the 2017 tax legislation have remained a force. Even Bruce Bartlett concedes that there is "absolutely no evidence at the state and local level or the federal level, of any tax cut that I have ever looked at, of it coming anywhere close to paying for itself."[57] What plenty of evidence does show is that wealthy Americans tend to be more conservative than the average American when it comes to policies such as taxation, regulation, and social insurance programs—and increasing economic inequality makes it easier for their views to hold sway. This constitutes a crisis, and nothing short of reforming our democracy to ensure that policymakers are accountable to the citizens of the republic at large will resolve it.

# 4

# Market Structure

A T FIRST GLANCE, the beer industry in the United States would seem to prove Adam Smith's point that, when brewers compete with many others to sell their wares, an invisible hand pushes the economy toward mutually beneficial outcomes. Thousands of new businesses have successfully entered the US market over the past several decades, following the path blazed by Jim Koch, the cofounder of the Boston Beer Company, which produces Sam Adams beer. Beer aficionados point to a craft beer revolution, with many upstart brands touting new flavor profiles produced locally. In 1978, just prior to the deregulation agenda put in place under President Ronald Reagan, there were eighty-nine breweries nationwide; by 2017, there were more than 6,300. Just in Washington, DC, where I live, a variety of breweries have opened over the past decade within the city limits, among them DC Brau Brewing Company, 3 Stars Brewing Company, Atlas Brew Works, and Bluejacket. Craft brewers now account for almost 13 percent of all beer sold in the United States by volume and over 23 percent by revenue.[1]

While the craft revolution has injected competition, quality, and innovation, these upstart breweries have a fragile foothold in the industry. Consumers who read the fine print learn that most brands sold are owned by one of two giant beer corporations: Anheuser-Busch InBev of Belgium or Molson Coors Brewing Company of the United States. Together, these two corporations account for roughly two-thirds of beer shipments in the United

States. The big beer corporations have eliminated their competition by merging with erstwhile competitors, buying up popular upstarts, and acquiring the firms that distribute beer—and limiting those distributors' ability to carry independent brands. AB InBev, which sells five hundred brands of beer globally, has gone so far as to invest in the websites that review beer—including *RateBeer*, *October*, and the *Beer Necessities*—making it that much harder for independent brewers to get their products to customers.[2]

The two big brewers are using their market power to crush their competition. They subvert the workings of the invisible hand by exercising their significant power in the marketplace to dictate the price of beer and the conditions for suppliers and people who work in the industry. The economic outcomes have been consistent with what theory would predict: after the joint venture between Molson Coors and SABMiller was consummated in 2008, beer prices rose by six percent, reversing decades of decline. The acquisition of Anheuser-Busch by InBev in 2008 led to 1,400 US workers being laid off, and following its agreement to merge with SABMiller in 2016, AB InBev announced plans to cut at least 5,500 jobs.[3]

Where the beer industry goes from here depends on whether we protect competition. But this story isn't just about beer. Competitive markets have been eroding in industries across the United States—and across the world—to similar effect. Two other everyday examples are cable television and mobile phone service. Both are basic features of our digital age, but most customers have only a few providers to choose from—and in some neighborhoods only one. Economists traditionally assumed that, for the most part, so-called perfectly competitive markets—where no one firm has the power to influence prices or market conditions—were close enough to the norm that they could provide the basis for economic models that guide antitrust policies. Situations where one monopoly firm—or an oligopoly of a few firms—has enough market power to set prices, limit competition, or dictate conditions for suppliers were considered outliers. Now, that exception seems to be the rule.[4]

Monopoly power tends to exacerbate inequality in income and wealth. A monopoly or oligopoly has enough market power to set prices, limit competition, and dictate conditions for suppliers. These firms can and do charge higher prices than they would in competitive markets and, as a result, they bring in higher profits, which are spent on higher pay for the firms' managers and larger payouts to shareholders in the form of dividends and share buybacks. All of this makes income inequality worse. At the same time, even as they dole out more money to executives and shareholders, firms in highly concentrated markets face less competition in hiring workers, which means they can pay non-executive employees lower wages and provide worse working conditions without losing staff. To the extent that industry concentration affects incomes, in short, it increases them for executives at the tops of firms while tamping down the salaries of everyone else, distorting both demand and the deployment of corporate savings into new investments—topics we'll tackle in Part III.

Additionally, dominant economic power reinforces itself in the political world. Those at the top of the wealth and income ladders are deploying their economic power to affect policy outcomes to benefit themselves rather than the nation overall. Beyond making it difficult for innovative startups to get a toehold on the economic ladder, this makes it hard for democracy to flourish. With a high degree of market power, those already at the top can afford to lobby hard for policies that will keep them there, and block others from entering. Corporations and wealthy elites in the United States spend more on lobbying than their counterparts in comparable democracies do, using money that, too often, they gain through their enormous market power. Thus, one way or another, concentration sits at the core of the economic problems created by economic inequality.

Over a century ago, our nation came together and enacted a body of legislation to prevent any given firm—or a handful of firms—from gaining enough market power to limit competition and raise prices. The Sherman Antitrust Act of 1890 made it illegal for businesses to collude with each other and form cartels or to monopolize markets on their own. The Clayton Antitrust Act of 1914 protected competition by limiting a firm's ability to merge with or acquire another firm if the effect would be to eliminate competition, by addressing interlocking corporate directories, and by forbidding price discrimination, among other things. The Federal Trade Commission Act, also of 1914, specifically dealt with competition and mergers by establishing a federal agency with the power to study industries and declare acts or practices to be unfair competition.

The original objectives of these pieces of legislation were to curb the outsized political power of concentrated firms, prevent wealth transfers from consumers and suppliers to these firms, and keep markets open and competitive. The laws were little used at first, during the Gilded Age in the late

1800s, but presidents Teddy Roosevelt and Woodrow Wilson later wielded them to good effect, keeping firms from amassing disproportionate market power for many years. Today, too many policymakers sit idly by as the dynamics of our competitive marketplaces benefit behemoths rather than preserving level playing fields. While these laws have not changed, their application has.[5]

## Too Little Competition Means Too Much Profit

The story of the beer industry is emblematic of market concentration and what it means for prices, revenues, and who gains from higher profits. Beer is an important product, but the industry accounts for only 0.7 percent of the US economy. Far more economically important is the health care industry, which is arguably even less competitive. It accounts for more than one-sixth of the US economy and employs more people than any other single industry. Typical families spend about 8 percent of their annual income on health care, and employers spend about 8 percent of payroll for their employees' health insurance. It is also an important source of technological innovation. Over the past decade, alongside the long-standing technological frontiers in pharmaceuticals and medical devices, there's been a sharp rise in use of electronic health records that may become a data and population-health tool for the future. What happens in the health care industry affects us all.[6]

Leemore Dafny has spent her career investigating the competitiveness of various aspects of the health care industry. While people may see the health care industry as unique because it provides goods and services that are fundamental to human well-being, Dafny believes that health care can be looked at like any other industry. "There are a lot of industries out there that sell outputs and have complicated institutions," she reminded the crowd at a recent *New England Journal of Medicine* conference in Boston, "and the same rules of business apply. And the same is true for health care."[7] Across a series of papers, she and her coauthors have made use of cutting-edge data and methods and found that much of the health care industry can be described as monopolistic. This helps to explain why health care costs are rising so much faster than other costs of living. In many communities, health care providers—doctors and nurses and aides—work for the same corporation. There are also only a few manufacturers for most medicines and medical devices, and few if any choices when it comes to choosing an insurance company.

Dafny's findings are important because US policymakers have long presumed that most people in our country will purchase both health insurance and medical services in the market. While well over a third of Americans receive health care through one of the two major public programs—Medicare for the aged or Medicaid for poor and very low-income families—and there are regulations on what insurers can offer, most people continue to rely on the private market for health insurance. Policymakers have promised the public that the way to ensure top-quality health care at the lowest cost is to rely on the invisible hand. Only competitive markets can deliver the innovations that will keep improving health outcomes at the lowest prices—medical advances that can then be exported around the world. Or so the story goes.[8]

The Affordable Care Act, President Obama's signature achievement, passed into law in 2010, embraces this philosophy. To achieve its goal of covering everyone while pushing down prices—"bending the cost curve"—this law established health insurance exchanges, which are marketplaces where those who don't have employer-provided health insurance can choose from (ideally) many companies to buy coverage at comparable rates. States can establish their own exchanges—as sixteen states and the District of Columbia have done—or use the federal exchange. Essential to the design of these exchanges was the assumption that sufficient numbers of insurance companies would compete for customers to drive prices down and provide enough insurance capacity—conditions that Dafny has found do not always exist.[9]

While Dafny's research is often credited with being critical to the development of the public exchange system in the Affordable Care Act, she didn't set out to become one of the nation's top experts on the health care industry. She told me that she began looking into this industry because she had found "a fantastic data source, a proprietary dataset that had information on the health plans offered by a very big sample of very big firms," covering almost five million employees per year between 1998 and 2005.[10] She relied on this data source in a paper she published in 2010 in the *American Economic Review*, where she showed that, compared to health care companies in competitive markets, those in concentrated markets are able to set prices so as to extract higher revenue. Dafny found that employers in more concentrated markets had to pay more when switching employee health insurance plans than employers did in more competitive markets. She concluded that "the strong bargaining position of insurers in concentrated markets enables them to capture more of the extra surplus generated by profit shocks."[11] Lack of competition allowed health insurance firms to rack up outsized revenues and profits.

In later work, Dafny went on to show how consolidation in the health insurance market hurts consumers. In 1999, Aetna and Prudential Health-Care merged, creating the bigger Aetna which is now the nation's third-largest health insurer and covers about 22 million people nationwide. Along with Stanford University's Mark Duggan and UCLA's Subramaniam Ramanarayanan, Dafny compared prices in the 139 geographic markets where both firms sold plans before and after the merger. After the merger, they found, people had fewer choices in what kind of insurance to buy and the new behemoth could charge more. In 2006, after the merger, the cost of buying health insurance was about seven percent higher than before the merger in 1998. The researchers translated this into hard household numbers: people with employer-sponsored health insurance paid about $250 extra per year (in 2018 dollars).[12]

Dafny is now seeking to understand whether there is sufficient competition for the new health insurance exchanges to serve their function. In April 2016, UnitedHealth Group's Stephen Hemsley, in his role as CEO of the nation's largest health insurer, announced that the conglomerate would not participate in most of the exchanges set up by the Affordable Care Act. This decision sparked the Kaiser Family Foundation—a nonprofit health policy research organization—to warn that "if United were to exit from all areas where it currently participates and not be replaced by a new entrant, the effect on insurer competition could be significant in some markets—particularly in rural areas and southern states."[13] Two months later, UnitedHealth announced plans to pull out of the federal exchange and only remain in three state exchanges—those in Nevada, New York, and Virginia (which handles plan management while relying on the federal health insurance exchange). Dafny, along with economists Jonathan Gruber at the Massachusetts Institute of Technology and Christopher Ody at Northwestern University, saw the health insurer's decision as an opportunity for them to study what reduced competition means for the price of health insurance. They examined prices nationwide before and after UnitedHealth's exit, and confirmed the law's premise: exchanges with more insurers have lower premiums. The exit of this insurer increased the premium for the second-lowest cost "silver" plan by 5.4 percent.[14]

Dafny has found it difficult to draw many conclusions from the exchanges' performance as markets because the situation has been so dynamic. "The exchanges have fluctuated dramatically over the years in terms of market participation, with some early entrants—and then, as everyone is well aware, a lot of legislative uncertainty," she told me. "I would say, we didn't let the exchanges perform by giving them a clear set of rules and then seeing what the market did. We kept mucking with the rules, and also saying we *might* muck with the rules." As a researcher, she concluded: "I find the actual experience to be of much more limited value than you might think." In short, the jury's still out on whether this system can work effectively.[15]

Insurance is by no means the only corner of the health care sector where a small number of firms have a high degree of monopoly power. We see consolidation in hospitals, as well. In many markets, only one corporation owns all the hospitals (as a monopoly) and in others there may be two—or less likely, three—corporations who own all the hospitals (as an oligopoly). Regardless of whether it's a monopoly or oligopoly, market concentration creates enormous market power and, with it, rising prices and less access to quality care. Dafny, in research with Robin S. Lee, also at Harvard, and Kate Ho at Princeton, found that when hospitals merged—in the same state but not in the same geographic market—greater market concentration led to price increases of about 7 percent to 10 percent. The clear conclusion is that having hospitals all owned by one corporation raises prices.[16]

Of course, the pharmaceutical industry is the classic case study for students of monopoly power—which is compounded in its case by the importance of intellectual property. For years, these firms have found new and creative ways to abuse their patent rights and manipulate regulations, leaving consumers to pay the bills. Beginning in the 2000s, for example, some pharmaceutical companies initiated patent infringement litigation against producers of generic versions of their branded offerings, then settled by paying those potential competitors to delay entry—a practice known as "pay-for-delay." According to a 2010 study by staff at the Federal Trade Commission, deals of this type from 2004 to 2009 delayed generic competition by seventeen months, increasing drug costs by $3.5 billion a year. Although a 2013 Supreme Court decision has, for the moment, limited this

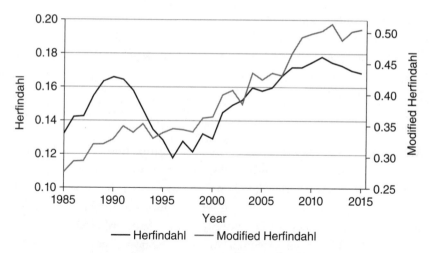

Figure 4.1   Market concentration has risen in recent decades
Mean Herfindahl across industries in the United States, 1985–2015.

*Source:* Germán Gutiérrez and Thomas Philippon, "Declining Competition and Investment in the US"; US Census Bureau; Compustat.

practice, marketers of branded drugs have turned to other tactics to stifle competition.[17]

What's happening in the health care industry is very much a part of a much larger trend. The evidence is all around us—think airlines, or the online platforms operated by the likes of Amazon and Google. Researchers document declines in competition across a wide array of industries. Figure 4.1 offers a summary of their findings, using two common measures: the Herfindahl Index, which indicates the level of industry concentration, and the Modified Herfindahl Index, which accounts for anticompetitive effects due to common ownership. Along both lines, concentration has risen sharply since the mid-1980s.[18]

As a particularly vivid case, antitrust experts Gene Kimmelman and Mark Cooper have looked into the telecommunications sector, which has experienced extreme consolidation since the enactment of the 1996 Telecommunications Act. Across wireless service, business data services, broadband, and video distribution services, the top four telecommunications firms now have overwhelming market share. This dominance is likely to increase in the wake of US District Judge Richard Leon's June 2017 ruling in federal court that the merger between AT&T and Time Warner could go through. That added concentration could catastrophically subvert the market by enabling the company to manipulate prices to the detriment of both consumers and the workers in this industry.[19]

## How Monopoly Power Crimps Innovation
## and Economic Growth

When companies plow their profits into innovating, this leads to the kinds of productivity gains that drive long-term improvements in living standards. This raises another fundamental question in economics: What kinds of firms are more likely to invest in innovations—ones in a competitive market or ones with monopoly power? Stanford University economist and Nobel laureate Kenneth Arrow came down on one side of this debate: building on his work on how competitive markets create the conditions for general equilibrium (and the corollary that general equilibrium is socially optimal), he concluded that, when there's less competition, there's less innovation. Oligopolies simply face less pressure to invest in it. Or, as he put it, "preinvention monopoly power acts as a strong disincentive to further innovation."[20]

The alternative view was developed decades before by Austrian economist Joseph Schumpeter. Schumpeter took up the question of innovation as his life's work, famously developing the idea of "creative destruction"—the process by which, in a market economy with free entry and exit of firms, new and better offerings continually displace old ones. As he put it, this is the "process of industrial mutation . . . that incessantly revolutionizes the economic structure *from within*, incessantly destroying the old one, incessantly creating a new one."[21] In his view of the marketplace, monopoly power can spur innovation in two ways. First, it creates a stronger incentive to innovate because a large, monopolistic firm has the opportunity to reap bigger rewards from a product that is superior to the alternatives customers could choose. Second, when a firm's greater market power raises its profits, it has the financial cushion to make longer-term investments in research and developing new products. Schumpeter developed these ideas during the 1930s and 1940s, when large-scale capital investments drove economywide changes across a variety of industries.[22]

Neither economist is entirely wrong; over time, there is evidence pointing in both directions. There are examples of concentrated industries fostering innovation—think of the industry dominated by Boeing and Airbus and its long-term success in producing ever more efficient jet airliners, or the constant upgrades made to the operating systems on our smartphones, controlled by Apple's iOS and Google's Android. But there also are examples of big corporations stifling innovation. In the 1970s, Eastman Kodak invented the digital camera, but its executives consciously decided to shelve the new technology because they recognized it would be the end of their photographic film monopoly. Today, dominant pharmaceutical companies acquire innovative competitors and quash some of their drug development projects, especially if they overlap with the acquirer's own initiatives.[23]

Looking at the US economy today, the evidence is accumulating from a wide array of sources that higher industry concentrations are doing more to impede investments in the development of new products and services than to foster them. Economists Thomas J. Holmes at the University of Minnesota, David K. Levine at the European University Institute, and James A. Schmitz at the Federal Reserve Bank of Minneapolis tested the hypothesis that firms with monopoly power are less likely to lead technological changes because the transition to the new technology is costly. In their words, one of the costs of adopting new technology is "the forgone rents on the sales of those 'lost' units, and these opportunity costs are larger the higher the price on those lost units."[24] Other scholars have found that price markups increased significantly after horizontal mergers or acquisitions, but there is no corresponding evidence that productivity increased within plants in the newly created firms.[25]

On the question of investment generally, compelling new evidence comes from research by New York University economists Germán Gutiérrez and Thomas Philippon. Their research questions why economywide investment is down even though firms have a lot of cash on hand. To understand what the investment levels should be, they predict investments based on the ratio of the value of a company—calculated by its market value—relative to the value of all the assets of the company were they to be purchased at current prices. This is called "Tobin's Q," named after Yale economist and Nobel laureate James Tobin who developed the idea in 1969. The higher the value of Q—the market value of the company relative to the cost of rebuilding the company—the more the company should invest. Their analysis shows that, since 2000, the financial valuations of firms relative to their assets have increased, but business investments haven't increased nearly as much. Indeed, market concentration—including common shareholder ownership—and corporate short-termism (financial market-speak for executives who focus on quarterly earnings and the short-term price of their companies' shares at the expense of long-term investments) explain about 80 percent of the difference between actual business investment and what they predict investment should have been. (Note, however, that these conclusions cannot establish causality as they are based on simple regressions.)[26]

Other economists asking these questions are coming to similar conclusions. Gauti Eggertsson, Jacob Robbins, and Ella Getz Wold, all at Brown University, find that a rise in the market power of firms can explain a number of puzzles in the current economy. These include firms having a lot of financial wealth but not investing it; the cost of capital being fairly constant but the real interest rate (the cost of borrowing) falling; and the increasing share of national income going to the owners of capital rather than to the salaries of workers. Their conclusion is that the rise in market power slows down economic growth because heightened price markups result in lower wages—and thus a lower supply of labor—and lower investment.[27]

One unique aspect of this era—which might explain why Schumpeter's view is less correct today than Arrow's—is how the monopoly power of many of today's most profitable firms stems from the creation of innovative platforms. A "platform firm" is an intermediary, connecting buyers and sellers of goods and services in one or multiple different markets. Think of an auction house—either the old-fashioned type where everyone shows up on a certain day and bids on items up for sale, or the new, online version run by eBay. The auction house and eBay aren't producing any of the goods being sold on their platforms. They add value by creating a streamlined marketplace that brings together buyers and sellers in a convenient way. We see much the same in platforms operated by companies such as Amazon, Uber, Lyft, Postmates, Airbnb, and the multitudes of other firms that are providing people a place to buy and sell transportation, groceries, home improvements, dry cleaning, and more—all of them taking their cut of the transactions.

There also is evidence that, as in the case of the big brewers, online platforms are doing everything they can to pull up the ladder behind them, which has the effect of reducing innovation and, with it, long-term productivity and growth. Antitrust experts Jonathan Baker and Fiona Scott Morton looked at online platforms and found that they increasingly demand that any supplier using a platform not offer its services or products at a lower price on a competitor's platform. By doing this, they limit the ability of new platform firms to enter the market; it's a practice that re-

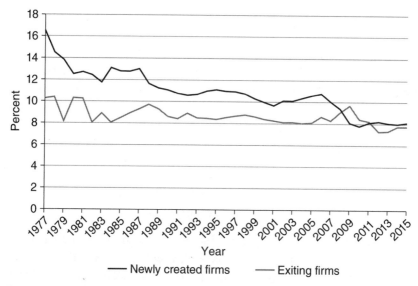

Figure 4.2    Startup rates are declining
Startup and exit rates for US firms, 1979–2015.

*Source:* Jay Shambaugh, Ryan Nunn, and Patrick Liu, "How Declining Dynamism Affects Wages," Brookings Institution, February 27, 2018.

duces competition. If all the hotels on Booking.com agree not to make rooms available for lower prices on other websites, it becomes much more difficult for new online travel agents to enter the market, and thus hotel room rates are kept artificially high.[28]

One metric of the effects of high market concentration on innovation is the reduction in the number of startups. The television series *Silicon Valley* portrays the internet-based startup culture as a ruthless environment in which established firms try to frustrate the show's entrepreneurial heroes by any means necessary—sabotage, stealing, or buying them up. Evidence shows the portrayal is not far off from reality. Jay Shambaugh, Ryan Nunn, Audrey Breitwieser, and Patrick Liu, all part of the Hamilton Project at the Brookings Institution, document that there's been a marked decline in startups since the late 1970s. As they point out, there may be a variety of causes, but one important one is that "increased market concentration is making the environment for startups inhospitable."[29] They point to research in another Brookings report, by economists Ian Hathaway and Robert E. Litan, showing that greater consolidation is associated with fewer startups.[30] (See Figure 4.2.)

The fall-off in startups has economywide consequences—not least among them that it contributes to lackluster productivity gains. Economists Titan Alon and David Berger of Northwestern University, Robert Dent of Nomura Securities, and Benjamin Pugsley of the University of Notre Dame estimate that since 1980, the decline in startups and accompanying aging of incumbent firms have dragged down aggregate productivity by 3.1 percent. An economy that pulls in new ideas and talent should not be seeing a decline in startups.[31]

### Market Concentration Enriches Those at the Top, But Not Everyone Else

Fatter profit margins from greater industry concentration means that a rising share of national income is going to the owners of capital rather than the workers doing the labor. Economists Loukas Karabarbounis at the University of Minnesota and Brent Neiman at the University of Chicago document the global shift away from labor income toward capital. The share of national income going to labor in the United States appeared to be stable around 65 percent through the 1970s, but since 1980, has fallen to below 60 percent. (See Figure 4.3.) Until recently, a trend like this would have surprised experts because, for a long time, economists assumed that the share of national income going to capital and labor was fixed. Cambridge University economist Nicholas Kaldor included this in what he called the "stylized facts," or conditions that are generally true about the modern economy. He argued that, looking across places and eras, the share of national income going toward wages was generally stable. It was an idea that most economists accepted—up until now.[32]

Economists are finding evidence that this change in the distribution of national income toward profits is connected to rising economic concentration and increased monopoly power. The most concentrated firms are able to increase their markups and enjoy higher revenues and profits. Economists Jan De Loecker of Princeton University and Jan Eeckhout of University College London look at price markups across all publicly traded US firms and find that between 1980 and 2014, across industries in the United States, markups more than tripled, rising to 67 percent from 18 percent above marginal cost of production—significantly increasing costs to consumers. If markup is a proxy for market power, companies that started

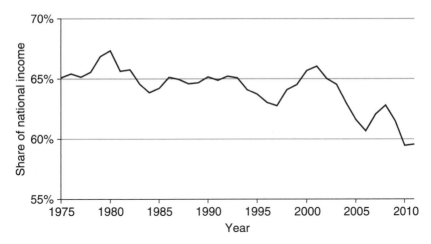

Figure 4.3  Share of income going to labor has declined over time
US labor share of income, 1975–2011.

*Source:* Loukas Karabarbounis and Brent Neiman, "The Global Decline of the Labor Share," *Quarterly Journal of Economics* 129, no. 1 (February 2014).

with more market power strengthened their lead over other companies. The authors argue that this increase in market power helps explain the decline in the labor share of income, declining wages for low-skilled workers, and slowing output growth.[33]

This is especially important because in multiple industries, the share of revenue going to the largest firms has increased. During the Obama administration, the Council of Economic Advisers summarized the trends on market concentration and revenue. They pulled together data showing that, from 1997 to 2012, the largest increases were in transportation and warehousing and retail trade, each experiencing over ten percentage points of growth in revenue concentration, challenging the common view that concentration is rare—only something to worry about among the internet giants.[34] (See Table 4.1.)

Instead of pumping profits into new investments to ensure future corporate growth, firms are lining the pockets of their top management and shareholders, exacerbating economic inequality—producing the opposite of the mutually beneficial outcomes that Smith predicted from a competitive market. Indeed, given that the top 10 percent of wealth holders own 84 percent of all stock shares, having firms funnel their profits into higher

Table 4.1   Share of revenue earned by the largest US firms is on the rise

| Industry | Revenue Earned by 50 Largest Firms, 2012 (Billions $) | Revenue Share Earned by 50 Largest Firms, 2012 | Percentage Point Change in Revenue Share Earned by 50 Largest Firms, 1997–2012 |
|---|---|---|---|
| Transportation | 307.9 | 42.1 | 11.4 |
| Retail Trade | 1,555.8 | 36.9 | 11.2 |
| Finance and Insurance | 1,762.7 | 48.5 | 9.9 |
| Wholesale Trade | 2,183.1 | 27.6 | 7.3 |
| Real Estate Rental and Leasing | 121.6 | 24.9 | 5.4 |
| Utilities | 367.7 | 69.1 | 4.6 |
| Educational Services | 12.1 | 22.7 | 3.1 |
| Professional, Scientific, and Technical Services | 278.2 | 18.8 | 2.6 |
| Administrative/Support | 159.2 | 23.7 | 1.6 |
| Accommodation and Food Services | 149.8 | 21.2 | 0.1 |
| Other Services, Non-Public Admin | 46.7 | 10.9 | −1.9 |
| Arts, Entertainment, and Recreation | 39.5 | 19.6 | −2.2 |
| Health Care and Assistance | 350.2 | 17.2 | −1.6 |

Note: Concentration ratio data is displayed for all North American Industry Classification System (NAICS) sectors for which data is available from 1997 to 2012. Data source: Economic Census (1997 and 2012), US Census Bureau.

Source: "Benefits of Competition and Indicators of Market Power," Council of Economic Advisers Issue Brief, April 2016, https://obamawhitehouse.archives.gov/sites/default/files/page/files/20160414_cea _competition_issue_brief.pdf.

dividends for shareholders can only lead to higher economic inequality. Gutiérrez and Philippon found that instead of investing their profits, firms are using them to buy back corporate stock or pay out dividends—both of which tend to raise their short-term stock valuations. Thus, higher revenues and profits aren't being reinvested but instead are enriching shareholders and managers paid in stock.[35]

Alongside this rise in the share of national income going to profits, we've seen a rise in pay among those at the top, with evidence that this is also due to market concentration. CEO pay has been rising faster than productivity and is a key reason for the rise of incomes in the top 0.1 percent of the income distribution. In the mid-1970s, the typical CEO earned about twenty-five times the income of the typical worker. Today, the typical CEO earns 270 times what the typical worker brings in, including compensation in the form of capital income such as stocks and options and other executive perks. In a study of tax returns from 1979 to 2005, Jon Bakija of Williams College, Adam Cole of the US Treasury, and Bradley T. Heim of Indiana University found that compensation gains by executives, managers, supervisors, and financial professionals accounted for 70 percent of the increase in share of national income going to the top 0.1 percent. This group also accounted for about 60 percent of the top 0.1 percent earners in recent years; the remaining 40 percent include lawyers and medical professionals who also benefit from market concentration and professional protectionism.[36]

In theory, this could be justifiable labor compensation, but there's evidence that this is not the case. In *Capital in the Twenty-First Century*, Thomas Piketty argues that rising CEO pay looks more like an economic rent (with earnings well in excess of what market conditions would normally permit) than earnings reflecting the marginal product of labor (that is, based on the amount of effort put into producing a good or service). Even though the top earners are managers who work for their income, they are a new class of rentiers both because their high incomes come from the economic rents their firms are earning (including pay in the form of shares and options that most workers do not receive, plus other forms of corporate compensation, including retirement health care plans, corporate jets, and other such perks) and because they themselves are extracting rents (by "earning" much higher pay than their multitude of coworkers). To the extent this compensation is a pure rent, this is antithetical to what economic theory teaches us about how wages are set—recall that economist John Bates Clark argued that in a competitive economy, every factor of production is paid its marginal product. To the extent that talented CEOs are scarce, higher pay may be reasonable. But it's hard to see how that's the case.[37]

## Market Concentration Lowers Earnings for Those Not at the Top

Monopoly power not only means that firms have power in the marketplaces where they sell their goods and services. They also have it in labor markets.

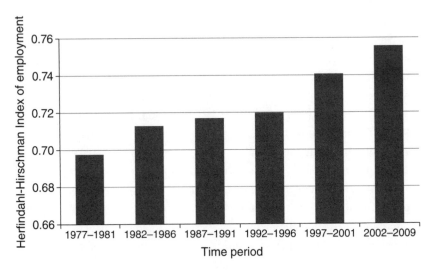

Figure 4.4  Employment is increasingly concentrated
US county level average of the Herfindahl-Hirschman Index of employment,
1977–2009.

*Source:* Efraim Benmelech, Nittai Bergman, and Hyunseob Kim, "Strong Employers and Weak Employees: How Does Employer Concentration Affect Wages?," National Bureau of Economic Research, February 2018.

When there's only one buyer for something, like labor, economists call this a monopsony. The mirror image of monopoly, it means there's a lack of options for those who seek to sell their services, ideas, or time. Economists have tended to devote little attention to monopsony problems, regarding them as so rare as to be limited to the old "company towns" of the late nineteenth and early twentieth centuries—built by factory owners who also owned all the houses, the store, and the church. Now, there's a growing body of research showing that monopsony markets are widespread and growing—subverting the markets for those selling their labor. (See Figure 4.4.)

In a 2018 speech to the world's top central bankers, the former Council of Economic Advisers chair Alan Krueger argued: "Although economists' go-to model of the labor market is often one with perfect competition . . . in many applications I think it is more appropriate to model the labor market as imperfectly competitive, subject to monopsony-like effects, collusive behavior by firms, search frictions, and surpluses that are bargained over."[38] Krueger concluded that greater monopsony power stemming from employer concentration could be suppressing wages, amid the erosion of forces that have traditionally counterbalanced monopsony power and boosted worker bargaining power over the past several decades.

There are more and less extreme examples of monopsony. It used to be that if you were trained as an astronaut, your only real employer option was NASA (now, of course, you might be able to get a job with SpaceX). If you're a nurse, you may have a variety of hospitals to choose from in your community, but it is increasingly likely that they are all owned by the same firm, reducing your bargaining power. In Massachusetts, for example, Partners HealthCare is the largest private employer in the state. In recent years, Partners has been able to ignore the demands of workers because of its enormous market power. Indeed, a meta-analysis by economists Todd Sorensen and Anna Sokolova of the University of Nevada–Reno finds that monopsony is especially prevalent in the health care industry. Monopsony labor markets mean employers can push down wages and provoke frustration among workers.[39]

These trends are economywide. Looking across nonfinancial firms since the 1970s, Massachusetts Institute of Technology sociologist Nathan Wilmers finds that firms that rely on large buyers—such as suppliers to Walmart—tend to pay lower wages to their employees and that this alone accounts for 10 percent of wage stagnation in nonfinancial firms since the 1970s. In other research, scholars have found that, on average, a firm operating in a labor market in which it is the only employer pays wages about 3.1 percent lower than a firm operating in a less concentrated labor market. Most of the decline occurs as the labor market gets closer to a pure monopsony. (There is evidence that in monopsony conditions, suppliers see lower prices for the goods and services they sell as well.)[40]

There is some emerging evidence that the effects of market concentration on labor markets arise in part for social and geographical reasons. People find a good job, settle into a community, and soon confront the fact there are high personal and economic costs to moving again. Employers can make the most of people's reluctance to move. Firms without competitors for potential employees don't see the need to offer higher wages. According to economists José Azar at the University of Navarra, Ioana Marinescu at the University of Pennsylvania's School of Social Policy and Practice, and Marshall Steinbaum at the Roosevelt Institute, communities that moved from the twenty-fifth percentile to the seventy-fifth percentile in concentration of firms saw a 5 percent to 17 percent decline in posted wages.[41]

Some researchers, however, find that monopsony is less prevalent for low-skilled—and low-wage—workers. We can look to the natural experiment of

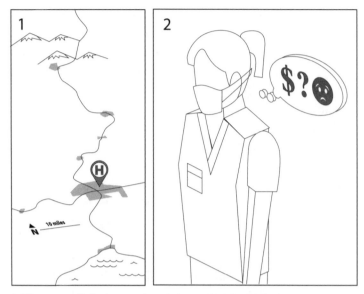

1. When a small city has one hospital or multiple hospitals that are owned by the same firm... 2. health care workers are left with little bargaining power.

what happened when California implemented a law in 1999 requiring nursing homes to have a minimum level of staffing. This rule change meant that 75 percent of firms were looking to ramp up their hiring of nursing assistants at about the same time. Columbia University economist Jordan D. Matsudaira found that nursing homes that were out of compliance with the new law did not have to increase wages in order to increase staffing compared to nursing homes that were already in compliance. He concludes that his findings are ambiguous: "The results provide no evidence that monopsony is an important feature of the labor market, at least for less skilled nurses in the long-term care industry."[42] Yet Temple University economist Doug Webber examines the near-universe of firms across the United States with linked employee-employer data from the US Census and finds that, while there is little evidence of monopsony impacting low-skill workers, the downward pressure on wages from the prevalence of monopsony impacts the income distribution by widening earnings inequality compared to what would exist in a competitive labor market.[43]

Economists have documented a rise in so-called lean production as firms have been increasingly focusing on their core competencies—that is, the basic function they do—shedding other aspects and outsourcing those. Economist David Weil calls this the "fissured workplace" and documents how increasingly people are working for a firm that supplies many companies with a specific product—such as janitorial services or basic legal research. This means that in many markets with rival firms there may be only one or two employers for a particular occupation across those firms. Imagine, for example, a market with multiple hotels. That might seem to guarantee competition for workers, but these new trends in how product markets are organized are creating a different sort of problem even where there appear to be many competing firms. Many of the workers inside the hotels are likely to be employed not by the individual hotels but by companies that specialize in providing employees to do certain types of work. Guests may see all workers wearing the same hotel uniform, but one contractor is probably providing the front-desk staff and another the janitorial services as the hotel has outsourced these jobs to other firms. A janitor would be working for the same company and probably for the same wages at a hotel across the road.[44]

Among other things, this means that the old story of the mailroom boy rising into management and eventually taking over the company doesn't reflect the new economy as it is more difficult in these settings for employees to work their way up the wage ladder by switching jobs. And given this new reality, when a firm sees its profits go up, there are no longer as many direct employees on site who can reasonably expect—or have the institutional capacity to demand—a share of the economic gains. Evidence for this comes from US Bureau of Labor Statistics economist Elizabeth Weber Handwerker. She has measured outsourcing by calculating the variety of occupations employed at a place of business. She found that establishments that employ low-wage workers tend to work in occupationally concentrated workplaces, limiting workers' opportunities to climb up the ladder.[45]

At the beginning of this chapter, we learned about how the merger of health insurance giants Aetna and Prudential into Aetna led to higher prices for those buying health insurance. It turns out that it also led to less bargaining power for the suppliers to the newly created firm. In a formal complaint, the US Department of Justice expressed concern that the merger would "give Aetna the ability to depress physicians' reimbursement rates in Houston and Dallas, likely leading to a reduction in quantity or degradation in quality of physicians' services."[46] Sure enough, Dafny and her colleagues found that the merger reduced physicians' earnings in a typical market by approximately 3 percent between 1999 and 2002. If a doctor's office or hospital doesn't like Aetna's terms, it may not have any other options—it either accepts them or chooses to forgo accepting payments from the insurer, denying it access to Aetna's customers.[47]

There is evidence that this merger led to distortions in the market not just for doctors but for other health care workers, too. In communities where both firms had provided insurance prior to the merger, Dafny and her colleagues found that three years after the merger, employment in the health care sector had fallen. It turned out that employees who didn't like the pay or working conditions at Aetna had few options; there was no place else to go because now the firm was the only health insurance employer in the area. The merger led to a situation where, for health insurance workers, it was like looking for work in a company town.[48]

The upshot: market concentration exacerbates economic inequality and—at least for now in the United States—there's evidence that this inequality across firms is leading to less investment and fewer startups, which in turn could be a factor behind the slowdown in US productivity. To the extent that market concentration also keeps wages low, this dynamic adds to the drag on growth because it reduces the buying power of US consumers and distorts demand and savings, as laid out next in Chapter 5. And to the extent that it reduces investment, market concentration lowers productivity and distorts growth, as laid out in Chapter 6.

### Ensure that the Marketplace Truly is Competitive

For several years after the Affordable Care Act became law, Dafny served as the deputy director for health care and antitrust in the Bureau of Economics at the Federal Trade Commission. At one point, representatives of hospitals planning to merge came in with their economists to defend a deal that the commission was investigating, making a long argument that the provisions in the Affordable Care Act encouraged hospital consolidation. Without missing a beat, Dafny looked at the parties' economist and asked: "Didn't you actively advocate for that provision?"[49]

This is a question that policymakers once asked on a regular basis and should pose more often to firms today. Back in 1913, as Progressive Era leaders sought to rein in monopoly power, President Woodrow Wilson wrote: "If monopoly persists, monopoly will always sit at the helm of the government. I do not expect to see monopoly restrain itself. If there are men in this country big enough to own the government of the United States, they are going to own it."[50] This rings true today. We are living in an era where the wealthy—those titans of industry at the top of concentrated firms—have access to political power far above and beyond a democratic ideal of one person, one vote. Emblematic of this is how CEOs get more time with policymakers. A May 2017 *New York Times* article pointed out that, in just the first four months since Inauguration Day, President Trump had "met with at least 307 chief executives of American companies."[51]

Not coincidentally, in our current era of rising inequality, there has been a concerted effort among firms to subvert existing antitrust laws meant to curb the outsized political power of concentrated firms, prevent wealth transfers from consumers and suppliers to these firms, and preserve open markets. At the same time, competition theory—so important to enforcement decisions—also took a different turn. These efforts have proceeded hand in hand since the 1980s.

Economists had long debated the issue of how to empirically measure concentration. In the late 1960s, the Chicago School view gained ascendance: Adam Smith's invisible hand would promote competition far better than the government. Indeed, Chicago School economists began to argue that antitrust enforcement itself was too much interference in the natural laws of the market. Instead of government regulators ensuring that there would be an open and competitive market, the assumption was that most mergers were economically efficient and beneficial. Unless a firm engaged in obvious and egregious conduct—such as price-fixing, bid rigging, and merging into an actual monopoly—policymakers assumed that firms could not behave anti-competitively. If a firm could earn extra-normal profits, this would only entice others to enter that industry, so those gains would be temporary. The implication was obvious: the first principle of antitrust law should be to not intervene, unless consumer welfare is threatened.[52]

The evidence accumulated by scholars presented in this chapter makes it clear: the US marketplace requires rules that ensure that those with the most economic power cannot subvert the market to benefit themselves at the expense of their competitors, workers, and consumers. In light of this, Congress needs to clarify that the antitrust laws protect competition in all of its forms, not simply where it affects prices. Antitrust laws should prevent the improper use and abuse of monopoly power when the victims are consumers as well as when it threatens competition and the economic well-being of employees. In cases of uncertainty, the laws should favor competition over concentration. The conversation on this score has already begun. In September 2017, Senator Amy Klobuchar of Minnesota, ranking member of the Senate Judiciary Antitrust Subcommittee, introduced two bills that would increase funding for antitrust agencies and restore the vigor of antitrust laws to prevent concentration.[53]

Attending to the issue of monopsony would be a new step for antitrust regulators. The evidence leads to the conclusion that, as a way to start, policymakers should consider how mergers affect labor markets. A merger between two companies that are ostensibly in different markets (and thus would be swiftly approved) might in fact be anticompetitive because they compete for the same employees. It would be reasonable for example, to think that eBay and Intuit—which developed and sells TurboTax—don't compete in the same market. Yet, the two companies found it profitable to enter a non-poaching agreement not to hire each other's computer engineers and scientists—suggesting that they are competitors in this segment of the labor market and that consolidation between them would have negative consequences for these workers, including suppressing wages. This limits the free flow of labor—a core assumption for the basic economic model to work. As a first step to address this, the Congressional Antitrust Caucus has sponsored a series of bills to clarify that anticompetitive activity harming workers is illegal. The Federal Trade Commission and Department of Justice are both newly committed to focusing on this issue. The question is whether they will live up to their promise.[54]

Economist Suresh Naidu at Columbia University, E. Glen Weyl at Microsoft Research, and legal scholar Eric A. Posner at the University of Chicago lay out three steps that the Federal Trade Commission and Department of Justice should take to address the ways that mergers subvert labor market power. They recommend updating the Horizontal Merger Guidelines to provide a detailed legal framework for evaluating the effects of a merger on labor markets. Then, they want regulators to calculate effects on wages. And once a merger is flagged as potentially having effects on the labor market, they argue regulators should engage in a detailed analysis of the likely effects—just like they do for product markets.[55]

Of course, another way to do this is to increase worker power by ending abusive treatment by employers, encouraging collective action, and making it easier to organize into a union. It's no accident that, back when unions were strong, the fruits of economic growth in our nation were more broadly distributed to unionized and non-unionized workers alike. While addressing concentrated capital has gained support from the legal community, restoring worker bargaining power has not. Beginning in the 1970s, a variety of legal hurdles and policy changes, many at the state level—along with the demise of US manufacturing—led to fewer and fewer private-sector workers in unions as a share of the total labor force. Solutions will require not only reinvigorating civic institutions—be they in formal unions or other kinds of worker solidarity organizations as laid out in the prior chapter—but also addressing how the legal landscape has become increasingly hostile to civic engagement. Business associations and their conservative allies in politics and policymaking pushed through so-called right-to-work laws that restrict collective bargaining, and filed serial lawsuits designed to cripple unions' ability to fund their activities. Restoring balance will require rethinking these policies.[56]

On top of everything else, in recent decades, federal antitrust enforcers have not had the resources they need to do their job of preventing anticompetitive consolidation. Since 2010, the number of mergers filed has increased by more than 50 percent, but appropriations to the agencies that enforce the antitrust laws have been flat in nominal terms. Not surprisingly, despite the wave in mergers, there has been no increase in merger enforcement. John Kwoka of Northeastern University examined FTC data from 1996 to 2011 and found that merger enforcement has narrowed its focus to mergers at the highest levels of concentration and permitted more consolidation. Between 2008 and 2011, there were exactly zero enforcement actions taken for mergers that would result in more than four significant competitors in the industry. Congress should ensure that enforcers have the resources they need to do their job.[57]

Getting to these fixes, however, will require coming to terms with the subversion of the political process. We don't have to dig deep to see the role of concentrated industries in promoting policies that improve their profits but are not in the interest of the nation overall. During the 2009 health care debate that led to the enactment of the Affordable Care Act, there were

3,300 registered health care lobbyists working on Capitol Hill—meaning there were six lobbyists for every lawmaker in Congress.[58]

There are many other examples of industry lobbyists' power. Two of the most egregious are the big pharma and big telecom industries. In 2016, the pharmaceutical industry's top lobbying group, known as PhRMA, gave $6.1 million to the American Action Network, a conservative "dark-money" group that isn't required to disclose the identities of its donors. A year later, American Action Network backed the failed Republican health bill that would have repealed the Affordable Care Act and eliminated a fee that pharmaceutical companies pay the federal government, potentially saving PhRMA's clients $28 billion over a decade. The telecommunications industry also lobbies hard—successfully—against federal rules that take away their power to dictate what content goes through their fiber optic cables. This debate over what are called net neutrality rules would not have happened without the huge influence of concentrated sources of money and powerful, concentrated interests over our political system.[59]

The flow of corporate money doesn't end there. Corporations also use charitable donations to influence federal agencies on regulatory decisions through nonprofit organizations—often perceived as entities that provide more neutral input into the lawmaking process. Marianne Bertrand at the University of Chicago and her coauthors find that when a *Fortune* 500 company donates to a nonprofit group, the nonprofit is more likely to submit a comment on proposed rules that the firm has commented on and more likely to support that corporation's views. This matters because the researchers show that when a nonprofit grantee of a corporate donation submits a comment, the final rule is more closely aligned with the corporation's comments.[60]

To counter corporate influence, we need changes in how we finance elections and political engagement. The Supreme Court's ruling that corporations have the status of a person has led to a rapid increase in both the cost of elections and the amount of dark money flowing through campaigns. Without a constitutional amendment, it is difficult to limit the money flowing into our democracy. So, instead, reformers are looking for ways to help regular citizens' voices rise to match those of the wealthy.

# III

# HOW INEQUALITY DISTORTS

Since the first economist put quill to parchment, one of the most fundamental economic debates has been the question of which comes first: the capitalist investing money in a new firm or idea, or the consumer spending money on goods and services? In the early 1800s, the French businessman and economist Jean-Baptiste Say argued that once a product was made and ready for market, it would be sold. Otherwise, he argued, the product had no value. "Thus the mere circumstance of creation of one product immediately opens a vent for other products," he noted. Say's logic was that making something in itself creates demand for the goods and services that go into producing that item.[1]

Say's Law is embedded in former Kansas Governor Sam Brownback's view that if investors (or potential investors) have money, they'll invest it to make new products and services—and thus create jobs. All government needs to do is make sure they have the money. When Senator Mitt Romney speaks of the "job creators" and Kevin Hassett, chair of the Council of Economic Advisers under President Donald Trump, says that cutting taxes on capital will spur blockbuster economic growth, they are both arguing, like Brownback and Say before him, that supply creates its own demand. If policymakers create the conditions for firms to invest, then businesses will do so and everyone will gain from the resulting economic growth. In the world that this view assumes, businesses do not sit on cash.[2]

Yet they do, and today's largest corporations are. The past decade has seen business investment fall even as profits have risen. US firms are sitting on record-high piles of cash, which have been steadily accumulating since the 1980s.

Understanding the dynamics of this cycle is key to fostering sustainable economic growth. And key to that is understanding how economic inequality affects
both consumer demand and private investment. The next two chapters will delve
into recent, data-rich evidence to answer that question. People's spending drives
business investment as consumers—you and I—account for nearly 70 cents of
every dollar spent in the United States. While some firms produce for government or export, these products and services combined account for a negative
contribution to total output in the United States, because we import much more
than we export.

But, people who don't have money cannot spend it. Today and for the past
several decades, the fact that US families in the bottom half of the income distribution have seen no income gains, and the gains for those families not among
the top 10 percent of income earners have been meager to negligible, means
that if firms were to invest more, they may not be able to sell their additional
goods and services—there might not be consumers in positions to buy them.
Many businesses, eyeing demand, have understandably not invested much over
this period. Others have found customers willing to purchase their wares, but
only because of the financially unstable expansion of household debt—as seen
especially in the run-up to the Great Recession in the middle of the last decade,
and as is occurring again today.

■ ■ ■

The next two chapters examine empirical evidence that the number of everyday
consumers who either don't have enough money to spend or are borrowing beyond their means to buy what they need is increasing; that this growing economic inequality destabilizes spending; and that the reduction in stable spending
is dragging down and distorting the US economy overall. When inequality distorts everyday decision-making by consumers and businesses, the outcomes
show up at the macroeconomic level. We see incentives directing resources
away from what could be their best use for our society and our economy.

Chapter 5 examines how inequality distorts how much is bought and by
whom. Karen Dynan, a Harvard University economist and veteran of the DC policymaking community, finds that inequality affects how much money is used for
consuming versus saving. Overall, people spend about 80 cents of every new
dollar in income, but the top 1 percent spend only 51 percent of their income,
while those in the bottom quintile spend 99 percent. This finding is generally con-

firmed in work by other scholars. As inequality rises, this difference translates to reduced consumption—again, the largest component of our nation's gross domestic product.

At the same time, high inequality increases the savings available. In the simplistic model, when there's more wealth available to invest in productive endeavors, investment follows. Yet many businesses have understandably not invested much over this period—and when they have, they've invested more in goods and services for high-end consumers, not the middle-income earners in our society. This has long-term implications for economy-wide productivity and inflation. Even as top tax rates have fallen, private investment still lags behind the pre-recession peak.

With consumption dragged down by flagging middle-class income, too much money in the hands of those at the top, and investors sitting on the sidelines, conditions are ripe for an increase in the supply of credit. Over the past forty years, US policymakers have made this even more likely by easing regulations governing the financial sector, making it easier to lend to households—in no small part due to the political power conferred on the financial industry by great wealth.

Chapter 6 highlights the work of finance economists Atif Mian at Princeton University and Amir Sufi at the University of Chicago, who have spent the past decade documenting the consequences of these distortions and showing how credit-driven economic growth both increases economic instability and leads to lost economic opportunity. The macroeconomic implications of rising inequality have long been ignored but, based on this new body of empirical research, we can see it as a key factor affecting both economic growth and stability.

# 5

# The Economic Cycle

IN FORMER Governor Sam Brownback's view, investors drive the economic growth responsible for creating the jobs that make the American Dream come alive. High barriers to private-sector investments were holding back economic growth in his home state of Kansas, he believed. Every extra dollar in taxes, every extra regulatory hoop for businesses and investors to jump through—no matter how small—lowered the chances of investment happening. This is why he set up the Office of the Repealer soon after taking office. Indeed, in his worldview, investment drives growth and ultimately improvements in living standards to such a degree that it is essentially the only proper concern of policymakers.

The claim that incentives—and the wherewithal—to invest are the keys to driving the economy toward broadly shared prosperity is commonly made. Yet this represents only one side of the most fundamental relationship in economics. An alternative view is that having a customer base with enough money to buy goods and services is even more important. From this perspective, business investors put their money at risk only when the opportunity for profits is clear—and that is only clear when there is a big enough market of potential buyers. This view of how the economy grows emphasizes that the purpose of an economy is to meet human needs and what's important are broad-based economic gains that leave no one behind and support a strong middle class.

This alternative perspective is summed up by venture capitalist Nick Hanauer. He likes to say that the economy can't keep growing if all its gains are going to people like him—because "there are only so many shirts" a person can buy. He's a billionaire and happy to spend money, but as he points out, the demand for basic goods from him and the rest of the top 0.01 percent income earners cannot keep the economy moving. "Only consumers can set in motion this virtuous cycle of increasing demand and hiring," he explained in a 2012 TED talk. "In this sense, an ordinary middle-class consumer is far more of a job creator than a capitalist like me."[1] When only incomes at the top are growing—that is, when there's more economic inequality—there tends to be insufficient consumer demand.

Economist Karen Dynan, now at Harvard University, is among an important group of researchers producing the evidence to answer Hanauer's implied question: Does inequality affect demand? A 2004 paper by Dynan (then at the Federal Reserve Board) and economists Jonathan Skinner at Dartmouth University and Stephen P. Zeldes at the Columbia Business School shows that while Americans on average spend about eighty cents of every dollar they earn and save about twenty, this varies widely depending on age and whether a household is rich or poor. The very richest households—the top 1 percent—save 51 percent of their income, while those in the bottom 20 percent save just 1 percent. Their findings are so conclusive that Dynan and her coauthors end the paper saying, "we believe that our work has established one fact: The rich do, indeed, save more."[2]

Dynan's study implies that, as income and wealth inequality rise, less money makes its way through the economy as income that turns into consumption, which implies that there's less overall consumer demand. Her work remains among the best we have on how inequality affects how much money is spent or saved up and down the income ladder. She and her coauthors assembled data in new ways and used cutting-edge research methods, giving us a high degree of confidence that their answers are as close to truth as possible. Once again, newly available data and methods may finally be making it possible to close the door on a theoretical economics question. The study has inspired others to follow similar lines of inquiry.

Still, many puzzles remain. If Dynan's research is correct, then consumer spending on goods and services should have slowed as inequality

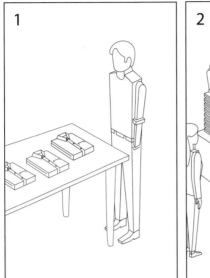 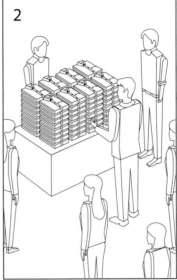

1. When most income is earned by a small number of people, demand suffers.
2. A strong middle class means strong demand for the goods businesses supply.

rose. As Hanauer said, the rich can buy only so many shirts. Yet the overall level of personal consumption in the United States—that is, the sum total of all the goods and services people buy—has risen in tandem with the total national income. This trend doesn't necessarily undermine her conclusions. There's strong evidence that many people left out of the gains from economic growth have turned to borrowing more to make up for that lost income. Middle-class families have been especially likely to take on new debt for education and other investments in their children's future, such as homes in better public-school districts. Other research corroborates this idea: for example, economists Joel Slemrod and Matthew Shapiro at the University of Michigan found that many low-income taxpayers used the income tax rebates of 2001 and those of 2008 to pay down debt.[3]

Both less consumption and more debt have serious repercussions for growth and stability. To be sure, when savings rise, more money is available for investment. But without a strong consumer base, where does it go? Rising debt combined with non-rising or stagnant incomes is a recipe for greater family economic instability that quickly spills across the broader economy. We'll tackle this question in the next chapter; here, the focus is on the demand side.

The question of how inequality affects consumption may be even more important in an era of greater economic insecurity, fiscal austerity, and political polarization. As people switch jobs—or are downsized—it can be hard to plan for the future. Most families are earning higher incomes than those working in the late 1950s and 1960s, yet that earlier era featured jobs that moved more steadily up the job ladder, offering real prospects of regular promotions while income and wealth inequality were on the decline. The fact that family incomes tend to be more volatile today affects how families consume and plan for the future.[4]

Rising income inequality affects consumption in a simple way: less income means less spending on immediate needs and desires. But there are also implications in the medium- and long-term, because rising inequality affects customers' choices among alternative offerings. When people head to the mall—or, increasingly, browse their favorite retailer's website—they're making decisions about what and how much to buy. Lots of things are known to affect these decisions—price, quality, design, time of day, even whether the shopper is hungry. Now, economists are finding that the growing gap between the haves and the have-nots affects these decisions, too. As people switch to lower-cost items—substituting generics for brand-name consumer items or shaving off a purchase here and there—this sends signals to firms about what merchandise and services to sell and how much they should invest to develop these people as customers. These developments in the marketplace lead to economywide effects on productivity and the kinds of jobs created—all of which affect the extent to which further economic growth is strong, stable, and broadly shared.

This chapter will examine all of these implications of income and wealth inequality on consumption. But first, it is useful to take a stroll through the history of recent economic thinking on the role of consumption and investment on economic growth. As will become clear, the weight of economic theory on today's economic policy debates matters—a lot—even as more data-driven, evidence-based research points to economic policies that recognize and address the realities of rising income and wealth inequality in the US economy.

## The Rich Do Act Differently

Dynan is an economist to watch. She's one of a new breed of scholars bringing rigorous empirical analysis to the most fundamental questions in macroeconomics. She spent most of her career in Washington, DC's policy-making circles before becoming a professor of practice in the Department of Economics at Harvard University in March 2017. Between 2014 and 2017, she served as chief economist and assistant secretary for economic policy at the US Department of the Treasury. There, she led the team that analyzed economic conditions and came up with new ideas to solve the nation's most pressing economic challenges. It was no surprise when Dynan was appointed to this government position. She was well prepared, having spent a couple of decades as an economist at the Federal Reserve and co-directed the Brookings Institution's Economic Studies Program.[5]

One specific reason I wasn't surprised by her appointment to a job at the US Treasury was that I had heard that President Barack Obama was eager for answers to the questions her research addressed. I learned this in the spring of 2011 when I was surveying economists about whether they saw evidence that the strength of the middle class affects economic growth and stability. One of my interviewees was Alan Krueger, who returned my call as he rode the train home from the nation's capital. As the Amtrak conductor's voice blared in the background, he told me something of his own experience at the Treasury Department, in the same job Dynan was later appointed to. He had been in "no less than five meetings" where President Obama had asked about what economics could show about the importance of a strong middle class in driving growth. He added that, at the time, he was frustrated because he couldn't give the President what he felt was a "thoroughly satisfactory answer." What he knew for certain, though, was that the best evidence available came from research by Dynan and her colleagues.[6]

A few months after our conversation, Krueger was appointed chair of the Council of Economic Advisers and, in his first major speech, he used Dynan's data to estimate the size of the drag on demand from rising income and wealth inequality. He multiplied the estimated savings rates from her study by data from Thomas Piketty and Emmanuel Saez, which showed that in the United States between 1979 and 2007, about $1.1 trillion (in 2007 dollars) was annually shifted toward the very rich—an increase of

13.5 percentage points. Krueger then calculated a simple counterfactual: What would have happened to the economy had that $1.1 trillion gone to the bottom 99 percent instead of the top 1 percent of Americans? His math reveals a shocking number: Had income inequality not risen, aggregate consumption would have been about 5 percent higher each year. That adds up to about $480 billion (in 2018 dollars) in lost economic gains annually. Krueger concluded his speech forcefully: "these calculations make clear that the economy would be in better shape and aggregate demand would be stronger if the size of the middle class had not dwindled as a result of rising inequality."[7]

Dynan's paper is the latest chapter in the long-simmering debate between two schools of economic thought, pioneered by two towering economists of the past: Cambridge University's John Maynard Keynes and the University of Chicago's Milton Friedman. Both sought to explain how to keep the economy growing at a strong, stable pace. Both viewed people's consumption patterns as a core piece to solving this puzzle. And each developed what he presented as a commonsense story of how much people spend and save out of their income. Yet their theories and logic led them to very different conclusions. Their debate played out over much of the twentieth century. It has only been resolved in the twenty-first century, as economists have finally gained the data and the tools to discern the actual relationships among income, wealth, and saving.

Keynes laid out his view of how to keep the economy on track in his book *The General Theory of Employment, Interest, and Money*, first published in 1936. His motivating goal was to explain a third category of unemployment that the economists of his day had failed to acknowledge or address. He argued that *involuntary unemployment*—as opposed to frictional or voluntary unemployment—occurred when the economy became stuck in a situation where people and machines sat idle due to too little spending relative to the productive capacity of the economy. He concluded that, while a variety of factors could lead to this kind of economic crisis, once there, an economy could remain there indefinitely: the private sector would not come to the rescue because firms would not invest additional profits until they saw enough customers to warrant the extra work of doing so. Instead, the solution was for government to fill in the gap. By borrowing and spending, thereby pumping up demand for goods and services and reducing unemployment, it would lead firms to invest again. Each dollar of government spending would multiply as it worked its way through the economy and provided incentives to invest.[8]

A crucial piece of Keynes's argument was his theory of how people's spending responds to changes in income. He said it was "obvious" that, in seeking to boost demand, government should focus on getting money to lower-income households, because they are more likely to spend more of each new dollar than those with higher incomes: "For the satisfaction of the immediate primary needs of a man and his family is usually a stronger motive than the motives toward accumulation, which only acquire effective sway when a margin of comfort has been attained. These reasons will lead, as a rule, to a greater *proportion* of income being saved as real income increases."[9] Keynes called this measure of how much people will spend out of a new dollar the "marginal propensity to consume." Targeting people with a high marginal propensity to consume is the surest way to boost demand quickly and push the economy toward full employment, because the multiplier effect will be larger than if government dollars go to people who will save it instead.[10]

Keynes did not suggest that investment was unimportant for improving productivity and living standards in the long-term. His argument was that, without customers who had money in their pockets ready to spend, there was no *incentive* to invest. In the chicken-and-egg question of what propels economic activity, he came squarely down on the side that, without customers, things come to a standstill. Firms will not invest additional profits in their lines of business if they don't expect there to be enough customers to warrant doing so. "All production," he wrote, "is for the purpose of ultimately satisfying a consumer."[11]

Friedman rejected the idea that policymakers could boost employment by pumping up demand. He argued that when the government borrows and spends as Keynes recommended, people won't necessarily respond by spending more, because how much people consume depends on their expectations of how much they will earn over their lifetime. A one-time check from the government doesn't have much impact on people's lifetime income and therefore won't affect their consumption patterns. These responses undermine the government's objective. Underlying Friedman's view is the idea that the marginal propensity to consume does not vary by people's current income; for him, the idea that it does is an erroneous read of the data. Friedman would go on to win an economics Nobel for showing "that the 'permanent income' of individuals over time and not year-to-year income is the determining factor when assessing total consumption outlay."[12] (Keynes died before the Nobel Memorial Prize in Economic Sciences began being awarded in 1968, and it is not given posthumously. Otherwise, he also would surely have received one.)

The permanent income hypothesis is that a person's consumption in any given time period is based on her expectation about what her lifetime income will be. In Friedman's view, everyone has expectations of how their income will vary in the future, given their skills and lot in life. As he put it, "consumption is determined by rather long-term considerations, so that any transitory changes in income lead primarily to additions to assets or to the use of previously accumulated balances rather than to corresponding changes in consumption."[13] If a person has an unusually high income one year, she'll save some, if not most, of that extra cash—especially if it's a one-time windfall, such as a bonus, inheritance, or tax cut. In lean years, such as when a person has been laid off or is young and earning entry-level wages, she will consume a higher share of her annual income. She also may borrow, with the expectation of a higher income later in life to pay off the debt, or dip into savings expecting to be able to replenish her nest egg in the future.

This theory led Friedman to conclude that once we consider time, there is no difference in the savings rates of rich and poor. Where Keynes had concluded that "obviously" there is "a greater proportion of income being saved as real income increases," Friedman argued that was a misconception.[14] In Friedman's view, if researchers look at a cross-section of people at one point in time, those with higher incomes will appear to spend a smaller share of their incomes. This only shows the propensity to consume out of current income, however; lifetime consumption patterns won't show up in that kind of data. To know how much a person actually spends out of new income, economists would need to track people's income and wealth over a lifetime—their permanent income. In Dynan's words, Friedman's hypothesis "basically yields sensible predictions for a world in which people are patient, forward-looking, able to borrow freely, and good at doing complicated calculations about optimal consumption, and then also good at sticking with the plan."[15] Whether the world is really populated by such people is the empirical question.

It's a question, moreover, that turns out to be absolutely critical for economic policy. In Friedman's view, unemployed workers and low- and middle-income families cannot be helped by government intervention in the short run because people will undo that added government spending by saving more—a view in complete opposition to Keynes's policy recommendations. The right policy prescription hinges on an empirical question that neither Friedman nor Keynes could answer because they lacked the data and computing power to tackle it. It would take another few decades for those to appear.[16]

## What We Demand—and What We Get

Academic debates over theory can be never-ending. Without access to data on people's lifetime of economic circumstances, researchers could not come to consensus on how income and wealth inequality affect consumption and savings rates. This led to a lack of interest in the question. Dynan and her colleagues note this at the outset of their paper: "Despite an outpouring of research in the 1950s and 1960s, the question of whether the rich save more has since received little attention."[17] We had to wait for the data to be compiled and available to researchers to know which theory was correct, which is why Dynan's study is so important. Further, her research required what used to be considered significant computing power. Today, we carry around powerful computers in our pockets, but even up until the early 2000s, this kind of research had to be done in computer labs or on servers capable of processing and storing large quantities of data.[18]

To test Friedman's idea that there are differences in savings out of temporary and permanent income, Dynan and her colleagues developed a set of measures of people's average income over a lifetime by looking at education, past and future earnings, the value of vehicles purchased, and food consumption. They made use of three national surveys, as well as data from Social Security and pension contributions, which, combined, allowed them to track people's income and wealth over time. One of the national surveys they used, the Survey of Consumer Finances, began tracking income and consumption in 1983 but, because it does not follow the same families over time, it needed to be paired with other data. They also used the Panel Study of Income Dynamics, the first large-scale US survey gathering income data over time. This survey began in 1968 with five thousand families who are regularly revisited. By the early 2000s, there were nearly four decades of data following the same families, enough to provide an estimate of permanent income, finally allowing researchers to see how savings patterns change relative to lifetime income, not just a short-term jump in income.[19]

As Krueger told me, compelling as Dynan's work is, he wanted to be able to cite more than one study to feel confident about telling the president that the strength of the middle class does affect consumption. This kind of work is now being done. Take, for example, research by Johns Hopkins University economist Chris Carroll and his colleagues confirming that those at the bottom of the income spectrum spend more than those at the top. They look at how much families up and down the income and wealth ladders spend out of new income. Using a model to generate a wealth distribution which matches the inequality shown by the Survey of Consumer Finances data, they can estimate the marginal propensity to consume. Their analysis finds that families spend about 20 cents to 40 cents out of every new dollar of income, but those with the highest wealth spend much less, meaning they have a lower propensity to consume, even accounting for their wealth. Other research using the same panel data Dynan used also finds that the marginal propensity to consume is lower at higher wealth quintiles—6 percent for those in the top 20 percent of the wealthy to 15 percent for the lowest. The authors infer that a transfer of wealth from the top 20 percent to bottom 80 percent of households would boost consumption and growth by four percentage points.[20]

While this research generally confirms Keynes's position, it turns out that Friedman was right that what people spend today out of their current income may be affected by how much they have in assets. Economists Atif Mian at Princeton University, Kamalesh Rao, now a senior data scientist at the French financial services giant Société Générale, and Amir Sufi at the University of Chicago found that lower-income households are more likely to spend down their wealth by selling assets or, more often, by borrowing against their assets or taking on unsecured debt that they then have to service out of their income. Between 2006 and 2009—from near the apex of the US housing bubble into the depths of the Great Recession—households in the bottom 20 percent of zip codes by average income spent roughly three times as much of every additional dollar of housing wealth as did those households in the highest quintile of zip codes.[21]

Even if people do behave as Friedman surmises, an important piece of information is whether they actually can tap into their assets to smooth their consumption. It turns out that many assets cannot be easily transformed into cash—think of real estate or other assets that cannot be sold quickly, or where borrowing against the asset may be impossible or prohibitively costly. Economists Greg Kaplan and Justin Weidner, both of Princeton University, and Giovanni L. Violante of New York University have a term for families who own assets they cannot easily access: they are "the wealthy hand-to-mouth." Even though they have high assets, these families have high propensity to consume out of new income. In contrast, households that have a lot of liquid assets, such as investments in the stock market that can be easily sold, tend to have much lower marginal propensity to consume out of income, because their spending is not constrained. When they want to consume more, they can easily convert their assets into cash. This observation that high-wealth households act differently, depending on how quickly and easily they can leverage their assets, adds a layer of complication to Friedman's hypothesis.[22]

A second issue for Friedman's hypothesis is whether people today have a clear sense of what their future income will be. This is a question that Dynan also has investigated. Along with Douglas Elmendorf (now dean of the Harvard Kennedy School) and Wellesley College economist Daniel Sichel, Dynan finds that income volatility is rising. According to their estimates, the share of US households experiencing a 50 percent drop in income over a two-year period increased from about 7 percent in the early 1970s to more than 12 percent in the early 2000s, before falling slightly to 10 percent before the Great Recession. Income volatility makes it difficult for people to internalize what economic trends mean for their own futures and may hamper people's ability to plan in the logical, rational way that Friedman suggests people do. It also has other economic outcomes. It can lead people to save and invest in assets that are easier to access but yield lower returns—choosing, for example, savings accounts over stocks or real estate—and it can discourage savings as people stop believing that saving is possible.[23]

It may also be the case that the United States is now in a situation where incomes at the tippy-top of the ladder are so high that Friedman's theory no longer applies (to the extent it ever did) to the wealthiest segment of households. It is inconceivable that those at the very top of the US income distribution can consume all their income. As the UK's *Business Insider* points out, today's wealthy have more money than one could spend in a lifetime. In 2017, Amazon's Jeff Bezos earned over $107 million and Microsoft's Bill Gates brought home $11 million—both *per day*. Overall, the top 0.1 percent of US income earners had average incomes of $6 million in 2016 and captured nearly 9 percent of all US income. This alone may have changed the marginal propensity to consume at the top in ways that affect investment and productivity.[24]

What the rich and non-rich buy also has macroeconomic implications. Income and wealth inequality are changing the way US consumers shop—and what is on offer at what price point. Retailers have increasingly become bifurcated into ones who seek out high-end consumers and those who focus on appealing to discount shoppers. With consumption accounting for just under 70 percent of economic growth, shifts in the way products and services are produced, delivered, and priced will have significant ramifications for future productivity and growth.

What's happening to America's shopping malls illustrates these trends. Long-standing department stores that once anchored these malls, such as Macy's, Sears, and J. C. Penney, all of which catered to middle-class customers, have registered plummeting sales. Macy's announced in August 2016 that it would close a hundred stores nationwide—about 15 percent of all its outlets. Sears filed for bankruptcy in November 2018 and added 142 more stores to its growing list of planned closures. And J. C. Penney, not profitable since 2010, shuttered about 140 stores in 2017. At the other end, as middle-class income mainstays fall by the wayside, malls that cater to high-end customers are accounting for a larger share of total mall shoppers.[25]

While part of this cascade of troubles for brick-and-mortar store chains is that people are shopping more online, the hollowing out of the middle class is another culprit, especially considering that discount retailers are doing quite well. Take Dollar General, whose target customers are families with incomes below $35,000, which reportedly plans to grow sales to $30 billion by 2020. According to *Bloomberg Businessweek*, at a 2016 shareholder meeting of Dollar General, Chief Executive Officer Todd Vasos said his company's strategy is to expand into small towns where families are strapped for cash and dependent on government assistance.[26]

Changes in spending patterns are driving changes in what firms are producing, with a number of economic implications. Xavier Jaravel at the

London School of Economics finds that businesses are investing in new products targeted at high-end consumers while developing fewer products for those in the lower end of the market. This means that there are now more buying options for those at the top of the income ladder, but fewer for those at the bottom. For those at the bottom of the income spectrum, this shift in whom businesses are producing for leads not only to fewer choices but also to higher costs. More competition among those businesses competing for high-end dollars is leading to more productivity growth in high-end products and lower prices for those at the top of the income ladder. For those at the low end, however, there's less competition for their business, which means lower productivity and higher prices. This shows up in the data: Jaravel found that between 2013 and 2014, families with incomes greater than $100,000 per year saw prices rise by 0.65 percent less than for families earning below $30,000.[27]

## Consuming Puzzles

While the evidence presented above indicates that income and wealth inequality distorts consumption, there are lingering puzzles in the data. Key among them is that over the period from the late 1970s to today, income for the bottom half of the US income distribution hasn't grown—and has actually fallen for those at the very bottom—yet aggregate consumption, as measured by the national accounts, did not fall in tandem. The solution to this puzzle lies in understanding debt. Many US families seemed to treat credit just like it was cash, maintaining their spending by tapping into home equity as house prices rose and taking on more consumer credit.[28]

Up until the 1980s, across all US families, total debt was about 60 percent of annual income. Over the following three decades, families' debts rose significantly. By the time the housing bubble burst in 2008, debts of households and nonprofits were equal to 100 percent as a share of GDP. Even at the end of 2018, a decade after the last recession began, household and nonprofit debt was equal to 77 percent of GDP and total household debt in the United States amounted to $13.5 trillion, 7 percent above the peak in the third quarter of 2008. (See Figure 5.1.) Indeed, the savings rate among the bottom 90 percent fell steadily throughout the past few decades into negative territory by the late 1990s,

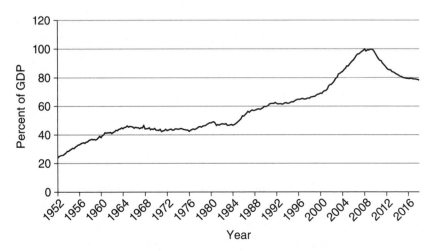

Figure 5.1   Household debt has grown significantly since the 1950s
US household and nonprofit liabilities relative to GDP, 1952–2018.

*Source:* Board of Governors of the Federal Reserve System, Bureau of Labor Economic Analysis, Federal
Reserve Bank of St. Louis.

according to data from Piketty, Saez, and their frequent coauthor Gabriel
Zucman.[29]

Over the course of the first decade of the twenty-first century, mortgage
debt, both for new homes and refinances, grew faster than other kinds of
debt. Between the first quarter of 2000 and the first quarter of 2008, before the housing bubble burst, mortgage debt increased by $8.4 trillion.[30]
This debt allowed people to buy ever more expensive homes. The S&P/Case-
Shiller US National Home Price Index, which measures changes in home
prices at the national level, rose to an all-time high in the first quarter of
2007, then fell 26 percent to its most recent low in early 2012. Since then,
home prices have recovered to the point that they have now surpassed their
pre-recession peak. Families still need to take on high levels of debt to buy
a home.[31] (See Figure 5.1.)

A second reason that mortgage debt grew was that homeowner families
leveraged the equity they had accumulated in their homes. This shows up
in the data on home refinancing. Between the fourth quarters of 1991 and
2008, the refinance rate of single-family homes through which homeowners
cashed out value from their homes nearly tripled, from 19.8 percent to
53.7 percent. This trend is repeating itself today as home prices are again

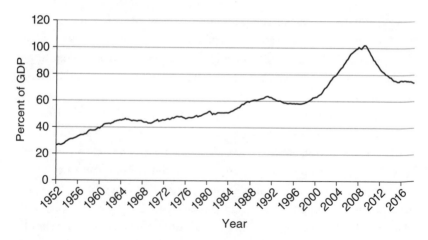

Figure 5.2 Mortgage debt has grown over time
US mortgage debt outstanding as a share of GDP, 1952–2018.

*Source:* Board of Governors of the Federal Reserve System and Bureau of Economic Analysis.

on the rise. According to data from the credit-reporting firm Equifax, home equity loan originations increased by 8 percent in the second quarter of 2017 to nearly $46 billion, the highest level since 2008. In tandem with lower prevailing interest rates—and a rise in easy-to-get-loans as the housing crisis subsided—the refinances mean that families are able to tap into their homes' rising values. People use their home equity for home improvements, funds for their children's college tuition, and other types of consumption.[32]

Other kinds of debt grew, as well. Revolving consumer credit, which is mostly credit card debt, hit an all-time high of $1.004 trillion in December 2008. By late 2018, even as unemployment held below four percent, consumer credit had risen to $1.041 trillion. And, year after year, students and their parents (and grandparents) take on ever higher levels of debt to pay for college. Between 2006 and the end of 2018, student debt outstanding increased by more than $1 trillion, from $480 billion to $1.57 trillion.[33]

The idea that many Americans borrowed more to make up for declining or stagnant income gains is compelling, but the question for policymakers and economists is whether that is indeed the biggest factor in rising debt. Some scholars point to the role of income and wealth inequality itself to explain why people are so willing to take on such high levels of debt. Federal Reserve economist Jeffrey Thompson has identified a strong correlation

between higher incomes among the top five percent of income earners at the state level and increased mortgage borrowing. He also finds evidence of increases in the ratio of housing debt payments to incomes. Importantly, these increases are strongest for middle- and upper-middle-income households.[34]

Cornell University economist Robert Frank argues that, as the rich have gotten richer and those at the very top of American society shift their kids to the very best public and private schools, families just below them in society struggle to keep up. Frank and his coauthors, Adam Seth Levine and Oege Dijk, call these *expenditure cascades* and say they have serious repercussions. University of Chicago (Booth School of Business) economist Marianne Bertrand and University of California–Berkeley (Haas School of Business) finance professor Adair Morse argue that, to keep pace with more well-to-do peers and neighbors, people with a little less wealth and income have started saving less, consuming more, and getting into financial trouble more often and more severely. According to their findings, the savings rate among average Americans would have been 2.6 percent to 3.2 percent higher had income growth at the middle of the distribution stayed in line with income growth at the top.[35]

Let's step back for a moment here to consider all of this new data-derived evidence in light of Friedman's idea that people have foresight into their future incomes. It may be that the rise in borrowing before and after the Great Recession is evidence of people's faith that their incomes would soon begin rising as they had for previous generations. After all, the late 1990s saw the strongest labor market in decades. In that period, the typical male wage-earner began to see his earnings rise after more than a decade and a half of inflation-adjusted declines, while women's employment rates hit an all-time high of 58 percent. With the typical family income growing by an average annual rate of nearly 2 percent, it seemed that the middle class was finally growing again. People entering the new century might have been optimistic that the 2001 recession would be short and shallow (as it was) and that the recovery from that dot-com recession and the Great Recession would eventually look like the late 1990s. Polling data suggests they were. At the turn of the century, both Gallup and the University of Michigan's Survey of Consumers found people fairly positive about economic conditions. Around 2000, Michigan's Current Economic

Conditions Index was the highest it had ever been, going back to the early 1960s.[36]

Of course, that optimism was misplaced. Now, we're left with the question of whether consumption can continue to grow in the face of slow- or no-growth incomes. But there are other important questions, as well. Compounding the troublesome dynamic in income trends are financial institutions that encourage borrowers to take on more debt than they can safely service with their incomes—at times with the implicit or explicit backing of policymakers, which is an issue we'll examine in the next chapter.[37]

## A Perfect Storm, The Perfect Case Study

How we answer the question of whether and how inequality distorts consumption directly affects what policy levers—if any—policymakers can pull to reduce widespread unemployment in the short run. The past decades provide the perfect case study. Starting with the collapse of the housing bubble in 2006 and the ensuing financial crisis in late 2007, the US economy fell into what would be known as the Great Recession. By the end of 2008, the Federal Reserve was taking increasingly bold steps to address the crisis through monetary policy, lowering the federal funds rate to effectively zero and embarking on what would be the first of three rounds of quantitative easing—that is, buying up assets to increase liquidity and spur economic activity. As President Obama took office in January 2009, the US economy appeared to be in a free fall, with twenty thousand more people becoming unemployed every day. A few weeks into his first term, he signed into law the American Recovery and Reinvestment Act of 2009, which pumped more than $830 billion into the US economy.[38]

Empirically-oriented economists have looked at this as a real-world test of Keynes's and Friedman's theories about spending and savings. The Recovery Act included a variety of efforts to address the lack of demand; many targeted lower-income families by increasing funding for programs that help low-income families, such as food assistance and Medicaid. Others cut taxes for families across the income distribution. This was standard Keynesian policy. Dynan, who worked in the US Treasury during the slow-growth recovery from the Great Recession, offers this rationale: "when the economy is in a slump, you want to target fiscal support to households with higher propensities to consume in order to provide the biggest boost to demand, so as to get the economy back to full employment sooner. Likewise, we want to make sure that countercyclical monetary policy can reach people with high propensity to consume." She adds that this turned out to be challenging during the Great Recession "because many people that probably had high propensities to consume were underwater with their mortgages, and had difficulty refinancing their mortgage loans into lower-rate loans that would increase their discretionary monthly cash flow."[39]

Economists Alan Blinder (former member of the Council of Economic Advisers under President Bill Clinton and now at Princeton) and Mark Zandi (former advisor to presidential candidate and US Senator John McCain, and now chief economist at Moody's Analytics) evaluated the effectiveness of the Recovery Act, alongside the extraordinary steps that monetary policymakers at the Federal Reserve took to bring down interest rates. They compared what would likely have happened had the government not acted. They concluded that, in 2009, US gross domestic product was 1.6 percent higher than it would have been without the fiscal stimulus, and by 2010 the cumulative boost to GDP generated by government spending grew to 3.6 percent. The accompanying steps by the Fed to shore up the financial sector also were important. Their simulation shows that without them, US gross domestic product would have fallen by 6.5 percent from the peak of the recovery that ended in 2007 to the trough of the recession in 2009, and the US economy would have shed more than 12.5 million jobs. Combined, in 2011, the fiscal and financial policy responses kept unemployment almost seven percentage points lower than it would have been, reduced the number of jobs lost by about ten million, and pushed inflation-adjusted gross domestic product 16.3 percent higher.[40]

Particularly compelling evidence for Keynes's view comes from analysis of the effects of the extensions of unemployment benefits. In June 2008, Congress passed legislation to provide additional federal benefits to unemployed individuals who had exhausted their regular state unemployment benefits. This Emergency Unemployment Compensation program was amended eleven times through January 2013, when Congress made the extended benefits available until the end of that year. Unemployment benefits go directly to workers who lose their jobs through no fault of their own. These benefits make it possible for the unemployed to maintain their consumption, at least partially, while they search for work.[41]

There is ample evidence that unemployment benefits not only help families but also are effective in moving the economy toward full employment. Researcher Wayne Vroman of the Urban Institute did an extensive analysis of both the regular benefit programs and the extensions and found that they reduced the severity of the Great Recession. He found that the regular unemployment insurance program closed about one-tenth of the shortfall in real gross domestic product from the second half of 2008 to the first half of 2010 (after accounting for inflation), while the extended benefits closed about one-twelfth of that shortfall—meaning that the unemployment insurance program overall closed more than a sixth of the total gap. Those differences may seem small but this amounted to more than $180 billion (in 2018 dollars) over that period, about 0.9 percent of US gross domestic product. Economists Peter Ganong and Pascal Noel at the University of Chicago confirm that an important reason why unemployment benefits are such a powerful policy tool is because they boost spending by those lower down the income ladder. Their analysis shows that spending on nondurable goods and services drops on average by 6 percent when a person loses a job, yet the fall in spending is much smaller in states with high unemployment benefits compared to those with low benefits.[42]

The effectiveness of the policy responses to the Great Recession notwithstanding, the focus on pumping up demand ended too soon. One compelling piece of evidence that this was too early comes from the Congressional Budget Office. Every year, it issues projections of what national income will be in the decade to come. If the projection it made in 2007, before the crisis hit, had come true in 2017, the US economy would have generated about 13 percent more income than it actually did. The implication is that our nation is on a permanently lower growth path.[43]

The downward shift in the nation's path was a preventable policy tragedy. Even at the time of the passage of the Recovery Act, many economists had come to the conclusion that it would not be sufficient and there would need to be other such policy endeavors. Instead, additional spending on the programs targeted at those at the low end of the income spectrum was mostly phased out by 2011 and the US federal government tacked toward austerity, exacerbating trends in the states. Analysis that excludes Social Security and Medicare—thus the effects of an aging population and rising health care costs—shows that federal program spending is in fact below its forty-year average of 11.9 percent of GDP. This is not to say that spending hasn't increased in nominal dollars, but it does show that the shares are lower. Moreover, spending on federal low-income programs outside of health care—including the Earned Income Tax Credit and the Child Tax Credit—has dropped since 2010 as a share of GDP to an average of 2 percent and is projected to decline further. On top of this, most states have constitutional requirements that prohibit them from spending more than they collect in revenue. This often means that spending is reduced, not increased, when an economy is already hurting. Lacking additional help from the federal government, many states responded to the Great Recession with deep cuts to education, health care and social services—and the funding for these remains below historic levels.[44]

Part of the reason the federal government stopped supporting demand is that this policy agenda was viewed through a highly partisan lens and political polarization meant that there was not strong bipartisan support for these steps. The legislation did not receive a single vote from Republican members of the House of Representatives and got only three Republican votes in the Senate—from Olympia Snowe, Susan Collins, and Arlen Specter (who switched to the Democratic Party later in the year). The addition of supply-side policy inducements in the form of tax breaks for new investment by businesses did not win additional Republicans over, but this also meant that the legislation wasn't as targeted as many would have liked—of the total funding, only about 36 percent was explicitly targeted at those with a high marginal propensity to consume. Many now argue that it was the failure of the US economy to recover quickly that sparked the rise in populism and ongoing political polarization.[45]

We're learning from evidence that broad prosperity for those on the bottom and middle rungs of the income ladder not only reduces inequality but also can create better overall economic outcomes. While addressing the Great Recession was an urgent crisis, there are also now long-term implications for investments in our nation's future.

### Accounting for Inequality's Distortions in Our Macroeconomic Policy

Policymakers need to be more aware of how economic inequality distorts consumption, savings, and investment. One way to begin would be for them to consider just what level of inequality is acceptable or ideal. With a sense of what the right ratio of incomes at the top and bottom is, they can better plan how to raise pre- and post-tax incomes for the non-wealthy. This could then inform the implementation of a more progressive "tax and transfer" system—the catch-all phrase for government policies that collect tax revenue and distribute that revenue throughout the economy— or policies encouraging higher wages and incomes across the board or encouraging those with jobs to put in more hours, assuming that leads to more pay. Adopting a better measure of where national income goes is another important input to policymaking—as I'll lay out in the Conclusion.

It's clear that when unemployment is high, policymakers should be attentive to how inequality may affect the effectiveness of both monetary and fiscal policy. Yet in the current divided political climate, effective active fiscal policy by Congress seems unreliable. That leaves an important role for so-called automatic stabilizers, such as unemployment insurance, which are triggered to ramp up when the economy worsens. When unemployment insurance kicks in, workers who are laid off through no fault of their own can collect diminished but steady income for set periods of time. Or consider the Supplemental Nutrition Assistance Program, which workers under a certain income threshold can tap to help sustain their families. In general, automatic stabilizer programs have been underfunded and without action, when the next recession happens, they may be unable to play their historic role in mitigating the damage. Policymakers should identify how automatic stabilizers can be strengthened and take these steps now, before the next crisis hits. This should happen at the federal level, in no small part because states often act pro-cyclically in recessions and are bound by the need to balance their budgets while the federal government is not so constrained.[46]

In terms of directly addressing economic inequality more generally, the most straightforward path is through the tax and transfer system. Policymakers should provide more income support to raise the standard of living of families lower down the income ladder. The Earned Income Tax Credit (EITC), which provides tax credits to low-income workers with jobs, is a long-standing policy with bipartisan support, having been expanded by both Republican President Ronald Reagan and Democratic President Bill Clinton. The EITC is the most progressive tax expenditure in the income tax code and is also designed to encourage work: credit increases with each additional dollar of earnings. Because the EITC is refundable—meaning that, if the credit is larger than a worker's tax liability, she receives a refund—it is a powerful antipoverty program. Expanding the EITC to fully incorporate single earners and increasing eligibility and benefits for families are straightforward ways to increase living standards and encourage more people to enter the labor market.[47]

Along these lines, new work by journalist Annie Lowrey and Facebook cofounder Chris Hughes points to the importance of a universal basic income—that is, a program by which the government gives all Americans some set amount of money, with no strings attached. This concept has created unlikely bedfellows from the left and the right, from labor leaders to conservative think tanks in Washington to libertarian Silicon Valley executives. Many see the need for such a cash distribution to cushion against job loss due to automation, to boost wages by strengthening workers' bargaining power, to eliminate poverty, and to reduce race and gender biases. Trial experiments, including several in Northern California, will provide additional evidence, especially relating to legitimate concerns about the full costs of such a program, and whether it would result in fiscal starvation of traditional safety-net programs.[48]

Another way to raise incomes for more Americans is take out of their household budgets some of the biggest-ticket items they now purchase on their own, such as health care, retirement, and higher education. Even with the Affordable Care Act, many moderate-income families struggle to afford health care, so instead of undermining the ACA, policymakers could adopt a plan that would allow everyone to tap into the efficiencies of Medicare either through a public option on the health care exchanges or through a Medicare-for-all-type system, as many are proposing. Whatever the means, the goal should be to provide universal coverage that families can afford, using the tax system to subsidize as necessary. Similarly, addressing the need for childcare as laid out in Chapter 1 would address a large family budget item.

Another way to do this is to evaluate the extent to which families must take on the risk of debt. Take higher education: student-loan debt has now reached sky-high levels, and over the past decade, its growth has outpaced other forms of debt. In 2010, in a now rarely acknowledged piece of legislation that passed in conjunction with the Affordable Care Act, the student loan industry was overhauled and lending operations were fully transferred from commercial banks to the Department of Education. This allows the government to set better terms and repayment options for a large portion of student-loan debt, giving people more flexible options to repay their loans than private lenders would offer. Still, with so much debt outstanding, and with very few people able to have their loans discharged, most people with student loans are stuck using significant portions of their income to serve this debt. Policymakers could revisit student loan policies—or lower the cost of college in the first place—to relieve families of economic anxiety and stabilize demand.[49]

Policymakers can also address incomes before tax and transfers—what Yale political scientist Jacob Hacker calls "pre-distribution"—with policies that ensure that those at the top of the ladder share the gains of economic productivity. The most straightforward way to support the incomes of middle- and lower-income families and encourage greater distribution of the gains of economic growth is to support people's right to have a voice at work. The rising share of business income accruing to the owners of capital in those firms, relative to the share of income going to their workers, indicates that there is room for unions or other workforce-friendly institutions to push for higher wages. Unions historically played a significant role in creating America's middle class and fostering widespread wage gains, particularly in the immediate postwar era. As laid out in Chapter 3, we need to find new ways to boost worker power to ensure this happens again.

The economics profession also has to broaden its ambit to include the impact of inequality across the US economy. Traditionally, macroeconomists haven't taken inequality into account in their forecasting models, but they should. Most macroeconomic models start with a so-called representative agent—that is, they assume that all people in the economy act the same, regardless of whether they are low- or high-income earners. In a recent essay, Moody's Analytics' Zandi—who oversees one of the most well-respected forecasting models—integrated inequality into his model for the United States. Adding inequality to the traditional models did not change the short-term forecasts very much, but he concluded that higher inequality increases the likelihood of instability in the financial system when looking at the long-term picture or considering the potential for the system to spin out of control. The truth is that people do not all behave in the same way in response to events and trends, so economists' models should no longer be built on the premise that they do. As Gabriel Zucman recently put it, "Goodbye, representative agent."[50]

Government entities are coming to similar conclusions. The Bank of England has released a series of papers showing that agent-based models—which take into account inequality and assume actors will behave in varying ways—have strong predictive power. There's even a team inside the International Monetary Fund's research department doing work that shows reducing inequality can improve macroeconomic stability. Economists Jonathan Ostry, Andrew Berg, and Charalambos G. Tsangarides find that, when policymakers lower inequality through the tax and transfer system via redistribution, productivity or economic growth are not hampered. The next step is for policymakers to take actions consistent with these findings.[51]

# 6

# Investment

**W**HEN SAM BROWNBACK set up the Office of the Repealer during his first month as Kansas Governor in 2011, the sole purpose of this new state government office was to eliminate "unreasonable, unduly burdensome, duplicative, onerous, and conflicting laws, regulations, and other governing instruments." His reasoning was that government regulation tends to discourage business investment—and thus economic growth—and should be kept to a bare minimum: "The top priorities of my administration are to grow the state's economy . . . . With the help of Kansans, the Office of the Repealer is working to identify laws and regulations that are out of date, unreasonable, and burdensome. State laws and regulations shouldn't hinder opportunities for Kansans and Kansas businesses."[1]

Brownback is hardly alone in this view. Over the past four decades, many others have argued (by and large, successfully) that a wide array of business activities in the US should not be regulated—or should be regulated very lightly. Since the 1970s, in industry after industry, from transportation to energy to telecommunications, rules have been relaxed in the name of fostering greater economic efficiency and growth. But few sectors have been targeted as clearly as financial services—commercial banking, investment banking, mortgage underwriting, financial futures, and options trading. Firms in these industries match people who have money saved up and ready to invest with people who want to put money to good use making and selling goods and services. This makes finance a special industry—it's a business that creates capacity for productive investments. According to those who favor deregulation, the financial sector is better able to match money to productive investments when there are fewer rules governing the sector and the services it provides. That may sound plausible in theory. The problem is, the financiers in our country have both encouraged and taken advantage of waves of deregulation over the past few decades to invest other people's money (and sometimes their own) in ways that have not promoted the interests of the larger economy—or our society—and that have instead led to economic destabilization and growing economic inequality.[2]

Case in point: Starting in the 1980s, states began to rethink how they regulated banks. The 1927 McFadden Act allows states to decide for themselves the conditions under which national banks can operate within their borders. Up until the early 1980s, no state allowed an out-of-state bank—or its holding company—to own a bank within its borders. That all changed in the course of a decade. By 1990, forty-six states had rewritten their laws to let out-of-state banks in to do business. The argument was that changing these rules would increase the efficiency of banking operations and reduce costs to borrowers, leading to more investment. At first, this seemed like a success. There was an increase in banking assets and, as banks branched out across markets, they became more accessible. Both effects led to lower loan costs. But the fact that banks increased their assets tells us nothing about whether more savings were funneled into productive investments, or whether businesses had more access to the financing they needed to run their businesses.[3]

These were the questions that economists Amir Sufi at the University of Chicago's Booth School of Business and Atif Mian and Emil Verner, both at Princeton University, set out to answer in a 2017 working paper. They looked at whether eliminating state-level rules for how banks conducted their business led to more investment in businesses—and thus more job creation and productivity growth. They found that, once banks could open branches across state lines, they increased lending—mostly to households in the form of home mortgages, home equity loans, and revolving credit-card lending, and, less so, to firms. At first, this new lending tended to foster increased aggregate demand and resulted in an economic boom, with the greatest growth occurring in places that saw the largest increases in household credit. But when the states' economies turned from expansion to contraction, those same places also tended to experience recessions that were deeper and more protracted. As Mian told me, this "suggests that while credit can have short-term positive impacts, there is a tradeoff to think about, which is that it can lead to an ultimately stronger downturn. That essentially means that credit can generate an amplification of the cycle, both on the upside as well as on the downside."[4] Their conclusion: eliminating rules on cross-state banking led to more loans but—contrary to proponents' promises—not to stronger, more stable, broad-based economic growth. While Mian and Sufi are careful in their paper to "avoid normative claims," it seems that removing rules created distortions, not the other way around.[5]

This study about money and where it flows is just one piece of a larger body of research produced by Mian and Sufi on these topics. It is emblematic of how they are employing the latest data and evidence to examine how economic inequality affects economic growth and stability. In Chapter 5, we learned that one outcome of high income inequality is that more savings are sloshing around in the economy. The question this chapter addresses is: What happens to that money? In the simplistic story that Brownback and others tell, as long as there's money available to invest—and not too many rules about what firms can or cannot do—then investment will happen. Yet the evidence shows the story isn't so simple. Examining the data to understand when and how savings translate into productive, socially beneficial investments is fundamental to determining whether inequality and the set of rules governing finance are distortionary.

This chapter examines in detail how the effects of rising inequality combine with financial deregulation's failures to propel productive business investment. They leave us in a highly unusual situation—with an economy of too much savings but not enough income flowing into the hands of families outside the very top of the income spectrum. Investment is a key driver of economic growth because it leads to job creation and productivity increases. Yet there seems to be an erroneous view of the incentive structure; there's a presumption that those who control the surplus will direct it toward investments that do the most for the general economy. In fact, the surplus of savings from both the household and corporate sectors, combined with deregulation, gave financial institutions greater leeway to concoct an array of consumer loans for income-strapped families into a highly toxic brew. This wasn't an accident—the financial industry used its extensive resources to lobby for relaxing the rules governing firms' activities, distorting economic gains toward their profits and away from uses that would be more beneficial for the economy overall.

As income inequality rises, more capital becomes available for investment. Yet no more demand materializes, so no additional goods and services are sold. In the end, it appears that high inequality results in either too little consumption or too much debt—from either consumers, which this chapter discusses, or corporations—neither of which encourages strong and stable growth. While today's low interest rates mean low debt service burdens and low delinquency rates, the evidence shows that relying on debt to keep the economy afloat can be destabilizing. Further, in the current US economic climate, policymakers have limited bandwidth to use interest rate policy to spur investors to put that money to good use.

This was predicted by Keynes. He argued that, in the long term, high inequality leads to the perverse outcome of having more savings available for investment but less incentive to invest. The implication is that places and eras with large gaps between rich and poor will see too little investment: "the richer the community, the wider will tend to be the gap between its actual and its potential production; and therefore the more obvious and outrageous the defects of the economic system," Keynes wrote. "Not only is the marginal propensity to consume weaker in a wealthy community, but, owing to its accumulation of capital being already larger, the opportunities for further investment are less attractive unless the rate of interest falls at a sufficiently rapid rate."[6]

Lawmakers who would like to change all this face an uphill battle, as the financial industry has become steadily more powerful in the policy realm. Stripping away rules that govern how firms go about their business turns out to have created opportunities for rent-seeking—recall that's the economic term for businesses pursuing undue profits—and pulls resources away from productive investments. It increases inequality but does not necessarily grow the economy. In short, financial firms have used their greater economic power to rewrite the rules so that they earn even more money, and reduce their risk while increasing risk for everyone else. The underlying causes of the twin housing and financial crises in the twenty-first century detailed in this chapter are testament to this power dynamic. So, too, are more recent moves by the industry and its supporters in Congress and the executive branch to renew the push for more deregulation amid a new wave of subprime lending.

## The Distortion of Credit and the Great Recession

Mian and Sufi are both finance economists, which means they study how money, prices, interest rates, and asset prices affect the macroeconomy. They met at Chicago Booth as junior faculty at the height of the mortgage boom in 2006, and realized they shared a passion for understanding why credit has expanded toward households. While it may be surprising to many readers, this is not a question that economists had traditionally asked. Their evidence leads to the conclusion that the rise in credit supply—made possible both by the additional savings flooding the economy and the deregulation of finance—was the leading cause of the Great Recession.[7]

The economic crisis of the late 2000s was the single most important economic event in decades and Mian and Sufi's groundbreaking research on it has catapulted their careers. They've published their findings in top economics and finance journals and also presented them to general audiences. As of this writing, their collaboration, nearly a decade long, has yielded over fifteen academic articles and working papers, some with additional coauthors. *House of Debt*, written for lay readers, made the short list for the 2014 award given by the *Financial Times* and McKinsey to the "best business book of the year." (That was the year the award went to Thomas Piketty's *Capital in the Twenty-First Century*.) The International Monetary Fund put both on their list of twenty-five young economists who it expects "will shape the world's thinking about the global economy in the future." In 2017, Sufi was awarded the American Finance Association's Fischer Black Prize, a biennial award given to the top financial economics scholar under the age of forty.[8]

The Great Recession provided them with a perfect case study. It's both economically meaningful and provides a rich set of tough academic questions. Sufi is from Topeka, Kansas, and he compares the force of the 2008 financial crisis to a tornado because of the way it tore through the economy, laying waste to $12 trillion in household wealth and 8.7 million jobs. Between 2007 to 2011, the typical American family lost an average of $6,000 in annual income and it took eight years—until 2015—for their income to recover to its pre-recession peak. Initially, wealthy households lost as much or more as a percentage of their income and wealth as others, but this group quickly regained their footing, recovering nearly all their lost wealth by 2012.[9]

To understand the crisis, Mian and Sufi start with the data. They trace the expansion of credit and follow that money as it flowed throughout the economy—and what happened when the bills came due. To do this, they compiled detailed information on borrowing, spending, housing prices, and defaults by county and zip code level. In their 2009 paper in the *Quarterly Journal of Economics* and in subsequent work, they use these and other data to show how the expansion of credit took place mainly for borrowers in low-net-worth communities and how this accelerated the collapse of the housing bubble. Their first surprising finding was that, during the run-up to the housing bubble, credit expanded unevenly, flowing to neighborhoods with low credit scores and declining incomes. Basically, banks were making loans that were not tethered to borrowers' abilities to pay them back. Mian and Sufi found that over the years from 2002 to 2005, mortgage credit expanded more than twice as fast per year in neighborhoods with low credit scores as in neighborhoods with high credit scores. By the peak of the bubble, places with low-net worth were also the most highly leveraged. This was highly unusual; it was the only period over nearly two decades that they studied where this was true.[10]

To illustrate what happened in many low-income communities across the country, Mian and Sufi point to the experience of the westside neighborhoods of Detroit. Detroit is the biggest city in a state that had already suffered more than a decade of stagnation and recession, and most of its westside neighborhoods had low average credit scores. About two-thirds of households had a credit score below 660, compared to about one-third nationwide. If a borrower has a score below 660, lenders typically flag that borrower as a relatively high risk of default, and consider issuing only what they call a "subprime" loan. Yet, even with the high share of people at risk of being unable to pay back loans, mortgage-denial rates fell dramatically during the run-up of the housing boom. While average income in the zip codes of west Detroit fell by 1 percent during these years, mortgage origination rates jumped 22 percent per year. Of course, this wasn't happening only in Detroit; it was happening in low-net-worth communities across the nation. In Chicago, for example, mortgages for home purchases in zip codes with low credit scores grew by 36 percent per year from 2002 to 2005, more than double the 15 percent growth for the zip codes with high credit scores.[11]

At the height of this lending frenzy, the growth in mortgage credit across the country was unglued from any semblance of financial fundamentals. Economists Yuliya Demyanyk at the Federal Reserve Bank of Cleveland and Otto Van Hemert at New York University note that, by the peak of the housing bubble, home loans were so disconnected from prudent lending practices that "an unusually large fraction of subprime mortgages originated in 2006 and 2007 [became] delinquent or in foreclosure only months later." Between 2005 and 2007, the rate at which loans that were twelve months old entered delinquency more than doubled, from roughly 10 percent to more than 20 percent.[12]

At the time, this made financial sense for mortgage brokers because they were able to sell the loans to investors and thus didn't need to worry about potential repayment problems. Subprime loans were being bundled into bonds along with just enough low-risk mortgages that credit rating agencies rated them AAA. Investors bought these bonds, happy to find allegedly AAA-safe investments that had such high returns—driven, of course, by the subprime risk of the majority of the underlying assets. Investors were given even further (also false) sense of security because these bonds could be hedged in the financial futures markets with unregulated credit default swaps—a form of insurance offered by major companies including the global insurance giant at the time, American International Group.[13]

The fact that the highest-indebted households were also disproportionately low-income magnified the implications when the housing bubble popped. As discussed in Chapter 5, families were using their home equity for consumption. When home prices began falling in 2006, counties that had both high household-debt burdens and large declines in house prices cut back sharply on spending. From 2006 to 2009, in counties with the largest declines in net worth, consumption fell by almost 20 percent. For the entire US economy, it fell 5 percent. The drop rippled through the retail sales data: in the second quarter of 2006, home-related products and services (called residential investment in government economic data compilations) dropped by an annual rate of 17 percent. Notably, this drop-off in consumption began a full two years before the dramatic collapse of two major Wall Street firms, Bear Stearns and Lehman Brothers, and the rescue of beleaguered insurance company American International Group, which many think of as the beginning of the crisis.[14]

Over the next two years, what started out as a consumption crisis among highly-leveraged, predominantly low-income communities was amplified across the nation. At first, counties that avoided the collapse in total net worth or experienced only small declines did not see lower spending. Families with the most net wealth were protected from having to cut back as much because they had sufficient money on hand to maintain their spending. This is why, nationwide, non-residential investment didn't begin to fall until late in 2008. But by 2009, spending declines spread beyond just those counties hit with large declines in net wealth. Consumer spending decreased by nearly 10 percent in counties that experienced the smallest declines in net worth.[15]

While the first unusual trend Mian and Sufi identified was that lenders were pumping money into communities where people would be unable to repay the loans, the second was that many of the new loans went to people who already owned and lived in their homes. As family income failed to rise during the early 2000s, rising home values and low interest rates led many families to leverage their homes to access much-needed income. Lenders were all too happy to help. In their 2011 paper in the *American Economics Review*, Mian and Sufi document how, as home values rose sharply during the bubble, lenders came up with more ways for borrowers to extract as much cash as possible through home equity loans or lines of credit, cash-out refinances, and mortgage refinances that deferred principal payments for years. This allowed homeowners to take advantage of rising home prices and created a situation where millions of families never moved, yet also became highly indebted. This also meant that the rise in lending in the run-up to the crisis wasn't driven by people seeking to afford their homes but by people accessing the capital already stored in the value of their homes.[16]

Notably, about four in ten mortgage defaults were among home equity borrowers—and we don't know how many of the other 60 percent were defaulting on cash-out refinances, by which they had taken on new mortgages bigger than their prior ones, to have some spending money. As Mian and Sufi document, these trends dragged down the net worth of neighborhoods with declining incomes. When the bubble burst, millions were left with homes worth substantially less than what they owed on their mortgages. Even at this writing, a full decade after the collapse of Lehman

Brothers and the rescue of American International Group, nearly one in ten mortgage holders in America remain underwater, according to a national real estate database.[17]

After researching decades worth of evidence, Mian and Sufi confidently declare that "debt is dangerous." Their evidence is hard to ignore—and they are not the only ones making these arguments. They are part of a new generation of economists using detailed microeconomic data and analysis to understand the macroeconomy. As they happily acknowledge in *House of Debt*, there has been "an explosion in data on economic activity and advancement in the techniques we can use to evaluate them."[18] These are the marks of a new movement in economics, distinguishing them from prior generations of macroeconomists who tended to rely more on theory and to use aggregate data in their analyses. In the past, the field did not generally consider the role of inequality—in income or in wealth—as a variable of interest.

## The Wealth Distortion

Mian and Sufi's evidence points to the cause of the Great Recession being the increase in the supply of credit rather than an independent surge in the demand for loans. In their view, this means that economists—and policymakers—need to pay much more attention to economic inequality and how it affects the dynamics of the macroeconomy. In the summer of 2018, Mian told me that, because the rise in inequality is largely a top 1 percent phenomenon and because the top 1 percent tend to have high savings rates, inequality has the effect of increasing gross savings, which has led to a rise in the supply of credit. "Now, the thing about gross savings is that when people save, they essentially channel that money through the financial sector," he noted. "So they leave it to the financial sector to decide where those savings go. And what has been happening globally is that this increased flow of savings coming into the financial sector has naturally led to the creation of credit—because that's what the financial sector does."[19]

While he and Sufi have focused their research agenda on understanding why and how a rise in the credit supply makes economic crises more likely, other economists are asking why savings have ballooned in the first place

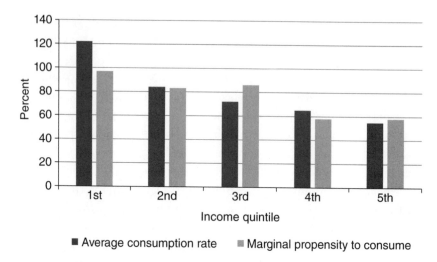

Figure 6.1   The wealthy are more likely to save their income
Consumption rates in the United States by income quintile.

*Source:* Author's calculation based on Lukasz Rachel and Thomas D Smith, "Secular Drivers of the Global Real Interest Rate," Bank of England, December 2015; and Karen E. Dynan, Jonathan Skinner, and Stephen P. Zeldes, "Do the Rich Save More?" *Journal of Political Economy* 112, no. 2 (April 2004): 397–444.

and yet investment is low. It turns out that you can have too much of a good thing.

Over the past four decades, savings have increased for the simple reason that the rich—who have become much richer—save more because they have more. New data compiled by Emmanuel Saez and Gabriel Zucman shows that the savings rate among the wealthiest one percent of households is 40 percent. Given that the incomes of the top 1 percent increased by about $19,000 annually since 1980, on average, this means an additional $7,600 in savings per family each year. This rise more than offsets the decline in savings rates for the bottom 90 percent, which have fallen since the 1970s from around 5 percent to around negative 5 percent in the mid-2000s, and 0 percent after the Great Recession. Bank of England economists Lukasz Rachel and Thomas D. Smith estimate that the shift in income from the bottom to the top of the income distribution accounts for an increase of forty-five basis points in the global savings rate. (See Figure 6.1.) That may not sound like much, but in a global economy of $75.9 trillion, it represents $340 billion annually.[20]

Other trends have been contributing to higher US national savings. First, the US population is aging. Just from 2000 to 2017, the median age in the United States went from 35.3 years old to 38 years of age. This means a larger share of the public is saving for retirement years, pushing up national savings and slowing growth—although this will change in the near future as the Baby Boomers retire and start spending their savings. Second, there's been an influx of additional savings from abroad since the late 1990s. The volatility in global markets—like during the Asian financial crisis in the 1990s—has left many emerging market governments wary and looking for safer investments. The United States remains an attractive destination for foreign capital because it has relatively high productivity growth and its deep capital markets can boast a disproportionate share of the world's marketable securities and financial assets. Despite a decline since the Great Recession, ownership of US government debt by foreign banks and private investors stayed consistently over 40 percent between 2004 and the end of 2017, and China, the largest foreign owner of US debt, held an average of $1.16 trillion in US Treasuries in 2018.[21]

High corporate profits are also contributing to high savings. While corporate profits experienced a sharp drop in 2008, they recovered quickly in 2009 toward the end of the Great Recession, and have stayed high since then. Inflation-adjusted corporate profits were 52.5 percent larger in June 2018 than in June 2009. Corporate profits have translated into disproportionate income gains from financial investments for wealthy households, which has contributed to the massive income and wealth inequality that has characterized the US economy over the past few decades. Among the top 1 percent of the income distribution, about 40 percent of income comes from earnings and 60 percent from capital income—rent, dividends, or interest. As firms distribute profits to shareholders through dividends and stock buybacks, this heightens inequality. From 2003 through 2012, the 449 companies that had been included in the S&P 500 over that entire time spent 54 percent of their earnings on share repurchases and an additional 37 percent of their earnings on dividends—a whopping 91 percent of all their earnings. Compare this to the early 1980s, when only about half of profits went to shareholders.[22]

Yet, even with the rise in wealth and savings, US investment has remained relatively low. In 2018, private residential investment hovered just below 4 percent of gross domestic product, which is at the low end of the

Corporate profits are high but they are being paid out to shareholders rather than going toward productive investments.

historical range of between 4 and 6 percent. Nonresidential investment, which economists sometimes prefer as a reading of overall economic health, is also stagnant. Investment in equipment is around 6 percent of gross domestic product, lower than the usual range since the 1970s of about 7 percent. Investment in structures remains below three percent, also down about one percentage point from its historic trend.[23]

This low level of investment is confounding both because corporate profits have been at historically high levels and because borrowing costs remain at near-historic lows. Corporations—and businesses more generally—are the largest investors, accounting for nearly all of US nonresidential investment. Typically, corporations find money for investment from either equity (stocks) or debt (bonds or loans). Since 2000, investments made by corporations have not increased by nearly as much as their financial valuations relative to their assets. Yet the amount of cash held by US corporations is at a historic high. The ratio of cash holdings to total assets was consistently below 6 percent between 1990 and 1995 but reached above a historic high of 12 percent by 2011.[24] (See Figure 6.2.)

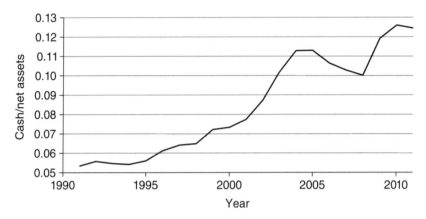

Figure 6.2  Firms are holding more cash as a share of net assets
Ratio of cash to net assets of publicly-traded US firms, 1991–2011.

*Source:* Juan M. Sanchez and Emircan Yurdagul, "Why Are Corporations Holding So Much Cash?," *Regional Economist* (Federal Reserve Bank of St. Louis), January 2013.

There also is accumulating evidence for another reason that savings are not translating into investment: the way US corporations are structured and financed is encouraging them to pay out profits in dividends or share repurchases rather than reinvest them in the firm. While the tax system favors capital investment or stock buybacks over dividends, there is mounting empirical evidence that other aspects of firm governance do not—especially for publicly traded firms. Economists John Asker of the University of California–Los Angeles, Joan Farre-Mensa of Harvard Business School, and Alexander Ljungqvist of New York University looked at short-termist behavior at public firms and how it affects investment decisions. They found that private firms face less intense pressure to undertake short-term decision-making than publicly traded firms, and that publicly traded firms pursue fewer investment opportunities. Other economists find that low interest rates also may be encouraging dividend payouts and stock buybacks rather than capital investment. And, as we learned in Chapter 4 from research by Thomas Philippon and Germán Gutiérrez, incentives to reinvest and innovate also drop with greater monopoly power.[25]

Economic inequality means lots of savings but too few attractive opportunities for profitable investments, which creates a long-term trajectory of slow growth. This is not a short-term problem; it's a medium- to long-term one tied to lack of income growth documented earlier. The term economists use to describe this combination of trends is *secular stagnation*. Harvard University economist Lawrence Summers, who served as treasury secretary in the Clinton administration, points to the role of economic inequality in secular stagnation and relatively low interest rates. We had a conversation in 2016, where he explained that "one aspect of that excess in saving over investments is that rising inequality has operated to reduce spending," since middle-income families spend more of their income than high-income families.[26] Paul Krugman argues that we are "facing persistent shortfalls of demand, which can't be overcome even with near-zero interest rates."[27] Part of this shortfall is due to the fact that incomes for the bottom 90 percent in the United States are failing to keep pace with average growth. Economists Adrien Auclert at Stanford University and Matthew Rognlie at Northwestern University also find that, if interest rates are already at zero and thus cannot be lowered anymore, then increases in income inequality can exacerbate the problem and lead to secular stagnation.[28]

Another Northwestern economist, Robert Gordon, sees secular stagnation as a supply-side issue, unlike Summers who sees it as mainly one of demand deficiency. To Gordon, structural headwinds such as aging populations lead to weaker potential growth. He argues that over the next decade, absent some sort of escape from the secular stagnation, growth will be well below 2 percent per year for the next two to four decades.[29]

Summers argues that secular stagnation is inherently unstable: "as the United States and other industrial economies are currently configured, simultaneous achievement of adequate growth, capacity utilization, and financial stability appears increasingly difficult."[30] Typically, when investment is too low, the Federal Reserve lowers the interest rate, hoping that cheaper borrowing will get people to invest more. This is not an option for policymakers today—rates were set at near zero for much of the Great Recession and subsequent slow recovery period. While interest rates have risen over the past two years, from essentially zero to between 2.25 percent and 2.5 percent (at the time of writing), they remain low, providing little room for policymakers to maneuver when the next recession hits. Historically, the Fed has lowered rates by about five percentage points during the last three recessions. At the same time, as laid out in the prior chapter, policymakers continue to work against expansionary fiscal policy.[31]

To be sure, not everyone agrees. Former Federal Reserve Chair Ben Bernanke argues that secular stagnation isn't likely in an economy open to international trade and capital flows. In his view, excess savings will flow abroad, and this will reduce the value of the dollar and discourage imports. This dynamic, in turn, will encourage exports and thus help grow the domestic economy. Bernanke's argument, however, presumes that the rest of the world is not also experiencing secular stagnation. That's an open question today among economists, given the fast-moving trade and investment fallout from the Trump administration's wide-ranging assault on the international rules of the road that have governed the global economy for decades. The same goes for Bernanke's argument that there is a worldwide savings glut, as it relies on similar mechanisms operating abroad.[32]

## The Financial Distortion

It turns out that having money available isn't enough to spur investment. Instead, with high profits and weak investment, we are seeing that savers increasingly finance credit for other parts of the economy. Prior eras did not see the expansion in the credit supply that we saw in the run-up to the Great Recession. In earlier eras, robust financial regulations kept financial institutions from making unsound loans to risky borrowers. Mian and Sufi, and many others, are looking at how financial deregulation, which by the early 2000s had been fully embraced by policymakers, allowed this change to happen in where savings go.[33]

Let's look at how—and why—the rules governing finance changed. Starting in the late 1970s, policymakers began a long path toward deregulating the financial sector. The goal was to free up money for investment. Proponents of *financialization*—a term that captures the growing role of complex financial products and services in everyday consumer and investment activities—argue that giving the financial industry greater leeway will make more money available for investment, which will drive up productivity and growth and create more and better jobs. The cornerstone was the Supreme Court's 1978 decision in *Marquette v. First of Omaha*, which allowed banks lending across state lines to export their home state law and apply maximum interest rates nationwide. This gave banks incentives to relocate to states like Delaware and South Dakota, with the most industry-friendly rules, and, as laid out at the beginning of this chapter, fueled a race among states to relax their regulations and attract these financial firms, effectively eliminating the rate ceilings set by the usury laws in prior decades.[34]

The capstone of these deregulatory efforts came in the form of three acts signed into law by President Clinton. In 1994, he signed the Riegle-Neal Interstate Banking and Branching Efficiency Act, which eliminated the last remaining restrictions keeping banks from operating across state lines. By that point, only Arkansas, Iowa, and Minnesota still had rules prohibiting banks from working across state lines. In 1999, he signed the Gramm-Leach-Bliley Financial Services Modernization Act, which repealed the last remaining barriers between commercial banks and investment banks and allowed deposit-taking commercial banks to engage in investment banking and debt underwriting. One of the last acts he signed as president was the 2000 Commodity Futures Modernization Act. This enabled the unregulated trading of so-called credit default swaps, which in turn enabled Wall Street financiers using them to "insure" the toxic mortgage backed-securities they packaged and sold to investors and ultimately led to the collapse and subsequent rescue of American Insurance Group, at the time one of the world's largest insurance companies. All three of these deregulatory decisions played an outsized role in the ensuing housing and financial crises to come in the 2000s, culminating in the 2007–2009 Great Recession.[35]

At the time these three laws were enacted, there was a robust debate among leading economists about whether this would increase investment and grow the economy or destabilize it. In 1998, Brooksley Born, then chair of the Commodity Futures Trading Commission, proposed that the multitrillion-dollar derivatives market be subject to regulatory oversight because of the economic risks it created. But her warning was met with fierce opposition from top economic officials. Congress instead passed legislation that prohibited her agency from regulating derivatives, relying on testimony from the president's economic team. President Clinton's treasury secretary, Robert Rubin, formerly head of Goldman Sachs, was a major advocate of financial deregulation. He told Congress that the Gramm-Leach-Bliley Act "takes the fundamental actions necessary to modernize our financial system by repealing the Glass-Steagall Act's prohibitions on banks affiliating with securities firms."[36]

The result of the decades-long deregulation of finance was to distort resources toward financial sector profits and away from their most productive use—the opposite of what the invisible hand is supposed to do. It turned
out that the proponents of deregulation were wrong: left without rules to
guide their behavior, financial firms focus more on short-term profits than
protecting the economy. One example of this distortion showed up in how
mortgages were financed. Wall Street came up with cleverer ways of pack-
aging up loans into securities; this is what created the incentive to separate
the financing of home loans from the mortgage brokers arranging the loans.
Making matters worse, banks themselves lost the incentive to ensure that
mortgages they bought from brokers were extended prudently, since the
banks turned around and sold most of the loans they had just bought to
Wall Street investment banks or to their own investment banking sub-
sidiaries. These buyers in turn packaged them into ever more complex
mortgage-backed securities to sell to investors around the country and the
world—financial products ostensibly insured against default via unregulated financial derivatives. This created additional supplies of money to
pump into new financial products to extend credit to more and more
people and the expansion of the subprime lending market.[37]

This was a marked departure from earlier decades, when banks made
loans and then mostly held onto them. In those years, banks cared a great
deal about whether loans would be repaid, as any defaults would directly
damage their profits. Under the relaxed rules, mortgage brokers got paid
when they sold the loan to the bank, eliminating most of their incentive to
make only those loans with high probabilities of being paid off. That, they
could conclude, was for the bank to worry about. This separation of the
original lender of the money from the organization that would hold the
loans while homeowners paid them back—or tried to—created perverse
incentives for Wall Street firms. They could apply the financial engineering
they had previously pioneered with asset-backed securities for businesses
into securitized home mortgages.[38]

Further, as laid out above, the expanded pool of people targeted for loans
included many who would be unable to repay. Economists Tobias Adrian
and Hyun Song Shin explain the explosion of subprime mortgage lending
by emphasizing the increased supply of loans, rather than any independent
increase in demand: "Someone has to be on the receiving end of new loans.
When all the good borrowers already have a mortgage, the bank has to

lower its lending standards to capture new borrowers. The new borrowers are those who were previously shut out of the credit market but who suddenly find themselves showered with credit."[39]

Outright fraud was also a culprit behind the expansion of subprime loans. In a TED talk in 2013 titled "How to Rob a Bank (From the Inside, That Is)," University of Missouri–Kansas City economist William Black described some of these practices. He showed how mortgage brokers engaged in widespread appraisal fraud and "liar's loans"—loans issued without confirming that the borrower is telling the truth about their income or ability to pay back the loan. (Black understands fraud: he took the notes during the Keating Five meeting that led to the exposure of the corruption in Congress during the 1980s savings and loan crisis.) Borrowers, often guided by lenders, inflated their incomes on mortgage applications to qualify for bigger loans. Academic research confirms these trends: Mian and Sufi found that income overstatement was highest in zip codes with low credit scores and low incomes—the places that experienced the strongest mortgage credit growth from 2002 to 2005. Another study found that in 2006, 49 percent of new mortgage originations were liar's loans—up from 18 percent in 2001. There is also evidence that, as early as 2000, banks began blacklisting appraisers who refused to inflate property values. In a 2007 survey by October Research, a financial real-estate analysis firm, nine in ten appraisers reported they had felt pressured to change their assessment of a property's value, usually by a lender, mortgage broker, or real estate agent.[40]

One clear outcome of deregulation of the financial industry is the rise in the size and profitability of the financial sector. According to research by Thomas Philippon, profits in the financial industry nearly doubled from 1980 to 2010, from about 5 percent of gross domestic product to about 9 percent, and the finance sector now accounts for about 27 percent of total US corporate profits, up from about 20 percent in the years prior to 2000. A larger financial sector means that fewer of our nation's economic resources go to their most productive uses but are instead directed to the top executives, shareholders, and "super managers" in the financial services industry.[41]

The high rates of pay in the financial sector have encouraged the best and the brightest coming out of colleges and universities to turn their own job-seeking efforts toward finance, adding to income (and wealth) inequality and distorting the labor market away from other endeavors, such as medicine and engineering. According to research by Philippon and Ariell Reshef at the Paris School of Economics on wages in the finance industry, workers in the financial sector once commanded average pay compared to their peers in other elite white-collar work, controlling for education and other components and indicators of human capital. By 2006, however, financial sector salaries had ballooned such that they were 50 percent higher than those in formerly comparable fields. As for executives, the growth is much more extreme. By the same year, executives in finance earned 250 percent more than executives in other industries.[42]

With a larger share of profits—and extremely well-paid jobs—the finance industry soon wielded significantly greater political power. One of Mian and Sufi's early papers focused on the role of this power in the deregulation of finance. In research with University of British Columbia economist Francesco Trebbi, they look at the political campaign contributions of the mortgage finance industry across congressional districts. They found that members of Congress from districts with higher campaign contributions from the financial services industry were more likely to vote for legislation that has the effect of transferring wealth from taxpayers to that industry. The researchers found that from 2002 to 2007—a period when mortgage industry campaign contributions increasingly targeted representatives from congressional districts with a large fraction of subprime borrowers— campaign contributions and the share of subprime borrowers in a district increasingly predicted how lawmakers would vote on housing-related legislation. These patterns are not reflected in the non-mortgage financial industry.[43]

This research echoes that of many other economists, political scientists, and other scholars who have been seeking to understand how financialization affects governance. Massachusetts Institute of Technology economist Simon Johnson, who also served as chief economist at the International Monetary Fund, and University of Connecticut law professor James Kwak make the case in their book *13 Bankers: The Wall Street Takeover and the Next Financial Meltdown*. They demonstrate that overconcentration of political power among a narrow band of elites is often associated with financial crises. As the financial sector pulls in more national income, it uses this economic power to encourage a regulatory environment favorable to further financial innovation, which may lead to excessive and unwarranted risk-taking—a precursor to a financial crisis. While the basic research behind Johnson and Kwak's conclusions examines emerging economies, they conclude that, in fact, the "financial sector and its political influence are a serious risk to our economic well-being" in the United States.[44]

Certainly, the conclusion reached by Johnson and Kwak maps neatly onto what actually happened in the Great Recession. Wall Street used its political and economic power to protect itself from the fallout amid the rolling collapse of the US housing market and the onset of the crisis, while many homeowners went belly up. The ways in which loans were structured prevented the vast majority of homeowners from getting relief, because their mortgages had been packaged up, then sliced and diced into myriad mortgage-backed securities owned by investors worldwide. No single investor had the incentive or legal right to restructure these loans, and therefore homeowners had no way to negotiate for mortgage payment relief. This increased foreclosures, which in turn reduced the value of nearby homes, amplified the decline in overall home prices, and led to the broader loss in wealth for most American families. This is all part of a larger story of how economic inequality subverts governance as discussed in earlier chapters.

In 2014, Mian and Sufi published a blog post about their book *House of Debt* in which they summarized the mechanism through which inequality affects the macroeconomy:

> When the wealthy save in the financial system, some of that saving ends up in the hands of lower wealth households when they get a mortgage or auto loan. But when lower wealth households get financing, it is almost always done through *debt contracts*. This introduces some potential problems. Debt fuels asset booms when the economy is expanding, and debt contracts force the borrower to bear the losses of a decline in economic activity.[45]

Debt can indeed be dangerous—and so can wealth with nothing productive to do.

### Pushing toward Strong, Stable, Broadly Shared Growth

Mian and Sufi argue that, all too often, macroeconomists have simply assumed that the financial sector provides credit as necessary. The pair's work shows that a rigorous understanding of how finance works in practice—and how it can distort economic outcomes and create unnecessary vulnerabilities—has too often been left out of macroeconomic analysis. Their conclusion: when macroeconomists take the actual behavior of finance into account, it becomes clear that economic inequality has played an important and arguably outsized role in the generation of profits within the financial services industry and destabilizing our economy. While it was common knowledge that too many people had amassed too much debt, focusing attention on why so many were able to do so—and on who held that debt and how economically vulnerable they were—is necessary to predicting and preventing future credit-driven economic crises.[46]

Mian and Sufi's evidence and new way of thinking contradicts the thinking of how to address a financial crisis that was prevalent during the Great Recession. In 2008, as that crisis unfolded, policymakers focused their energy on halting the sharp decline in credit flows as a number of financial institutions tried to cope with the large number of home foreclosures among the home mortgages they had not been able to sell when the crisis hit. While they bailed out the banks—through the Temporary Asset Relief Program implemented under President George W. Bush that pumped more than $800 billion into the financial markets—policymakers gave very few homeowners help. And research suggests the federal assistance that did go to homeowners was poorly designed and failed to prevent most defaults and foreclosures.[47]

Now we know more. Mian and Sufi's body of research shows that, in an era of high inequality when there was a lot of money looking for a place to go, deregulation led to financialization—and produced the Great Recession. Indeed, the credit boom resulting from deregulation and financialization fed the escalation of household borrowing, which contributed to the "strength, the depth, as well as the persistence of the recession that followed 2008."[48] Policymakers should in future ensure that the financial services industry is focused on supporting sustainable and productive investment, rather than enriching itself at the expense of the least well-off in our society. Ensuring that there's sufficient money in the US economy for productivity-enhancing investment—and that lax lending guidelines and poorly supervised financial institutions do not channel these funds into risky investments—should be considered important policy goals.

There's been movement in this direction. After the twin housing and financial crises roiled the US and global economy, the US Congress in 2010 passed the Wall Street Reform and Consumer Protection Act, more commonly known as Dodd-Frank, named after its two cosponsors, Senator Christopher Dodd and Representative Barney Frank. The new law reined in many of the deregulatory excesses of the previous decade. Dodd-Frank also established the Consumer Financial Protection Bureau as an independent agency to regulate financial products for consumer protection. The CFPB was authorized to enforce consumer protection laws and prohibit lenders from steering consumers to predatory loans or ones they could not reasonably repay.[49]

Yet, undeterred by the evidence, proponents of deregulation today continue to argue for even looser regulation of financial services. Dodd-Frank came under immediate assault from the financial services industry and conservative legislators who continued to argue that greater deregulation was good for the economy and investment. By 2017, after most of the country had recovered from the Great Recession, a different and more conservative Congress began chipping away at Dodd-Frank, requiring fewer and fewer financial institutions to adhere to the law's most prudent supervisory rules and regulations, and seeking to strip the CFPB of its authority and funding. Subprime lending is on the rise again across a range of consumer products, from car loans to credit card debt to, yes, mortgage financing, even as lending to businesses that should be engaged in productive investments remains moribund. The policy agenda should focus on strengthening, not undermining these protections.[50]

Focusing investment on its best use requires more than getting the rules right. We must also take actions to address the ways in which inequality has distorted demand and dulled the private sector's incentives to invest. Indeed, we must address secular stagnation head on. There are two ways to grow the economy when it's experiencing secular stagnation. One is to allow another asset bubble to form—not a sensible route. This, however, will become more likely if interest rates remain low and borrowing standards are lax, giving people access to capital to drive up asset prices.

Alternatively, government could tap into national savings and make greater investments in large-scale projects, such as upgrading the nation's failing transportation infrastructure, addressing climate change, and investing in people and families. There are myriad ways to do this. There are the traditional investments in transportation, as well as developing the technology to limit the emission of greenhouse gases and to address the consequences of climate change. Between the need for investments in the development and deployment of green energy, the need to mitigate the effects on our food supplies, and the need to assist communities upended by the rising prevalence of climate change-induced natural disasters, there's a comprehensive agenda to be enacted. At the same time, there's an unmet need for investments in health care, education, and the diverse needs of the elderly and families caring for young children or disabled family members that would lead to improvements in quality of life and sustain economic growth.[51]

It will likely remain a good environment for investment in large-scale projects for some time to come. At the 2018 Allied Social Science Association conference in Philadelphia, where more than ten thousand economists gathered to share research and ideas, I chaired a session on interest rates. According to the research presented there, interest rates in the United States will probably remain low for many years. Researchers from academia and government showed that a combination of low aggregate demand, technological change, and the shifting demographic composition of the United States is likely to leave interest rates dangerously close to zero. And of course, with that comes the risk of entering a recession, with Federal Reserve policymakers restricted in what traditional stabilization policies they can pursue. The low costs of borrowing, combined with the pressing social and environmental needs and an imperative to make sure savings is well spent, point in the direction of prioritizing new public investments.[52]

# Conclusion

## The Economic Imperative of Equitable Growth

THE EVIDENCE ILLUSTRATES that economic inequality constricts economic growth and stability. In the case studies explored, three basic dynamics play out: we see Smith's invisible hand being obstructed, subverted, and distorted as economic inequality translates into social and political power. When looked at as a whole, insights from cutting-edge research provide the outlines of a new vision for policymaking dedicated to broadly shared improvements in well-being and a stronger and more stable US economy. To unleash broadly shared growth, we need to break inequality's grip.

These findings conflict with misleading theories that the economy, left to its own devices, will deliver optimal outcomes. More than two hundred years ago, Adam Smith transformed how people thought about the economy, giving us the idea of dynamics pushing the market as though with an invisible hand toward mutually beneficial outcomes. If the desires for wealth that inspire the butcher, brewer, and baker guide free, competitive markets toward outcomes that are generally socially beneficial, then they act as forces for good. During the latter half of the twentieth century, however, Smith's ideas were stripped of nuance and turned into a widespread faith among policymakers that, if they left markets to their own internal logic, the nation would see broadly-shared improvements in well-being. The evidence is in: That bare-bones framework doesn't work.

The Introduction to this book argued that we are in the midst of what the philosopher of science Thomas Kuhn called a "paradigm shift." For a long time, economists did not consider economic inequality as fundamentally important to understanding the dynamics of the economy. This has changed. Now, cutting-edge economics research seeks to understand whether and how economic inequality affects economic, social, and political outcomes. Table C.1 summarizes what we've learned about how inequality obstructs, subverts, and distorts the processes that lead to economic productivity and growth, laying out both the direct effects of inequality and the consequences of those effects. The most direct effects of inequality are relatively straightforward and easy for economists to assess. Deep inequality, for example, gives the wealthy the power in the political realm to lobby successfully for low taxes, regulatory changes in their favor, and outsized electoral influence. The secondary knock-on effects are just as important yet often harder to identify in empirical research. How does lost tax revenue, for example, affect the economy and general well-being when consequent impacts on public policies are taken into account? A new generation of research is focusing on these trickier, second-order questions.

Armed with a better understanding of inequality's effects on our economy, we face the question of what to do with this knowledge. We can look to American history for inspiration. The Industrial Revolution of the nineteenth and early twentieth centuries created vast wealth and outsized political and social power for a small group of wealthy elites, but immiseration for many others. Like today, inequality's grip threatened our economy, our society, and our democracy. Political leaders responded by putting rules in place to contain inequality and ensure the marketplace delivered for the many, not the few. These institutions and new rules governing the market and expanding democratic accountability sought to thwart the concentration of wealth, generate more revenue for government to take necessary actions for the public good, protect people in the workplace, and guard against poverty. Decades later, the civil rights movement sought to ensure that everyone had the same rights before the law and that all could participate equally in our democracy.

This fundamental shift in the role of government worked to ensure that workers and their families gained from economic growth both in the workplace—in the distribution of earnings before taxes—and through the tax-and-transfer system that redistributed earnings through government programs. Many in that era's bottom 90 percent needed social insurance for times when they couldn't work due to sickness or old age, or because jobs weren't available. The push to rein in economic power gave government the capacity to tax and enact policies to cope with a changing economy, bringing forth pension systems, unemployment benefits, and new ways to support wages, such as the minimum wage and overtime regulations, as well as an administrative state focusing on pushing firms to act in the public interest. These policies that supported workers and their families brought forth strong productivity and growth and meant that the middle of the twentieth century marked the nadir of economic inequality.

These policy changes required policymakers to take bold action, including amending and reinterpreting the US Constitution and reimagining what tools a democratically elected government might use to rein in economic power. Legal scholars Joseph Fishkin and William Forbath of the University of Texas–Austin argue that previous generations were able to loosen the grip of economic elites on both the economy and society by making the case that equality was fundamental to our democracy: "From the beginning of the Republic through roughly the New Deal, Americans vividly understood that the guarantees of the Constitution are intertwined with the structure of our economic life."[1] The enactment of a federal income tax was initially overturned by the Supreme Court and it took advocates nearly two decades to organize the states to adopt the Sixteenth Amendment to the Constitution in 1913. Other early twentieth-century policies included the introduction of antitrust laws and laws that gave workers and their families greater bargaining power with respect to employers, and insurance against economic insecurity. With these came changes in how the legislative, executive, and judicial branches of government saw their role in economic policy.

We will need similarly bold action today. If we want to address the economic and social challenges posed by high inequality, we need to reclaim the idea that these are fundamental—even constitutional—issues. But the institutions we need to do this are in trouble. The scale of the challenges has grown just at the moment when unions have weakened and the federal government's enforcement of a competitive market is at a low point. Many of today's most profitable firms have become adept at limiting the extent to which they share their outsized gains with workers and communities. They've fissured their workplaces so that only the workers in the branded,

**Table C.1** What we've learned about how economic inequality affects economic growth and stability

| The effects of economic inequality on... | The knock-on effects on growth of the US economy |
| --- | --- |
| *Chapter 1: The Beginning of the End of Adam Smith's Invisible Hand* | |
| ...our understanding of economics | New data-driven evidence shows that rising economic inequality harms the economy |
| *Chapter 2: Learning and Human Capital* | |
| ...our children by obstructing too many from reaching their potential | No longer an intergenerational reboot, threatening the productivity of tomorrow's labor force |
| *Chapter 3: Skills, Talent, and Innovation* | |
| ...people with skills, talent, and new ideas by constricting pipelines into the economy | Reduces people's ability to freely participate in the economy and reduces productivity |
| *Chapter 4: Public Spending* | |
| ...taxes and democracy, by subverting fiscal responsibility and public accountability | The wealthy have a disproportionate say in who pays taxes—and they don't want taxes levied on them—leaving the government unable to make investments to foster productivity and growth |
| *Chapter 5: Market Structure* | |
| ...markets through rising monopoly and monopsony power | Limits opportunities for new firms and new ideas, reducing innovation and competition |
| *Chapter 6: The Economic Cycle* | |
| ...the level and composition of both consumption and investment | Skews investment away from products that would improve the lives of most in favor of those for the wealthy and reduces productivity over time |
| *Chapter 7: Investment* | |
| ...the flow of credit through the economy | More severe recessions and reduced economic opportunity for younger generations |
| *Conclusion* | |
| ...overall economic growth and stability, hindering equitable growth | Income and wealth inequality perpetuates economic inequalities |

Table C.1   (continued)

| The knock-on effects on US political and social power | Proposals for more equitable growth |
|---|---|
| Rising inequality is evident in the top 1 percent dominating political and social power | Disaggregate growth by income and wealth and design policies for more equitable growth |
| Leads to greater hoarding of opportunity at the top while limiting fiscal support for public investments that would benefit all children | Expand economic opportunity through policies such as universal early childhood education and care, better public education, and work-life policies |
| Erodes public trust in the American Dream | Eliminate economic discrimination and ensure true equal opportunity for all Americans |
| Citizens fear that others are not paying their fair share of taxes, generating frustration with government and undermining the common good | Ensure economic inequality does not subvert political debate and that government has resources to address social needs |
| Firms use their economic power to manipulate policies to benefit themselves, not the common good, through lax antitrust law and regulation and limiting worker bargaining power | A robust competition agenda that addresses monopoly power and monopsony labor markets and ensures that economic inequality does not translate into political power |
| Political polarization, reducing capacity to enact sound policies to address macroeconomic stability | Macroeconomic policies that account for inequality, including how inequality distorts fiscal and monetary policy and the political process |
| Undermines shared belief that the economy can deliver for the many, not just the few, threatening liberal democracy | Fiscal and financial regulatory policies that support sustainable and productive investment by encouraging savings toward public infrastructure and addressing climate change |
| Economic inequality subverts politics and society, reinforcing the grip of the top 1 percent on economic power | Measure what matters: Implement Distributional National Income Accounts and release disaggregated growth data each quarter alongside gross domestic product so that the public see the benefits of equitable growth |

core firm earn the highest wages, outsourcing as many functions as possible as a way to push down wages for everyone else. They employ small armies of accountants and lawyers to minimize their tax liabilities. They lobby effectively to limit regulations preventing them from polluting our waterways and unsustainably exploiting our natural resources.

To put the American Dream within reach of most Americans and reverse rising inequalities of income and wealth, the century-old progressive policy agenda for which our grandparents and great-grandparents fought must be updated for the twenty-first century. The preceding chapters laid out ideas to address this challenge; key elements of these are presented in the last column of Table C.1. These policies collectively address the problem of economic inequality across the income distribution—the bottom, middle, and top—and recognize the power of those with high incomes and wealth to subvert political processes away from the common good. There is no one magic policy solution; the path lies in a comprehensive agenda focused on addressing unbridled economic inequality and how it creates and reinforces social and political inequities.

Like policymakers sought to do a century ago, we must focus on removing obstructions with policies that ensure widespread access to the basics required to live a better life, such as high-quality childcare and preschool, well-funded public schools, and infrastructure investments that ensure the health of all, regardless of where one sits on the income spectrum. Removing obstructions will not only help people as individuals but boost our economy and society more generally.

A basket of policies designed to remove obstacles to social mobility will, however, serve as a band-aid more than real solution unless we also address the ways that inequality subverts both the market and our democracy. Today's high inequality gives some actors enormous political and economic power, making it that much harder to implement the policy agenda laid out in the preceding pages—and that much more urgent. As Raj Chetty and his colleagues show, in order to improve absolute upward mobility, we need to address inequality head-on. This means that policymakers must do more to ensure that economic incentives push the economy toward the most socially useful purposes, that competition is real, and that government has the resources and power to act on behalf of the many, not just elites. These challenges may be the toughest ones inequality poses for our political system, as well as the most imperative to fix. Only then can we correct the economic distortions inequality causes.

We can implement an agenda to revitalize income and well-being across the economic spectrum and strengthen the economy. Time and time again, both democracy and the market economy have delivered vast improvements in living standards. To deliver on their promises, both require a high degree of inclusiveness, and institutions and rules that balance the power of economic interests. While the competitive marketplace can contain economic inequality, it does not do so automatically. If some people can grab even just a little extra market power, that can set the stage for the erosion of competition, the unchecked pursuit of rent-seeking, and the shattering of any cap on rising income and power at the top.

To enact these changes, we need to revise our thinking about the economy and the role of inequality. One important—and relatively simple—step is to measure the success of the economy differently so that citizens understand how economic growth affects them directly. At present, we tend to rely on one measure: gross domestic product (GDP), an aggregate measure of what the nation produces. It's a very useful number to track, but it does not measure how the fruits of production are shared or say anything about human well-being more broadly. Fortunately, economists have been working on alternatives.

Like the revolution ushered in nearly a century ago to measure our economy in the aggregate, groundbreaking scholarship, now aided by increased computing power, is fundamentally changing our understanding of the importance of the distribution of economic growth. A measure of how national income is distributed among us would allow us to quantify inequality in our economy, and, in its most advanced format, let US statistical agencies disaggregate economic growth to see how the economy is performing for people according to their income, geographical location, gender, and more. While we have measures of income and inequality, up until now we haven't had access to data that directly connects how ordinary people are experiencing the economy to growth in national income. Being able to do so will enable policymakers at federal, state, and local levels to better understand the consequences of rising economic inequality and design policies that promote more equitable and sustainable economic growth. This starts with disaggregating our national income accounts.

## Measure what Matters

The National Income and Product Accounts—the data sources that enable the US government to produce its quarterly reports and monthly updates on growth in the US economy—are among the most important economic innovations of the twentieth century. They aggregate information from all the businesses, households, and governments across the economy to tally the total value of goods and services sold, the total incomes received, and the shares coming from various sources, such as earnings, interest, rent, and government payments. They show how much the United States sells to other countries and buys from abroad. They provide the Federal Reserve Board and other policymakers with critical tools to understand and manage the US economy toward full employment and sustainable growth. Prior to the introduction of the National Accounts in the 1940s, policymakers, business leaders, and citizens had to rely on a hodgepodge of data to infer what was going on in the economy.

The National Accounts allow us to calculate aggregate national income, commonly measured by GDP, which is the sum total of all the goods and services produced within the nation's borders. Every three months, the US Bureau of Economic Analysis releases new GDP data showing how much—and of what—was produced and indicating whether it was more or less than in previous quarters. As this book goes to press, it reports that, in the fourth quarter of 2018, GDP grew at an annualized rate of 2.2 percent.[2]

The data was first put together in the 1930s to help policymakers understand the Great Depression. The US Department of Commerce commissioned Simon Kuznets, who at the time was an economist at the National Bureau of Economic Research and a professor at the University of Pennsylvania, to develop estimates of aggregate national income for the United States. In 1934, he and his team of researchers in New York and at the US Commerce Department presented their findings to the US Senate. The report itself is nearly three hundred pages long and is filled with appendices. Its hundreds of tables offer painstaking detail for every line of information published, drawn from an immense number of independent sources and statistical abstracts across every major industry and government agency responsible for their oversight. Based on this work, the first US national income statistics were published in 1942. These accounts, specifically developed to help the United States effectively marshal its economic resources to fight in World War II, are what we have used since to measure economic progress and tabulate GDP. Kuznets would go on to win the third Nobel Memorial Prize in Economic Sciences for this work and his research on economic growth.[3]

Once the National Accounts were developed, they swiftly became the standard way for policymakers across the globe to measure growth. In the early 1960s, the member countries of the Organisation for Economic Co-operation and Development (OECD) adopted aggregate GDP as a standard to compare economic growth across all countries, making this the preferred metric of success. As one scholar makes clear in a history of the OECD, GDP was at the center of the organization's defining goal of economic growth, which led one of its most influential directors to describe it as "a kind of temple of growth for industrialized countries." The OECD's position as a club of the biggest economic players in the world helped cement GDP as a globally pervasive measure of social well-being—and GDP *growth* as a societal goal. Policymakers needed a simple, widely understood metric and GDP fit the bill.[4]

Yet the National Accounts and, in particular, aggregate GDP reveal nothing about whether growth is broadly shared and whether more people are reaching the American Dream. This makes GDP ill-suited to help policymakers address today's challenges. As Jason Furman, a professor of the practice of economic policy at Harvard University and former chair of the Council of Economic Advisers in the Obama administration, recently argued, policymakers' goal should be to deliver broadly shared economic gains, not simply growth. Fortunately, there are a number of economists in the United States and around the world pursuing a pathbreaking idea that addresses one of the key flaws in national income accounts—the lack of connection to ordinary people's well-being. This does not address all the problems, but it provides a course to significant improvement. It opens the door to a new conversation about economic progress.[5]

For the United States, a team of scholars—Thomas Piketty, Emmanuel Saez, and Gabriel Zucman—have been doing the hard work of matching survey data and administrative records to the National Accounts data in order to show how income growth looks across income groups. They call these Distributional National Accounts, and the three have created the data to show disaggregated US economic growth going back to 1913 (although the more detailed data goes back only to 1962). They focus on national income, which is closely related to GDP but adjusts for the decline in value of the capital stock and certain international transactions. Figure C.1a shows national income as we currently think of it; Figure C.1b shows it disaggregated by what portion is going to the top 1 percent, the next 9 percent, and the next 40 percent, alongside the rest—the bottom 50 percent. The striking trend is how much of total national income goes to those at the top of the income ladder and how the share of national income accruing to them has grown since the late 1970s.[6]

These scholars' work on Distributional National Accounts provides policymakers and economists with a better way of understanding economic growth—one that directly connects the analysis of aggregate economic data with the real-life circumstances of individuals. Gabriel Zucman sees this work as a continuation of the project Kuznets began: "We talk about growth, we talk about inequality—but never about the two together," Zucman told me. "Kuznets and others, in parallel, looked at tax data to study the description of income as reporting tax returns, but they never bridged the gap between GDP and income and taxes. So what we tried to do is to complete the Kuznets agenda of GDP looking at the description of income between these two things in a common and consistent conceptual framework." This research is part of the larger project, he explained, which is "an attempt at bridging the gap between macroeconomics, on the one hand, and inequality studies on the other hand."[7]

If policymakers could track this data alongside the GDP data each quarter, then there would be no question as to why Americans feel that the economy is on the wrong track. When they learned, for instance, that in the fourth quarter of 2018 GDP grew by 2.2 percent, they would also know who in the United States took home those gains. Policymakers and the public would then be able to understand how these gains or lack of gains look for families. When it comes to governing, the question isn't just whether GDP is growing, whether the stock market is growing, or whether unemployment is down, but rather what is happening up and down the income distribution and in communities across the country. This gives policymakers the right set of metrics to measure what matters. As Zucman told me, "there's a growing demand from the public everywhere around the world for this type of distribution of national accounts. People realize that it's not

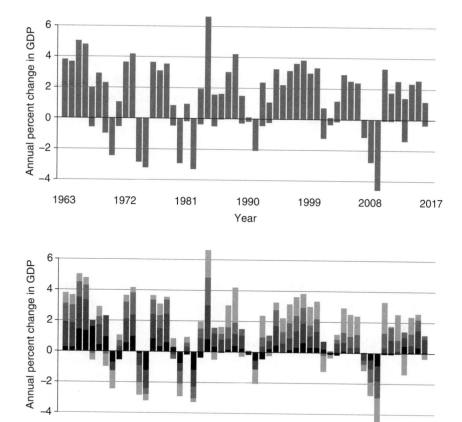

Figure C.1a and C.1b  Disaggregating national income is revealing
a. Aggregate numbers say nothing about how growth is distributed
Per-capita annual real US National Income growth, 1963–2016
b. Disaggregation shows growth flowing to high-income Americans
Per-capita annual real US National Income growth subdivided by amount of
growth earned by each income group, 1963–2016.

*Source:* Author's analysis of Thomas Piketty, Emmanuel Saez, and Gabriel Zucman, "Distributional
National Accounts: Methods and Estimates for the United States," *Quarterly Journal of* Economics 133,
no. 2 (May 2018): Appendix tables II: distributional series, available at http://gabriel-zucman.eu/usdina/.

enough to know GDP is growing—they want to know how income is growing for people like them."[8]

Using disaggregated economic growth figures rather than aggregate ones would go a long way toward changing the conversation about our nation's economic performance. While the media regularly report on newly released economic data—including GDP, inflation, trade deficits, daily changes on the stock market, and monthly changes in the unemployment rate—there are few government data releases each year that focus at all on family economic well-being, much less on what's happening to wealth inequality and the income share of families in poverty. The US Census Bureau releases statistics on income and poverty early each fall, tracking the trend line of family income growth, but the attention the media pay to these reports pales in comparison to the daily coverage of the business side of the equation.

To be sure, disaggregating growth doesn't solve all our problems. The National Accounts were never intended to measure economic well-being. Even at the time of their development, Kuznets was well aware of the limitations of what he'd worked so hard to create. He himself stressed that the data was incomplete. He was always careful to differentiate between the idea of aggregate economic output and "economic welfare," arguing that GDP was not a measure of welfare or well-being. In his 1934 report to Congress, there is a section titled "Uses and Abuses of National Income Measurements" which makes this clear: "The welfare of a nation can, therefore, scarcely be inferred from a measurement of national income."[9] Using growth in GDP as the basis for a metric of economic success means that anything that leads to increased output is measured positively. Perversely, this means that the production of a toxic chemical—or the clean-up of its spillage—adds to our measure of success alongside the building of schools and performing life-saving surgery.[10]

Disaggregating growth is a necessary step, even with these caveats. A century ago, economists defined the goal posts by giving us data for the first time that tracked the national economy. Our continued reliance on aggregate GDP as our primary metric of economic success has left us with a distorted view of what counts. It has allowed policymakers to present a false front to the world about our success and well-being. It was never enough and is growing increasingly inadequate by the day. Altering the data we rely on to understand economic performance will go a long way to ensuring that the paradigm shift happening in economics makes its way into our nation's economic policymaking.

## Shape a New Understanding of Inequality's Role in the Economy

Disaggregating growth is a relatively simple step we can take now that will have far-reaching implications for our understanding of economic performance. In many policy debates, one side argues that if policymakers give outsized incentives to those at the top or allow them to operate with little or no oversight, these gains will eventually benefit the economy overall. (Patent protection is a good example: it gives inventors the right to keep others from capitalizing on their ideas in the hope that this spurs innovations.) If the Bureau of Economic Analysis produced disaggregated growth data, we'd know whether any rise in GDP was shared across the income spectrum or only benefited those at the very top.

Having the right data will help us get to a new, more widely understood model of how the economy works. It will give us more clarity on how to hold policymakers accountable for delivering an economy that works for all. Helping the public and policymakers understand the economy is—and has been—the role of economists, something Adam Smith understood. He said that "political economy, considered as a branch of the science of a statesman or legislator, proposes two distinct objects: first, to provide a plentiful revenue or subsistence for the people, or more properly to enable them to provide such a revenue or subsistence for themselves; and secondly, to supply the state or commonwealth with a revenue sufficient for the public services. It proposes to enrich both the people and the sovereign."[11] This deep connection remains with us today. Economists provide advice to policymakers in a joint pursuit to advance the wealth of the nation.

When I earned my PhD in economics and moved to Washington, DC, seeking to contribute to economic policymaking, there were still many in that community who saw the job of the economist differently. It was simply to improve productivity and growth, and the presumption was that the rest would follow. We can now recognize the job of the advisor on economic policy as much more complex. We need answers about how to create the conditions to foster more sustainable growth and we must address questions about who benefits—and who does not. Disaggregating growth allows us to put these two ideas together and reframe national debates over not only the right measures of economic success but how to put them in place and use them.

The paradigm shift happening within economics needs to be part of the national debate over economic policy. The ideas discussed in the preceding chapters are not yet widely known outside of the economics profession—but they need to be. It's imperative that the policymaking community understand what economists know about how inequality constricts growth. One challenge in making that happen is that, over the past few decades, economics has become more scientific. This means that much of the most important research is hiding in plain sight, widely available but not actually accessible or knitted together so that the implications of this research are clear. More efforts to inform the policymaking community—including not just political leaders, but business leaders and the legal community, as well as the public more generally—about the shifts in economic thinking are undoubtedly necessary. Certainly, that is a goal of this book.

The policymaking community is ready for economics to propose new answers. Since the economic crisis that began with the collapse of the housing bubble in 2007, a new generation of thinkers and doers has begun questioning the market fundamentalism of past generations. They ask why we do not have an economy that works for all, and what policymakers can do to create one that does. The simultaneous moves toward the search for policies that work both inside and outside urban cores, and the increasingly progressive sentiments of those born after President Reagan took office, are changing the conversation. Cathy Cohen, a professor of political science at the University of Chicago, recently surveyed today's twenty- and thirty-somethings and reports that they "do not believe, in fact, that the free market alone can handle the economic issues that face the country, and in particular, face their generation."[12]

Policymakers are being encouraged by important institutions that are also asking a new question about the intersection between economic and political power. The Ford Foundation, led by Darren Walker, has put addressing inequality at the core of its grant-making. The Hewlett Foundation has embarked on a multiyear effort asking scholars to engage in finding what this new paradigm looks like. As its president, Larry Kramer, argues, "circumstances are ripe for the emergence of a new intellectual paradigm—a different way to think about political economy and the terms for a new twenty-first-century social contract."[13]

One audience that needs to hear more about the new ideas in economics is the media, which is especially where a framework that begins with disaggregated growth could help reshape the public's understanding of economic progress. The stories told in the public square about how the economy works remain wedded to simplistic and outdated models. This partly reflects how debates happen in today's media environment—an economist typically has only a few minutes on a broadcast news panel to explain an economic issue—but it's also because too many economists and policymakers fall back on tired tropes that are more ideology than economics. These stories may be easier for audiences to embrace, but many of them are inaccurate or misplaced.

As part of this effort, it will be important to ensure that the understanding of inequality's role in the economy isn't obscured by those who benefit from the status quo. One way to fix this is by creating more outlets for economic news that focus on the bottom 90 percent rather than those at the top. While there are whole cable news stations devoted to the stock market and business economics, there aren't stations devoted to how well the economy is delivering for ordinary people. Further, when inequality is covered in the media, it tends to be a special report or in-depth story, often anecdotal in its facts and not the day-to-day, data-driven updates on how well the economy is performing for individuals and their families.[14]

To this end, we need a wider array of voices in the economic debate. Most experts engaged in the public debate about the economy are not unbiased but are participants in the economy with a perspective—usually representing those at the top. A quick scan of *New York Times* coverage of the monthly release of data on US employment over 2018 reveals that the experts who represent the views of financial firms or the business community outnumber those representing organizations focused on the economic realities of US families by a factor of at least three to one. Furthermore, most of those commenting on economic news don't reflect the diversity of America's population, which means we too often hear less than the full story. We need to do more to ensure that the voices who shape our economic understanding also reflect the perspectives of the American people.[15]

■　■　■

In 1962, when Kuhn laid out how scientific revolutions happen, he argued that a paradigm changes when the consensus shifts. This is happening right now in economics. Behind the scenes, in academic conferences and journals across the nation, a new framework is emerging, one that seeks to explain how economic power translates into social and political power and, in turn, affects economic outcomes. As I hope the preceding pages have convinced you, this means that it is probably one of the most exciting times to follow the economics field. As some of the sharpest academics—Suresh Naidu, Dani Rodrik, and Gabriel Zucman—recently said, "Economics is in a state of creative ferment."[16]

It's now time for our national economic debates to reflect this shift. Let's take seriously the binding power of inequality and work to release our economy—and our society—from its grip, while retaining the vibrancy of a market economy so that we have an American economy that works for the many, not just the lucky few.

NOTES


ACKNOWLEDGMENTS


INDEX

# *Notes*

## Preface

1. Neil King, Jr. and Mark Peters, "Party Eyes 'Red-State Model' to Drive Republican Revival," *Wall Street Journal*, February 5, 2013, https://www.wsj.com/articles/party-eyes -aposredstate-modelapos-to-drive-republican-revival-1389363661; 13 News, "Office Of The Repealer To Tour Kansas," WIBW 13, September 30, 2011, http://www.wibw.com /home/headlines/Office_Of_The_Repealer_To_Tour_Kansas_130857783.html; Julie Bosman, Mitch Smith, and Monica Davey, "Brownback Tax Cuts Set Off a Revolt by Kansas Republicans," *New York Times*, June 7, 2017, sec. US, https://www.nytimes.com /2017/06/07/us/sam-brownback-kansas-budget-override.html; Peter Coy, "Kansas Tries to Shrink Its Way to Prosperity," *Bloomberg Businessweek*, April 18, 2014, https://www .bloomberg.com/news/articles/2014-04-17/kansas-governor-brownbacks-lab-for-steep-tax -and-budget-cuts; Sam Brownback, "Tax Cuts Needed to Grow Economy," *Wichita Eagle*, July 29, 2012, http://www.kansas.com/opinion/opn-columns-blogs/article1096336.html. See also Jonathan Shorman, "The Brownback Legacy: Tax Cut Push Led to Sharp Backlash," *Wichita Eagle*, July 26, 2017, http://www.kansas.com/news/politics-government /article163860323.html.

2. Scott Rothschild, "Brownback Gets Heat for 'Real Live Experiment' Comment on Tax Cuts," LJWorld.com, June 19, 2012, http://www2.ljworld.com/news/2012/jun/19 /brownback-gets-heat-real-live-experiment-comment-t/.

3. Brownback, "Tax Cuts Needed to Grow Economy." On the tax cuts, see Institute on Taxation and Economic Policy and Kansas Action for Children, "Kansas Governor Tax Proposal: Wealthy Kansans Pay Less, Poor and Middle-Income Kansans Pay More," press release, January 2012, https://itep.org/wp-content/uploads/ksbrownbackanalysis.pdf.

4. As of 2015, the top 1 percent of families control 15.6 percent of all income in Kansas. "Interactive: The Unequal States of America," *Economic Policy Institute* (blog), https://www .epi.org/multimedia/unequal-states-of-america/#/Kansas; Menzie D. Chinn, "Kansas and Missouri GDP Trends since Brownback | Econbrowser," *Econbrowser* (blog), December 11, 2017, http://econbrowser.com/archives/2017/12/kansas-and-missouri-gdp-trends-since -brownback; Michael Mazerov, "Kansas Provides Compelling Evidence of Failure of

'Supply-Side' Tax Cuts" (Center on Budget and Policy Priorities, January 22, 2018), https://www.cbpp.org/research/state-budget-and-tax/kansas-provides-compelling-evidence -of-failure-of-supply-side-tax-cuts.

5. Hunter Woodall, "Legislature Overrides Brownback's Veto of Bill That Rolls Back His 2012 Tax Cuts," *Kansas City Star*, June 6, 2017, http://www.kansascity.com/news/politics -government/article154691724.html.

The Congressional Budget Office estimates that the 2017 Tax Act will increase deficits by $1.9 trillion over ten years, after taking into account growth effects and net interest payments. The use of this score is not an endorsement of including macroeconomic feedback effects in official estimates of tax and spending policies. Congressional Budget Office, "Budget and Economic Outlook: 2018 to 2028," Congressional Budget Office, April 2018, https://www.cbo.gov/publication/53651.

6. Karl Polanyi, *The Great Transformation: The Political and Economic Origins of Our Time*, 2nd ed. (Boston: Beacon Press, 2001), 125.

7. See, for example, J. Bradford DeLong, "Karl Polanyi, Classical Liberalism, and the Varieties of 'Neoliberalism': Virtual Office Hours from Espresso Roma CCXXVI," *Grasping Reality* (blog), July 25, 2014, https://www.bradford-delong.com/2014/07/karl-polanyi -classical-liberalism-and-the-varieties-of-neoliberalism-virtual-office-hours-from-espresso -roma-ccxxvi-jul.html; Patrick Iber and Mike Konczal, "Karl Polanyi for President," *Dissent Magazine*, May 23, 2016, https://www.dissentmagazine.org/online_articles/karl-polanyi -explainer-great-transformation-bernie-sanders; Fred Block, "Learning from Karl Polanyi," *Institute for New Economic Thinking* (blog), April 9, 2015, https://www.ineteconomics.org /perspectives/blog/learning-from-karl-polanyi.

## Introduction

1. This fall in employment is from the height of Great Recession employment in January 2008 through February 2010, when employment fell to its then post Great Recession low. "All Employees: Total Nonfarm Payrolls," FRED, Federal Reserve Bank of St. Louis, March 9, 2018, https://fred.stlouisfed.org/series/PAYEMS; Household net worth dropped from a peak of over $69 trillion in the third quarter of 2007 to below $58 trillion in the first quarter of 2009. "Households and Nonprofit Organizations; Net Worth, Level," FRED, Federal Reserve Bank of St. Louis, December 16, 2018, https://fred.stlouisfed.org/series /TNWBSHNO; "Employed Persons and Employment-Population Ratio," US Department of Labor, Bureau of Labor Statistics, accessed January 17, 2019, https://www.bls.gov/web/empsit /cpseea08a.htm; Rakesh Kochhar and Rich Morin, "Despite Recovery, Fewer Americans Identify as Middle Class," Fact Tank, Pew Research Center, January 27, 2014, http://www .pewresearch.org/fact-tank/2014/01/27/despite-recovery-fewer-americans-identify-as-middle -class/; David Rosnick and Dean Baker, "The Wealth of Households: An Analysis of the 2016 Survey of Consumer Finance," Center for Economic and Policy Research, Washington, DC, November 2017, http://cepr.net/images/stories/reports/wealth-of-households-2017-11.pdf.

2. Data on household wealth is from Emmanuel Saez and Gabriel Zucman, "Wealth Inequality in the United States since 1913: Evidence from Capitalized Income Tax Data," *Quarterly Journal of Economics* 131, no. 2 (2016): 519–578, DOI: 10.1093/qje/qjw004.

3. Robert E. Lucas, "Macroeconomic Priorities," *American Economic Review* 93, no. 1 (2003): 1–14, DOI: 10.1257/000282803321455133.

4. Franklin Delano Roosevelt, Second Inaugural Address, January 20, 1937, https://www .presidency.ucsb.edu/documents/inaugural-address-7.

5. Michael Brocker and Christopher Hanes, "The 1920s American Real Estate Boom and the Downturn of the Great Depression: Evidence from City Cross-Sections," in *Housing*

*and Mortgage Markets in Historical Perspective*, ed. Eugene N. White, Kenneth Snowden, and Price Fishback, 161–201 (Chicago: University of Chicago Press, 2014); Herbert Hoover, "Annual Message to the Congress on the State of the Union," December 2, 1930, https://www.presidency.ucsb.edu/node/210889.

6. John F. Kennedy, "Remarks in Heber Springs, Arkansas, at the Dedication of Greers Ferry Dam," October 3, 1963, https://www.jfklibrary.org/Asset-Viewer/Archives/JFKPOF -047-015.aspx. On the OECD, see Matthias Schmelzer, "The Hegemony of Growth: The OECD and the Making of the Economic Growth Paradigm," Organisation for Economic Co-operation and Development, OECD History Department, Zurich, July 8, 2016, http://oecdinsights.org/2016/07/08/a-temple-of-growth-the-oecd-and-economic-growth-as -its-organisational-ideology/.

7. Economist Paul Samuelson, author of the best-selling economics textbook for many decades, declared of the discipline that it was "the oldest of the arts, the newest of the sciences—indeed the queen of the social sciences." Paul Samuelson, *Economics*, 8th edition (New York: McGraw-Hill, 1970), 8. For discussion, see William A. Lovett, "Economic Analysis and Its Role in Legal Education," *Journal of Legal Education* 26, no. 4 (1974): 385–421.

8. Thomas Piketty, Emmanuel Saez, and Gabriel Zucman, "Distributional National Accounts: Methods and Estimates for the United States," *Quarterly Journal of Economics* 133, no. 2 (2018): 553–609, DOI: 10.1093/qje/qjx043, Appendix Tables II: distributional series, available at http://gabriel-zucman.en/usdina/; Sarah Flood et al., "Integrated Public Use Microdata Series, Current Population Survey: Version 6.0 [Dataset].," IPUMS-CPS (Minneapolis, MN: University of Minnesota, 2018), www.ipums.org.

9. Gene Sperling, "How to Refloat These Boats," *Washington Post*, December 18, 2005. In 2016 the average post-tax income for the top 0.1 percent of US adults was $4.7 million. Piketty, Saez, and Zucman, "Distributional National Accounts."

10. Author's correspondence.

11. Emmanuel Saez, "Equitable Growth Along Three Dimensions: Measurement, mechanisms, and policies" (Speech, Washington Center for Equitable Growth 2018 Grantee Conference, Washington, DC, September 27, 2018).

12. See Thomas Kuhn, *The Structure of Scientific Revolutions*, 4th ed. (Chicago: University of Chicago Press, 2012).

13. Joseph E. Stiglitz, "Foreword," in Jonathan D. Ostry, Prakash Loungani, and Andrew G. Berg, *Confronting Inequality: How Societies Can Choose Inclusive Growth* (Columbia University Press, 2019).

Ultimately, looking across countries using econometric analysis, there aren't that many years or places, and nor is there consistent data to gauge these specific types of inequality. Researchers don't have much to go on. Still, we've learned a good deal from research that asks the overarching question of how inequality affects growth. First, while the evidence is mixed, it leans toward the conclusion that inequality is associated with less economic growth. In the 1980s and 1990s, most of the empirical research that looked across countries found that places with more inequality had lower growth. Over the late 1990s to mid-2000s, improved data and techniques led to conflicting results. Some found a negative relationship between economic growth and inequality, while others found the opposite. For a brief review of this literature, see Heather Boushey and Carter C. Price, "How Are Economic Inequality and Growth Connected? A Review of Recent Research," Washington Center for Equitable Growth, October 2014, http://equitablegrowth.ms.techprogress.org/ ?post_type=work&p=6900&preview=true.

14. Simon Johnson and James Kwak, *13 Bankers: The Wall Street Takeover and the Next Financial Meltdown* (New York: Pantheon, 2010); Raghuram Rajan, *Fault Lines: How Hidden Fractures Still Threaten the World Economy* (Princeton: Princeton University Press, 2010); Joseph Stiglitz, *The Price of Inequality* (New York: W. W. Norton, 2013).

15. Peter J. Walker, "The Challenger," *Finance & Development*, March 2016, https://www.imf.org/external/pubs/ft/fandd/2016/03/people.htm.

16. Harrison Smith, "Alan Krueger, Labor Economist Who Advised Clinton and Obama, Dies at 58," *Washington Post*, March 18, 2019, https://www.washingtonpost.com/local /obituaries/alan-krueger-labor-economist-who-advised-clinton-and-obama-dies-at-58/2019 /03/18/4d41942e-498e-11e9-93d0-64dbcf38ba41_story.html. See also David Card and Alan Krueger, *Myth and Measurement: The New Economics of the Minimum Wage* (Princeton, NJ: Princeton University Press, 1995).

17. Paul Krugman, "How Did Economists Get It So Wrong?," *New York Times*, September 2, 2009, https://www.nytimes.com/2009/09/06/magazine/06Economic-t.html.

18. Adam Smith, *The Essential Adam Smith*, ed. Robert L Heilbroner (New York: W. W. Norton, 1987), 150; See also E. P. Thompson, *The Making of the English Working Class* (London: Penguin, 1980).

19. Adam Smith, *An Inquiry into the Nature and Causes of the Wealth of Nations*, ed. Edwin Cannan (London: Methuen & Co., 1904), vol. II, p. 19.

20. Adam Smith, *The Wealth of Nations: Books I–III*, Penguin Classics (London: Penguin, 1999).

21. Smith, *The Essential Adam Smith*, 151.

22. Adam Smith, *The Theory of Moral Sentiments*, 6th ed. (London: A. Millar, 1790), 95–96; Anwar Shaikh has developed the idea of competition that is "antagonistic by nature and turbulent in operation." Anwar Shaikh, *Capitalism: Competition, Conflict, Crises* (Oxford: Oxford University Press, 2016).

23. Smith, *The Theory of Moral Sentiments*, 184–185.

24. Smith, *An Inquiry into the Nature and Causes of the Wealth of Nations*, bk. I, 18.

25. Oliver Stone, dir., *Wall Street* (Twentieth Century Fox, 1987).

26. John Clark, "Distribution as Determined by a Law of Rent," *Quarterly Journal of Economics* 5, no. 3 (1891): 289–318, 313.

27. Kenneth J. Arrow and Gerard Debreu, "Existence of an Equilibrium for a Competitive Economy," *Econometrica* 22, no. 3 (1954): 265–290, DOI: 10.2307/1907353.

28. Robert Solow, "A Contribution to the Theory of Economic Growth," *Quarterly Journal of Economics* 70, no. 1 (1956): 65–94, DOI: 10.2307/1884513; T. W. Swan, "Economic Growth and Capital Accumulation," *Economic Record* 32, no. 2 (1956): 334–361, DOI: 10.1111/j.1475-4932.1956.tb00434.x.

29. Stephanie Mudge has a nice exposition on this, calling modern-era economists "transnational, finance-oriented economists" who "speak for markets." Stephanie L. Mudge, *Leftism Reinvented: Western Parties from Socialism to Neoliberalism* (Cambridge, MA: Harvard University Press, 2018), 253–57.

30. Simon Kuznets, "Economic Growth and Income Inequality," *American Economic Review* 45, no. 1 (1955): 1–28. 26, https://www.jstor.org/stable/1811581.

31. Arthur M. Okun, *Equality and Efficiency: The Big Tradeoff* (Washington, DC: Brookings Institution Press, 1975), 1.

32. Okun, *Equality and Efficiency*, 89.

33. Thomas Piketty, *Capital in the Twenty-First Century* (Cambridge, MA: Belknap Press of Harvard University Press, 2014), vii. For their joint work, see Thomas Piketty and Emmanuel Saez, "Income Inequality in the United States, 1913–1998," *Quarterly Journal of Economics* 118, no. 1 (February 2003): 1–39.

34. In later research, Piketty and Saez gained approval from the US Treasury Department to use the microdata. For the process by which Emmanuel Saez and Raj Chetty gained access to IRS microdata, see Jeffrey Mervis, "How Two Economists Got Direct Access to IRS Tax Records," *Science*, May 22, 2014, http://www.sciencemag.org/news/2014/05/how-two -economists-got-direct-access-irs-tax-records. See also Daniel Hirschman, "Rediscovering the

1%: Economic Expertise and Inequality Knowledge," July 13, 2016, https://osf.io/228dt/ and Daniel Hirschman, "Inventing the Economy (Or, How We Learned to Stop Worrying and Love the GDP)," Dissertation, University of Michigan, 2016, https://deepblue.lib.umich.edu /bitstream/handle/2027.42/120713/dandanar_1.pdf?sequence=1&isAllowed=y.

While a census of the US population has been constitutionally required since the nation's founding, federal statisticians only began developing surveys tracking individual economic outcomes in the late 1930s. The Works Progress Administration developed a small-geography measurement of unemployment and later built a national survey called the Enumerative Check Census, administered for the first time in 1937. In 1942, this survey, along with a subsequent monthly Sample Survey of Unemployment, was transferred to the Census Bureau, laying the foundation for the US Current Population Survey, a nationally representative survey of households fielded monthly since 1948. In recent decades, scholars of incomes have mostly relied on surveys, such as the Current Population Survey, the Panel Study of Income Dynamics, or the decennial US Census. Surveys of the US population. "Current Population Survey: Design and Methodology," Technical Paper, US Department of Commerce, Economics and Statistics Administration; US Department of Labor, Bureau of Labor Statistics, March 2002, https://www.census.gov/prod/2002pubs /tp63rv.pdf.

35. Arthur M. Okun, *Equality and Efficiency*, 9.

36. The Conclusion to this book offers a more detailed description of the data. Piketty, Saez, and Zucman, "Distributional National Accounts: Methods and Estimates for the United States."

37. Piketty, Saez, and Zucman, "Distributional National Accounts: Methods and Estimates for the United States"; Kayla R. Fontenote, Jessica L. Semega, and Melissa A. Kollar, "Income and Poverty in the United States: 2017," US Census Bureau, September 2018, https://www.census.gov/content/dam/Census/library/publications/2018/demo /p60-263.pdf.

38. There are vast literatures on these issues. For a sampling, see Paul Krugman, "For Richer," *New York Times*, October 20, 2002, http://www.nytimes.com/2002/10/20 /magazine/for-richer.html?pagewanted=all&src=pm; David H. Autor, David Dorn, and Gordon H. Hanson, "Untangling Trade and Technology: Evidence from Local Labor Markets," Working Paper, March 2013, http://economics.mit.edu/files/8763; Sherwin Rosen, "The Economics of Superstars," *American Economic Review* 71, no. 5 (1981): 845–858.

39. Note that Saez and Zucman begin with the tax return data on incomes to compute their estimates of wealth, so the fact that the trends are similar may be because the underlying data source is the same. The assumptions of their method, of course, would adjust for this in theory, but in practice, it may be that it would be hard for this not to be the case. Emmanuel Saez and Gabriel Zucman, "Wealth Inequality in the United States since 1913: Evidence from Capitalized Income Tax Data," *Quarterly Journal of Economics* 131, no. 2 (May 2016): 519–578, DOI: 10.1093/qje/qjw004.

40. Gabriel Zucman, "How Corporations and the Wealthy Avoid Taxes (and How to Stop Them)," *New York Times*, November 10, 2017, https://www.nytimes.com/interactive /2017/11/10/opinion/gabriel-zucman-paradise-papers-tax-evasion.html. Of course, we gain data on wealth once it is turned into income that is subject to taxation. When stock holdings are sold, for example, this turns some of that wealth into capital gains, which are a taxable stream of income.

41. Lena Edlund and Wojciech Kopczuk, "Women, Wealth, and Mobility," Working Paper, National Bureau of Economic Research, June 2007, http://www.nber.org/papers /w13162.pdf; William Darity, William Darity Jr., Darrick Hamilton, Mark Paul, Alan Aja, Anne Price, Antonio Moore, and Caterina Chiopris, "What We Get Wrong About Closing

The Racial Wealth Gap," Samuel DuBois Cook Center on Social Equity, April 2018, http://socialequity.duke.edu/sites/socialequity.duke.edu/files/site-images/FINAL%20 COMPLETE%20REPORT_.pdf; Melany De La Cruz-Viesca, Zhenxiang Chen, Paul M. Ong, Darrick Hamilton, and William A. Darity Jr., "The Color of Wealth in Los Angeles," Federal Reserve Bank of San Francisco, 2016, https://www.frbsf.org/community -development/files/color-of-wealth-in-los-angeles.pdf; Tatjana Meschede, Darrick Hamilton, Ana Patricia Muñoz, Regine Jackson, and William Darity Jr., "Inequality in the 'Cradle of Liberty': Race/Ethnicity and Wealth in Greater Boston," *Race and Social Problems* 8, no. 1 (March 2016): 18–28, DOI: 10.1007/s12552-016-9166-9.

42. Raj Chetty, David Grusky, Maximilian Hell, Nathaniel Hendren, Robert Manduca, and Jimmy Narang, "The Fading American Dream: Trends in Absolute Income Mobility since 1940," *Science* 356, no. 6336 (April 28, 2017): 398–406, DOI: 10.1126/science. aal4617.

43. Raj Chetty, "Raj Chetty on 'The Lost Einsteins,'" January 11, 2018, https://www .brookings.edu/events/raj-chetty-on-the-lost-einsteins/.

44. Chetty and his coauthors show this using a thought experiment, comparing what the outcomes would have been if those born in the 1980s had lived through the same higher growth experienced by those born in the 1940s or, alternatively, the 1980 cohort had experienced the more equal distribution of income experienced by the 1940 cohort. In the first "higher growth" scenario, the share of children in the 1980 cohort earning more than their parents rises from 50 percent to 62 percent. In the second "more broadly shared growth" scenario, the share rises by more, to 80 percent. Raj Chetty et al., "The Fading American Dream."

45. Piketty has trenchant criticism for economists who only consider engineering problems without looking at how the system functions in the real world: "Economists are all too often preoccupied with petty mathematical problems of interest only to themselves. This obsession with mathematics is an easy way of acquiring the appearance of scientificity without having to answer the far more complex questions posed by the world we live in." Thomas Piketty, *Capital in the Twenty-First Century*, 32.

46. Heather Boushey, "A (Longer) Interview with Robert M. Solow," Washington Center for Equitable Growth, 2013, quote at 25:17, http://equitablegrowth.org/work/a-longer -interview-with-robert-m-solow.

47. Thomas Kuhn, *The Structure of Scientific Revolutions*, Preface. Hackling points out that British linguist Margaret Masterman identified "twenty-one distinct ways in which Kuhn used the word paradigm."

48. Claire Cain Miller, "Evidence That Robots Are Winning the Race for American Jobs," *New York Times*, December 22, 2017, https://www.nytimes.com/2017/03/28/upshot /evidence-that-robots-are-winning-the-race-for-american-jobs.html; Alex Williams, "Will Robots Take Our Children's Jobs?," *New York Times*, January 20, 2018, https://www .nytimes.com/2017/12/11/style/robots-jobs-children.html; Author's calculation based on US Bureau of Labor Statistics, "All Employees: Manufacturing," FRED, Federal Reserve Bank of St. Louis, May 4, 2018, https://fred.stlouisfed.org/series/MANEMP; US Bureau of Labor Statistics, "All Employees: Total Nonfarm Payrolls," FRED, Federal Reserve Bank of St. Louis, March 9, 2018, https://fred.stlouisfed.org/series/PAYEM; Andrew Hogan and Brian Roberts, "Occupational Employment Projections to 2024," US Bureau of Labor Statistics, December 2015, https://www.bls.gov/opub/mlr/2015/article/occupational -employment-projections-to-2024.htm; McKinsey & Company, "The Economic Impact of the Achievement Gap in America's Schools," 2009; *Wall Street Journal*, "Food-Delivery Robots Rolling in DC," video posted March 9, 2017, viewable at https://www.youtube.com /watch?reload=9&v=Rvlgmu7RVDU; Bureau of Labor Statistics, "Fastest Growing Occupa- tions: Occupational Outlook Handbook," https://www.bls.gov/ooh/fastest-growing.htm.

49. "Forbes 400," *Forbes*, https://www.forbes.com/forbes-400/list/.

50. Joseph Fishkin and William Forbath argue that the United States has a long history of using government—and the US Constitution—to thwart concentrated economic power and oligarchy and we will need to revive this kind of thinking. Joseph Fishkin and William Forbath, "Wealth, Commonwealth, and the Constitution of Opportunity," in *Wealth*, ed. Jack Knight and Melissa Schwartzberg, 45–124 (New York: NYU Press, 2017).

## I. How Inequality Obstructs

1. Heather Boushey, "In Conversation: Raj Chetty," June 8, 2018, https://equitablegrowth.org/in-conversation-with-raj-chetty/.

## 1. Learning and Human Capital

1. Amanda Holpuch, "Kansas School Funding Cuts Mean Summer Comes Uncomfortably Early," *Guardian*, May 5, 2015; Dayna Miller, "School Funding Is Key to the Future of Kansas," *Wichita Eagle*, December 29, 2017, http://www.kansas.com/opinion/opn-columns-blogs/article192028729.html.

This led the Kansas Supreme Court to rule the cuts to education funding unconstitutional. Hunter Woodall and Katy Bergen, "Kansas Supreme Court Rules New School Finance Formula Is Unconstitutional," *Kansas City Star*, October 2, 2017, http://www.kansascity.com/news/politics-government/article176606731.html.

2. Jeffrey Parks and Anurag Mantha, "Lead Testing Results for Water Sampled by Residents," Flint Water Study Updates, September 2015, http://flintwaterstudy.org/information-for-flint-residents/results-for-citizen-testing-for-lead-300-kits/; "Flint Water Crisis Fast Facts," *CNN*, April 8, 2018, https://www.cnn.com/2016/03/04/us/flint-water-crisis-fast-facts/index.html; "Disaster Day by Day: A Detailed Flint Crisis Timeline," *Bridge Magazine* (Michigan), February 4, 2016, http://www.bridgemi.com/truth-squad-companion/disaster-day-day-detailed-flint-crisis-timeline.

3. On the effects of lead, see "Lead Poisoning and Health," WHO Fact Sheets, World Health Organization, August 23, 2018, http://www.who.int/mediacentre/factsheets/fs379/en/; "Lead: Sources of Led, Water," Centers for Disease Control and Prevention, February 18, 2016, https://www.cdc.gov/nceh/lead/tips/water.htm.

4. On the situation in Michigan, see Louis Jacobson, "Who's to Blame for the Flint Water Crisis?," *PolitiFact*, February 15, 2016, http://www.politifact.com/truth-o-meter/article/2016/feb/15/whos-blame-flint-water-crisis/; Jonathan Oosting, "Fact Check: Did Michigan Gov. Rick Snyder Cut $1 Billion from Education or Add $660 per Student?," MLive.com, February 5, 2014, http://www.mlive.com/politics/index.ssf/2014/02/fact_check_did_michigan_gov_ri.html.

5. "Top 10% Authors (Last 10 Years Publications), as of January 2019," IDEAS bibliographic data base, Research Papers in Economics (RePEc), November 2018, https://ideas.repec.org/top/top.person.all10.html; Committee on the Status of Women in the Economics Profession, "Janet M. Currie Recipient of the 2015 Carolyn Shaw Bell Award," Press Release, American Economic Association, November 2015, https://www.aeaweb.org/content/file?id=471.

6. Jacob Mincer, *Schooling, Experience, and Earnings,* Human Behavior and Social Institutions Series, 2, National Bureau of Economic Research, 1974, https://www.nber.org/books/minc74-1; Thomas Lemieux, "The 'Mincer Equation' Thirty Years after Schooling,

Experience, and Earnings," in *Jacob Mincer A Pioneer of Modern Labor Economics, Economics,* ed. Shoshana Grossbard, 127–145 (Boston: Springer, 2006).

7. Janet Currie and Rosemary Hyson, "Is the Impact of Health Shocks Cushioned by Socioeconomic Status? The Case of Low Birthweight," *American Economic Review* 89, no. 2 (May 1999): 245–250, DOI: 10.1257/aer.89.2.245.

8. Claudia Goldin and Lawrence Katz, *The Race between Education and Technology* (Cambridge, MA: Belknap Press of Harvard University Press, 2010); J. Bradford DeLong, Claudia Goldin, and Lawrence Katz, "Sustaining US Economic Growth," in *Agenda for the Nation,* ed. Henry J. Aaron, James M. Lindsay, and Pietro S. Nivola (Washington, DC: Brookings Institution, 2003).

9. Douglas Almond and Janet Currie, "Human Capital Development before Age Five," in *Handbook of Labor Economics,* vol. 4, part B, eds. Orley Ashenfelter and David Card, 1315–1486 (Amsterdam: North Holland, 2011).

10. On the credibility revolution, see Joshua D. Angrist and Jörn-Steffen Pischke, "The Credibility Revolution in Empirical Economics: How Better Research Design Is Taking the Con Out of Econometrics," *Journal of Economic Perspectives* 24, no. 2 (2010): 3–30, DOI: 10.1257/jep.24.2.3.

11. Janet Currie and Duncan Thomas, "Early Test Scores, Socioeconomic Status and Future Outcomes," NBER Working Paper no. 6943, National Bureau of Economic Research, Cambridge, MA, February 1999, http://www.nber.org/papers/w6943.pdf.

12. Furthermore, at age forty, males who attended preschool reported less drug use than those who did not. Lawrence J. Schweinhart, Jeanne Montie, Zongping Xiang, W. Steven Barnett, Clive R. Belfield, and Milagros Nores, "The High/Scope Perry Preschool Study through Age 40: Summary, Conclusions, and Frequently Asked Questions" http://nieer.org /wp-content/uploads/2014/09/specialsummary_rev2011_02_2.pdf.

13. Since the experimental early-childhood research studies of the 1960s and 1970s, measures have been put in places to better protect human subjects participating in biomedical and behavioral research studies. See World Medical Association, "World Medical Association Declaration of Helsinki: Ethical Principles for Medical Research Involving Human Subjects," Helsinki, Finland, June 1964, https://www.wma.net/policies -post/wma-declaration-of-helsinki-ethical-principles-for-medical-research-involving-human -subjects/. "The Belmont Report," The National Commission for the Protection of Human Subjects, Department of Health, Education, and Welfare, April 18, 1979, https://www.hhs .gov/ohrp/regulations-and-policy/belmont-report/index.html.

14. James Heckman, Rodrigo Pinto, and Peter Savelyev, "Understanding the Mechanisms through which an Influential Early Childhood Program Boosted Adult Outcomes," *American Economic Review* 103, no. 6 (2013): 2052–2086, DOI: 10.1257/aer.103.6.2052; Eliana Garces, Duncan Thomas, and Janet Currie, "Longer-Term Effects of Head Start," *American Economic Review* 92, no. 4 (2002): 999–1012, DOI: 10.1257 /00028280260344560.

15. William T. Gormley, Deborah Phillips, and Sara Anderson, "The Effects of Tulsa's Pre-K Program on Middle School Student Performance," *Journal of Policy Analysis and Management* 37, no. 1 (2017): 63–87, DOI: 10.1002/pam.22023.

16. "Non-cognitive attributes are those academically and occupationally relevant skills and traits that are not specifically intellectual or analytical in nature. They include a range of personality and motivational habits and attitudes that facilitate functioning well in school. Non-cognitive traits, skills, and characteristics include perseverance, motivation, self-control, and other aspects of conscientiousness." Jeffrey A. Rosen, Elizabeth J. Glennie, Ben W. Dalton, Jean M. Lennon, and Robert N. Bozick, *Noncognitive Skills in the Classroom: New Perspectives on Educational Research* (Research Triangle Park, NC: RTI

Press, 2010), 1. James Heckman, "Policies to Foster Human Capital," NBER Working Paper No. 7288, National Bureau of Economic Research, Cambridge, MA, August 1999, https://www.nber.org/papers/w7288; James Heckman, "Schools, Skills, and Synapses," *Economic Inquiry* 46, no. 3 (2008): 289–324, 297, DOI: 10.1111/j.1465-7295 .2008.00163.x. See also Paul Tough, *How Children Succeed: Grit, Curiosity, and the Hidden Power of Character* (Boston: Houghton Mifflin Harcourt, 2012); Nick Tasler, "The Marshmallow Myth," *Psychology Today*, March 9, 2017, https://www.psychologytoday .com/blog/strategic-thinking/201703/the-marshmallow-myth; James Heckman and Tim Kautz, "Fostering and Measuring Skills: Interventions That Improve Character and Cognition," NBER Working Paper No. 19656, National Bureau of Economic Research, Cambridge MA, November 2013, http://www.nber.org/papers/w19656.

17. Heather Boushey, "In Conversation: Janet Currie," March 15, 2018, https:// equitablegrowth.org/in-conversation-with-janet-currie/. See also Lex Borghans, Angela Lee Duckworth, James J. Heckman, and Bas ter. Weel, "The Economics of Psychology of Personality Traits," *Journal of Human Resources* 43, no. 4 (2008): 972–1059.

18. Boushey, "In Conversation: Janet Currie."

19. Douglas Almond and Janet Currie, "Killing Me Softly: The Fetal Origins Hypothesis," *Journal of Economic Perspectives* 25, no. 3 (September 2011): 153–72, DOI: 10.1257/ jep.25.3.153.

20. Sandra E. Black, Paul J. Devereux, and Kjell G. Salvanes, "From the Cradle to the Labor Market? The Effect of Birth Weight on Adult Outcomes," *Quarterly Journal of Economics* 122, no. 1 (2007): 409–439, DOI: 10.1162/qjec.122.1.409; Douglas Almond, Janet Currie, and Valentina Duque, "Childhood Circumstances and Adult Outcomes: Act II," Journal of Economic Literature 56, no. 4 (December 2018): 1360, DOI: 10.1257/ jel.20171164.

21. Boushey, "In Conversation: Janet Currie."

22. "OECD Family Database," Organisation for Economic Co-operation and Development, Social Policy Division—Directorate of Employer, Labour and Social Affairs, accessed June 29, 2018, http://www.oecd.org/els/family/database.htm; Bridget Ansel and Matt Markezich, "Falling behind the Rest of the World: Childcare in the United States," Washington Center for Equitable Growth, January 25, 2017, http://equitablegrowth.org /equitablog/falling-behind-the-rest-of-the-world-childcare-in-the-united-states/.

23. Kerris Cooper and Kitty Stewart, "Does Money Affect Children's Outcomes? A Systematic Review" Report, Joseph Rowntree Foundation, York, UK, October 2013, 5, https://www.jrf.org.uk/sites/default/files/jrf/migrated/files/money-children-outcomes-full.pdf.

24. Greg J. Duncan, Pamela A. Morris, and Chris Rodrigues, "Does Money Really Matter? Estimating Impacts of Family Income on Young Children's Achievement with Data from Random-Assignment Experiments," *Developmental Psychology* 47, no. 5 (2011): 1263, DOI: 10.1037/a0023875.

25. Gordon B. Dahl and Lance Lochner, "The Impact of Family Income on Child Achievement: Evidence from the Earned Income Tax Credit," *American Economic Review* 102, no. 5 (2012): 1927–1956, DOI: 10.1257/aer.102.5.1927; Kevin Milligan and Mark Stabile, "Do Child Tax Benefits Affect the Well-Being of Children? Evidence from Canadian Child Benefit Expansions," *American Economic Journal: Economic Policy* 3, no. 3 (2011): 175–205, DOI: 10.1257/pol.3.3.175.

26. Heather Boushey, "In Conversation: Hilary Hoynes," March 8, 2018, https:// equitablegrowth.org/in-conversation-with-hilary-hoynes/; Hilary Hoynes and Diane Whitmore Schanzenbach, "Safety Net Investments in Children," Conference Paper, Brookings Papers on Economic Activity, Brookings Institution, March 8, 2018, https://www .brookings.edu/wp-content/uploads/2018/03/2_hoynesschanz1.pdf.

Janet Currie and Maya Rossin-Slater document the variety of programs for young childhood that have been shown to have long-term effects. They reviewed all the evidence available (as of 2015–2016) and found that some of the most effective are the Special Supplemental Nutrition Program for Women, Infants, and Children, which provides food to nursing mothers and their children; the Comprehensive Child Development Program, a program piloted in 1989 and 1990 in which nurses do make home visits to new mothers; and high-quality, center-based, early-childhood care and education. They do not find strong evidence that prenatal care or family leave have as much effect, although this evidence is less conclusive. Janet Currie and Maya Rossin-Slater, "Early-Life Origins of Life-Cycle Well-Being: Research and Policy Implications," *Journal of Policy Analysis and Management* 34, no. 1 (2015): 208–242, DOI: 10.1002/pam.21805.

27. In 2008, the Food Stamp program was renamed the Supplemental Nutrition Assistance Program. The authors used the Panel Study of Income Dynamics to assemble data linking family background and county of residence in early childhood to adult health and economic outcomes. The Food Stamp program was rolled out nationwide over fourteen years starting in 1961, which meant they could look at otherwise similar children—or siblings—across places as the roll out progressed. Hilary Hoynes, Diane Whitmore Schanzenbach, and Douglas Almond, "Long-Run Impacts of Childhood Access to the Safety Net," *American Economic Review* 106, no. 4 (2016): 903–934, 920, DOI: 10.1257/ aer.20130375.

28. Daniela Del Boca, Christopher Flinn, and Matthew Wiswall, "Household Choices and Child Development," *Review of Economic Studies* 81, no. 1 (2014): 137–185, DOI: 10.1093/restud/rdt026; Lawrence M. Berger, Christina Paxson, and Jane Waldfogel, "Income and Child Development," *Children and Youth Services Review* 31, no. 9 (2009): 978–989, DOI: 10.1016/j.childyouth.2009.04.013.

29. Ariel Kalil, Kathleen M. Ziol-Guest, Rebecca M. Ryan, and Anna J. Markowitz, "Changes in Income-Based Gaps in Parent Activities with Young Children from 1988 to 2012," *AERA Open* 2, no. 3 (2016): 1–17, DOI: 10.1177/2332858416653732; Garey Ramey and Valerie Ramey, "The Rug Rat Race," *Brookings Papers on Economic Activity* 41, no. 1 (2011): 121–199.

30. Heather Boushey, *Finding Time: The Economics of Work-Life Conflict* (Cambridge, MA: Harvard University Press, 2016).

31. Tricia K. Neppl, Jennifer M. Senia, and M. Brent Donnellan, "Effects of Economic Hardship: Testing the Family Stress Model over Time.," *Journal of Family Psychology* 30, no. 1 (2016): 12–21, DOI: 10.1037/fam0000168Ann Huff Stevens and Jessamyn Schaller, "Short-Run Effects of Parental Job Loss on Children's Academic Achievement," *Economics of Education Review* 30, no. 2 (2011): 289–299; Rucker C. Johnson, Ariel Kalil, and Rachel E. Dunifon, "Employment Patterns of Less-Skilled Workers: Links to Children's Behavior and Academic Progress," *Demography* 49, no. 2 (2012): 747–772, DOI: 10.1007/ s13524-011-0086-4.

32. Janet Currie and Erdal Tekin, "Is There a Link between Foreclosure and Health?," *American Economic Journal: Economic Policy* 7, no. 1 (2015): 63–94, DOI: 10.1257/ pol.20120325.

33. Raj Chetty, Nathaniel Hendren, Patrick Kline, and Emmanuel Saez, "Where Is the Land of Opportunity? The Geography of Intergenerational Mobility in the United States," *Quarterly Journal of Economics* 129, no. 4 (2014): 1553–1623, DOI: 10.1093/qje/qju022; Raj Chetty and Nathaniel Hendren, "The Impacts of Neighborhoods on Intergenerational Mobility II: County-Level Estimates," *Quarterly Journal of Economics* 133, no. 3 (2018): 1163–1228, DOI: 10.1093/qje/qjy006.

34. Boushey, "In Conversation: Janet Currie."

35. Janet Currie and Hannes Schwandt, "The 9/11 Dust Cloud and Pregnancy Out-comes: A Reconsideration," *Journal of Human Resources* 51, no. 4 (2016): 805–831, DOI: 10.3368/jhr.51.4.0714-6533R. See also: Austin Frakt, "How Pollution Can Hurt the Health of the Economy," *New York Times*, November 30, 2018.

36. Janet Currie, "Inequality at Birth: Some Causes and Consequences," *American Economic Review* 101, no. 3 (2011): 1–22, 17, DOI: 10.1257/aer.101.3.1.

37. Claudia Goldin, "America's Graduation from High School: The Evolution and Spread of Secondary Schooling in the Twentieth Century," *Journal of Economic History* 58, no. 2 (1998): 345–374, 347, DOI: 10.1017/S0022050700020544.

38. Jan Luiten van Sanden et al., eds., "How Was Life? Global Well-Being since 1820," Organisation for Economic Co-operation and Development, October 2, 2014, http://www.oecd.org/statistics/how-was-life-9789264214262-en.htm.; George P. Shultz and Eric A. Hanushek, "Education Is the Key to a Healthy Economy," *Wall Street Journal*, April 30, 2012. See also Eric A. Hanushek, Guido Schwerdt, Simon Wiederhold, and Ludger Woessmann, "Returns to Skills around the World: Evidence from PIAAC," *European Economic Review* 73 (2015): 103–130, DOI: 10.1016/j.euroecorev.2014.10.006; Flavio Cunha, James J. Heckman, Lance Lochner, and Dimitriy V. Masterov, "Interpreting the Evidence on Life Cycle Skill Formation," in *Handbook of the Economics of Education*, ed. Eric A. Hanushek and Finis Welch, 697–812 (Amsterdam: Elsevier, 2006).

39. "Public Education Finances: 2015," US Census Bureau, June 2017, https://www.census.gov/library/publications/2017/econ/g15-aspef.html.

40. Heather Boushey, "In Conversation: Diane Whitmore Schanzenbach," March 8, 2018, https://equitablegrowth.org/in-conversation-with-diane-whitmore-schanzenbach/; Julien Lafortune, Jesse Rothstein, and Diane Whitmore Schanzenbach, "School Finance Reform and the Distribution of Student Achievement," Washington Center for Equitable Growth, March 2016, http://cdn.equitablegrowth.org/wp-content/uploads/2016/02/29154351/School-finance-reform.pdf.

41. C. Kirabo Jackson, Rucker C. Johnson, and Claudia Persico, "The Effects of School Spending on Educational and Economic Outcomes: Evidence from School Finance Reforms," *Quarterly Journal of Economics* 131, no. 1 (2016): 157–218, DOI: 10.1093/qje/qjv036.

42. Some top-tier colleges enroll a sizable number of low-income students; at UCLA, Emory University, and Barnard College, at least 15 percent of the student bodies grew up in families from the bottom 40 percent. Even so, state universities tend to do better at delivering economic mobility. California State University, Los Angeles, the State University of New York at Stony Brook, the City University of New York, and the University of Texas at El Paso are all among those who move the most students into a higher income after graduation. Raj Chetty, John N. Friedman, Emmanuel Saez, Nicholas Turner, and Danny Yagan, "Mobility Report Cards: The Role of Colleges in Intergenerational Mobility," NBER Working Paper No. 23618, National Bureau of Economic Research, Cambridge, MA, July 2017, https://www.nber.org/papers/w23618; Gregor Aisch, "Some Colleges Have More Students from the Top 1 Percent Than the Bottom 60. Find Yours," *New York Times*, January 18, 2017.

43. Caroline Hoxby and Christopher Avery, "The Missing 'One-Offs': The Hidden Supply of High-Achieving, Low-Income Students," Discussion Paper, Brookings Papers on Economic Activity, Brookings Institution, 2013, https://www.brookings.edu/wp-content/uploads/2016/07/2013a_hoxby.pdf.; Susan Dynarski, C. J. Libassi, Katherine Michelmore, and Stephanie Owen, "Closing the Gap: The Effect of a Targeted, Tuition-Free Promise on College Choices of High-Achieving, Low-Income Students," NBER Working Paper No 25349, National Bureau of Economic Research, Cambridge, MA, December 2018, https://www.nber.org/papers/w25349.

44. Martha J. Bailey and Susan M. Dynarski, "Gains and Gaps: Changing Inequality in US College Entry and Completion," NBER Working Paper No. 17633, National Bureau of Economic Research, Cambridge, MA, December 2011, https://www.nber.org/papers/w17633.

45. Robert Kelchen, "How Much Do For-Profit Colleges Rely on Federal Funds?" Brookings Institution, January 11, 2017, https://www.brookings.edu/blog/brown-center -chalkboard/2017/01/11/how-much-do-for-profit-colleges-rely-on-federal-funds/; Tressie McMillan Cottom, *Lower Ed: The Troubling Rise of For-Profit Colleges in the New Economy* (New York: New Press, 2017); Terry Gross, "How For-Profit Colleges Sell 'Risky Education' to the Most Vulnerable," *Fresh Air*, March 27, 2017, https://www.npr.org/2017 /03/27/521371034/how-for-profit-colleges-sell-risky-education-to-the-most-vulnerable; David J. Deming, Claudia Goldin, and Lawrence F. Katz, "The For-Profit Postsecondary School Sector: Nimble Critters or Agile Predators?," *Journal of Economic Perspectives* 26, no. 1 (2012): 139–164, 158–159, DOI: 10.1257/jep.26.1.139.

46. Jesse Rothstein, "Equal Access to a Good Education Is Not Just about Sound School Budgets," Washington Center for Equitable Growth, April 23, 2018, https://equitablegrowth .org/equal-access-good-education-not-just-sound-school-budgets/.

47. Ben Bernanke, "Challenges for State and Local Governments," speech at the Annual Awards Dinner of the Citizens Budget Commission, New York, March 2, 2011, https://www .federalreserve.gov/newsevents/speech/bernanke20110302a.htm; Katharine B. Stevens, "Workforce of Today, Workforce of Tomorrow: The Business Case for High-Quality Childcare," US Chamber of Commerce, June 2017, https://www.uschamberfoundation.org /sites/default/files/Workforce%20of%20Today%20Workforce%20of%20Tomorrow%20 Report_0.pdf.

48. Boushey, "In Conversation: Janet Currie."

49. Rasheed Malik, "The Effects of Universal Preschool in Washington, DC," Center for American Progress, September 26, 2018, https://www.americanprogress.org/issues/early -childhood/reports/2018/09/26/458208/effects-universal-preschool-washington-d-c/.

50. Janet Currie, "Early Childhood Education Programs," *Journal of Economic Perspectives* 15, no. 2 (2001): 213–238, DOI: 10.1257/jep.15.2.213; Mariana Zerpa finds that children in states with early childhood education programs are 30 percent less likely to repeat a grade between ages six and eight—and that this effect lasts at least until age twelve. Pre-kindergarten programs also substantially reduce the probability of developmental and behavioral problems for children between ages four and eight, with approximately 60 percent of the effect sustained through age twelve. Mariana Zerpa, "Short and Medium Run Impacts of Preschool Education: Evidence from State Pre-k Programs," Washington Center for Equitable Growth, December 4, 2018, https://equitablegrowth.org/working -papers/short-and-medium-run-impacts-of-preschool-education-evidence-from-state-pre-k -programs/; Robert Lynch and Kavya Vaghul, "The Benefits and Costs of Investing in Early Childhood Education," Washington Center for Equitable Growth, December 2012, http://equitablegrowth.org/report/the-benefits-and-costs-of-investing-in-early-childhood -education/.

51. Claire Zillman, "Child Care Is Unaffordable in Every US State Except This One," *Fortune*, December 9, 2016, http://fortune.com/2016/12/09/child-care-cost-us/; Elise Gould, Lea J.E. Austin, and Marcy Whitebook, "What Does Good Child Care Reform Look Like?" Economic Policy Institute, March 29, 2017, https://www.epi.org/publication/what-does -good-child-care-reform-look-like/; Simon Workman, Katie Hamm, Rasheed Malik, and Cristina Novoa, "Top 10 Early Childhood Ideas for States in 2018," Center for American Progress, Washington, DC, March 14, 2018, https://www.americanprogress.org/issues/early -childhood/reports/2018/03/14/447867/top-10-early-childhood-ideas-states-2018/.

52. Heather Boushey and Bridget Ansel, "Modernizing US Paid Family Leave for 21st Century Families," Washington Center for Equitable Growth, June 18, 2018, https://

equitablegrowth.org/modernizing-u-s-paid-family-leave-labor-standards-for-21st-century
-families/; Heather Boushey and Elisabeth Jacobs, "Paid Family Leave: Looking to the
States," AEIdeas (blog), American Enterprise Institute, March 20, 2017, https://www.aei.org
/publication/paid-family-leave-looking-to-the-states/; Carrie Gleason, quoted in Heather
Boushey and Bridget Ansel, "Working by the Hour: The Economic Consequences of
Unpredictable Scheduling Practices," Washington Center for Equitable Growth, September 6, 2016, 16, http://equitablegrowth.org/research-analysis/working-by-the-hour-the
-economic-consequences-of-unpredictable-scheduling-practices/.

53. Lafortune, Rothstein, and Schanzenbach, "School Finance Reform."

54. Robert G. Lynch, "The Economic and Fiscal Consequences of Improving US
Educational Outcomes," Washington Center for Equitable Growth, January 2015, http://
equitablegrowth.org/wp-content/uploads/2015/02/10153405/0115-ach-gap-report.pdf.

55. Gary Becker, "Human Capital," in *The Concise Encyclopedia of Economics,* Library
of Economics and Liberty, 2008, 11–12, http://www.econlib.org/library/Enc/HumanCapital
.html.

## 2. Skills, Talent, and Innovation

1. Jodi Kantor and Megan Twohey, "Harvey Weinstein Paid Off Sexual Harassment
Accusers for Decades," *New York Times,* October 5, 2017; Sandra Gonzalez, "Ashley Judd
Suit Claims Harvey Weinstein 'Torpedoed' Career," *CNN,* May 1, 2018, https://www.cnn
.com/2018/04/30/entertainment/ashley-judd-harvey-weinstein-suit/index.html and Molly
Redden, "Peter Jackson: I Blacklisted Ashley Judd and Mira Sorvino under Pressure from
Weinstein," *Guardian,* December 16, 2017. Many others claim that rebuffing Weinstein's
sexual advances negatively affected their careers. See, for example: Mary Louise Kelly,
"Arquette: After Rejecting Weinstein, 'I Had a Completely Different Career,'" *All Things
Considered,* NPR, May 31, 2018, https://www.npr.org/2018/05/31/615911004/arquette
-after-rejecting-weinstein-i-had-a-completely-different-career.

2. Nellie Andreeva, "Seth MacFarlane Opens Up about His 2013 Harvey Weinstein
Oscars Joke, Condemns 'Abhorrent' Abuse of Power," *Deadline* (blog), October 11, 2017,
http://deadline.com/2017/10/seth-macfarlane-harvey-weinstein-oscar-joke-explained
-1202186425/.

3. Kenneth Arrow, "Some Mathematical Models of Race in the Labor Market," in *Racial
Discrimination in Economic Life,* ed. A. H. Pascal (Lexington, MA: Lexington Books,
1972); Warren Buffett, "Warren Buffett at Fortune's Most Powerful Women Summit,"
*Fortune,* October 4, 2011, http://fortune.com/2011/10/04/warren-buffett-at-fortunes-most
-powerful-women-summit/.

4. See: Chang-Tai Hsieh, Erik Hurst, Charles I. Jones, and Peter J. Klenow, "The
Allocation of Talent and US Economic Growth," unpublished manuscript, March 20, 2019,
http://klenow.com/HHJK.pdf; Janet Yellen, "So We All Can Succeed: 125 Years of Women's
Participation in the Economy," 125 Years of Women at Brown Conference, Brown
University, Providence, RI, May 5, 2017, https://www.federalreserve.gov/newsevents/speech
/yellen20170505a.htm.

The International Monetary Fund recently demonstrated that economies that do more
to include women experience stronger growth, and estimated that the United States could
boost gross domestic product by 5 percent if women's employment were as high as men's.
Katrin Elborgh-Woytek, Monique Newiak, Kalpana Kochhar, Stefania Fabrizio, Kangni
Kpodar, Philippe Wingender, Benedict Clements, and Gerd Schwartz, "Women, Work, and
the Economy: Macroeconomic Gains From Gender Equity," International Monetary Fund,
September 2013, http://www.imf.org/external/pubs/ft/sdn/2013/sdn1310.pdf.

5. Raj Chetty, interview by Heather Boushey, October 13, 2014. Notes available upon request.

6. Alexander M. Bell, Raj Chetty, Xavier Jaravel, Neviana Petkova, and John Van Reenen, "Who Becomes an Inventor in America? The Importance of Exposure to Innovation," NBER Working Paper No. 24062, National Bureau of Economic Research, Cambridge, MA, November 2017, rev. January 2019, 14, https://www.nber.org/papers/w24062.

7. "Report on Raj Chetty," American Economic Association Honors and Awards Committee, March 2013, https://www.aeaweb.org/about-aea/honors-awards/bates-clark/raj-chetty.

8. Bell et al., "Who Becomes an Inventor in America?"

9. Bell et al., "Who Becomes an Inventor in America?"

10. Asis Kumar Chaudhuri, "Einstein's Patents and Inventions," unpublished manuscript, September 5, 2017, Table 2, https://arxiv.org/abs/1709.00666; Bell et al., "Who Becomes an Inventor in America?," 1.

Chetty and his colleagues' finding is confirmed by other researchers. In a study of men in Finland, Philippe Aghion and his coauthors show that parental income affects an individual's probability of inventing, though to a lesser extent compared to parental education and its impact on the child's education. Nevertheless, while IQ plays a role in determining the level of education, family background and parental education matter—even in welfare states like Finland, where education is entirely free. The researchers find that highly talented individuals are disproportionately hurt by inadequate parental resources, carrying negative implications for the innovate potential of the economy. Philippe Aghion, Ufuk Akcigit, Ari Hyytinen, and Otto Toivanen, "The Social Origins of Inventors," NBER Working Paper No. 24110, National Bureau of Economic Research, Cambridge, MA, December 2017, https://www.nber.org/papers/w24110.

11. Kwame Anthony Appiah, "The Myth of Meritocracy: Who Really Gets What They Deserve?," *Guardian*, October 19, 2018. See also: Christopher Hayes, *Twilight of the Elites: America after Meritocracy* (New York: Broadway, 2012); Michael J. Sandel, *The Tyranny of Merit* (New York: Farrar, Straus and Giroux, 2020).

12. Heather Boushey, "In Conversation: Raj Chetty," June 8, 2018, https://equitable-growth.org/in-conversation-with-raj-chetty/.

13. "Raj Chetty on 'The Lost Einsteins,'" Brookings Institution, January 11, 2018, audio and transcript available at https://www.brookings.edu/events/raj-chetty-on-the-lost-einsteins/.

14. "Diana Project Overview," Diana Project, http://dianaproject.org/history/; Candida Brush, P. G. Greene, L. Balachandra, and A. Davis, "Diana Report: Women Entrepreneurs 2014: Bridging the Gender Gap in Venture Capital," Arthur M. Blank Center for Entrepreneurship, Babson College, Wellesley, MA, September 2014, 2, http://www.babson.edu/Academics/centers/blank-center/global-research/diana/Documents/diana-project-executive-summary-2014.pdf.

15. Gené Teare, "Announcing the 2017 Update to the Crunchbase Women in Venture Report," *TechCrunch*, October 4, 2017, http://social.techcrunch.com/2017/10/04/announcing-the-2017-update-to-the-crunchbase-women-in-venture-report/.

16. Valentina Zarya, "Venture Capital's Funding Gender Gap Is Actually Getting Worse," *Fortune*, March 13, 2017, http://fortune.com/2017/03/13/female-founders-venture-capital/.

17. Paul A. Gompers and Sophie Q. Wang, "And the Children Shall Lead: Gender Diversity and Performance in Venture Capital," NBER Working Paper No. 23454, National Bureau of Economic Research, Cambridge, MA, May 2017, https://www.nber.org/papers/w23454.

18. Robert W. Fairlie and Alicia M. Robb, "Disparities in Capital Access between Minority and Non-Minority Businesses: The Troubling Reality of Capital Limitations Faced by MBEs," US Department of Commerce, Minority Business Development Agency,

January 2010, https://www.mbda.gov/page/executive-summary-disparities-capital-access-between-minority-and-non-minority-businesses.

19. Alicia Robb, "Access to Capital among Young Firms, Minority-Owned Firms, Women-Owned Firms, and High-Tech Firms," Small Business Administration, April 2013, https://www.sba.gov/sites/default/files/files/rs403tot(2).pdf.

20. David S. Evans and Boyan Jovanovic, "An Estimated Model of Entrepreneurial Choice under Liquidity Constraints," *Journal of Political Economy* 97, no. 4 (1989), 808–827; Camilo Mondragón-Vélez, "The Probability of Transition to Entrepreneurship Revisited: Wealth, Education and Age," *Annals of Finance* 5, no. 3–4 (2009), 421–441, DOI: 10.1007/s10436-008-0117-3; and Kauffman Foundation, "Startup Density," May 2017, https://www.kauffman.org/kauffman-index/profile?loc=US&name=united-states&breakdowns=growth|overall,startup-activity|overall,main-street|overall#indicator-panel-se-index.

21. Lisa D. Cook and Chaleampong Kongcharoen, "The Idea Gap in Pink and Black," NBER Working Paper No. 16331, National Bureau of Economic Research, Cambridge, MA, September 2010, https://www.nber.org/papers/w16331.pdf.

22. Among inventors, 70 percent work at firms with more than one hundred employees. Bell et al., "Who Becomes an Inventor in America?," 31.

23. Malcolm Gladwell, *Blink: The Power of Thinking Without Thinking* (New York: Back Bay Books, 2007).

24. At the time of the paper's publication at the turn of the century, all five major orchestras had at least 20 percent female members; New York City's had the highest proportion at over 30 percent. Claudia Goldin and Cecilia Rouse, "Orchestrating Impartiality: The Impact of 'Blind' Auditions on Female Musicians," *American Economic Review* 90, no. 4 (2000), Fig. 1, https://pubs.aeaweb.org/doi/pdfplus/10.1257/aer.90.4.715.

25. Marianne Bertrand and Sendhil Mullainathan, "Are Emily and Greg More Employable than Lakisha and Jamal? A Field Experiment on Labor Market Discrimination," *American Economic Review* 94, no. 4, (2004): 991–1013, 992, http://www.jstor.org/stable/3592802.

26. Katie Benner, "Women in Tech Speak Frankly on Culture of Harassment," *New York Times*, June 30, 2017; Ruth Reader, "Uber Is Firing 20 People in Light of a Sexual Harassment Investigation," *Fast Company*, June 6, 2017, https://www.fastcompany.com/4040050/uber-is-firing-20-people-in-light-of-a-sexual-harassment-investigation-reports; Sheelah Kolhatkar, "The Tech Industry's Gender-Discrimination Problem," *New Yorker*, November 13, 2017.

27. Michele Madansky and Trae Vassallo, "Elephant in the Valley," January 2016, https://www.elephantinthevalley.com/.

28. Vivian Hunt, Dennis Layton, and Sara Prince, "Diversity Matters," McKinsey and Company, February 2, 2015, https://www.mckinsey.com/~/media/mckinsey/business%20functions/organization/our%20insights/why%20diversity%20matters/diversity%20matters.ashx.

29. Tyler Cowen, "My Conversation with Raj Chetty," *Marginal Revolution* (blog), May 24, 2017, https://medium.com/conversations-with-tyler/raj-chetty-tyler-cowen-inequality-mobility-american-dream-d5ea7f4742b1.

30. Raj Chetty and Nathaniel Hendren, "The Impacts of Neighborhoods on Intergenerational Mobility I: Childhood Exposure Effects," *Quarterly Journal of Economics* 133, no. 3 (2018), 1107–1162, DOI: 10.1093/qje/qjy007. On their data, see: Raj Chetty and Nathaniel Hendren, "How Do Neighborhoods Affect Economic Opportunity?," Equality of Opportunity Project, December 2017, http://www.equality-of-opportunity.org/neighborhoods/.

31. Cowen, "My Conversation with Raj Chetty."

32. Alexander M. Bell et al., "Who Becomes an Inventor in America?" See also Hans K. Hvide and Paul Oyer, "Dinner Table Human Capital and Entrepreneurship," NBER

Working Paper No. 24198, National Bureau of Economic Research, Cambridge, MA, January 2018, https://www.nber.org/papers/w24198.

33. Tatyana Avilova and Claudia Goldin, "What Can UWE Do for Economics?," *AEA Papers and Proceedings* 108 (May 2018), 186–190, DOI: 10.1257/pandp.20181103.

34. Ufuk Akcigit, John Grigsby, and Tom Nicholas, "Immigration and the Rise of American Ingenuity," *American Economic Review* 107, no. 5 (2017), 327–331, DOI: 10.1257/aer.p20171021; Ufuk Akcigit, John Grigsby, and Tom Nicholas, "The Rise of American Ingenuity: Innovation and Inventors of the Golden Age," Working Paper, Harvard Business School, June 7, 2017, https://www.hbs.edu/faculty/Pages/item.aspx?num=52130.

35. Abraham Lincoln, *Lincoln: Political Writings and Speeches*, ed. Terence Ball (Cambridge: Cambridge University Press, 2013), 238. On Lincoln's patent, see: Lily Rothman, "How Abraham Lincoln Became the Only US President to Hold a Patent," *Time*, May 20, 2016, http://time.com/4328119/abraham-lincoln-patent/.

36. John Majewski, "Not All Inequality Is the Same: Slavery versus Economic Creativity in Civil War America," Washington Center for Equitable Growth, December 10, 2015, 8, http://equitablegrowth.org/report/not-all-inequality-is-the-same/; See also: Birgit Brander Rasmussen, "'Attended with Great Inconveniences': Slave Literacy and the 1740 South Carolina Negro Act," *Publications of the Modern Language Association of America* 125, no. 1 (2010), 201–203, DOI: 10.1632/pmla.2010.125.1.201.

37. Raj Chetty, Nathaniel Hendren, Patrick Kline, and Emmanuel Saez, "Where Is the Land of Opportunity? The Geography of Intergenerational Mobility in the United States," *Quarterly Journal of Economics* 129, no. 4 (2014), 1553–1623, DOI: 10.1093/qje/qju022.

38. Alice Wu, "Gender Stereotyping in Academia: Evidence from Economics Job Market Rumors Forum," (Senior Thesis, University of California, Berkeley, August 2017), https://growthecon.com/assets/Wu_EJMR_paper.pdf.

39. American Economic Association's Committee on the Status of Women, "The 2017 Report on the Status of Women in the Economics Profession," American Economic Association, 2018, https://www.aeaweb.org/content/file?id=6388; Amanda Bayer and Cecilia Elena Rouse, "Diversity in the Economics Profession: A New Attack on an Old Problem," *Journal of Economic Perspectives* 30, no. 4 (2016), 221–242, DOI: 10.1257/jep.30.4.221. This lack of diversity is well known. Justin Wolfers wrote about Alice Wu's study in his *New York Times* column, and Olivier Blanchard, the former chief economist at the International Monetary Fund, posted to the Peterson Institute website urging the Economics Job Market Rumors (EMJR) to be "more aggressive in removing those posts 'that are too critical of someone's personal life,' or reflect 'racism, homophobia, and sexism.'" At the 2018 Allied Social Science Association meetings, several scholars presented papers examining why there are so few women in economics and what could be done about it. Anusha Chari and Paul Goldsmith-Pinkham found that the overall share of women participating in a prestigious annual economics conference hasn't improved in over fifteen years. Justin Wolfers, "Evidence of a Toxic Environment for Women in Economics," *New York Times*, August 18, 2017; Olivier Blanchard, "The Economics Job Market Rumors Site Needs to Clean Up Its Act," Peterson Institute for International Economics, Washington, DC, September 7, 2017, https://piie.com/blogs/realtime-economic-issues-watch/economics-job-market-rumors-site-needs-clean-its-act. Anusha Chari and Paul Goldsmith-Pinkham, "Gender Representation in Economics across Topics and Time: Evidence from the NBER Summer Institute," NBER Working Paper No. 23953, National Bureau of Economic Research, Cambridge, MA, October 2017, https://www.nber.org/papers/w23953.

40. Erin Hengel, "Publishing while Female: Are Women Held to Higher Standards? Evidence from Peer Review," unpublished manuscript, March 2019, http://www.erinhengel.com/research/publishing_female.pdf.

41. Heather Sarsons, "Gender Differences in Recognition for Group Work," unpublished manuscript, November 4, 2017, https://scholar.harvard.edu/files/sarsons/files/full_v6.pdf?m =1509845375.

42. Marion Fourcade, *Economists and Societies: Discipline and Profession in the United States, Britain, and France, 1890s to 1990s* (Princeton: Princeton University Press, 2010); Ann Mari May, Mary G. McGarvey, and Robert Whaples, "Are Disagreements among Male and Female Economists Marginal at Best?: A Survey of AEA Members and Their Views on Economics and Economic Policy," *Contemporary Economic Policy* 32, no. 1 (2014), 111–132, DOI: 10.1111/coep.12004; and Zubin Jelveh, Bruce Kogut, and Suresh Naidu, "Political Language in Economics," Columbia Business School Research Paper no. 14-57, October 31, 2014, DOI: 10.2139/ssrn.2535453. For a European perspective, see Ann Mari May, Mary G. McGarvey, and David Kucera, "Gender and European Economic Policy: A Survey of the Views of European Economists on Contemporary Economic Policy," *Kyklos* 71, no. 1 (2018): 162–183, DOI: 10.1111/kykl.12166.

43. Suresh Naidu, "Problems against Symptoms: Economic Democracy and Inequality," *Items* (digital forum), Social Science Research Council, September 6, 2016, http://items.ssrc .org/problems-against-symptoms-economic-democracy-and-inequality/.

44. Bell et al., "Who Becomes an Inventor in America?" This contradicts later research showing that the most successful inventors—those in the top 1 percent of all inventors— move if taxes are too high. Inventors who are employed by multinational firms "tax shop," living in locations with lower taxes. Ufuk Akcigit, Salome Baslandze, and Stefanie Stantcheva, "Taxation and the International Mobility of Inventors," *American Economic Review* 106, no. 10 (2016), 2930–2981.

45. Beronda Montgomery, "CSWEP Roundtables" January 8, 2018, https://www.aeaweb .org/about-aea/committees/cswep/programs/annual-meeting/roundtables.

46. Editeur officiel du Québec, "Pay Equity Act, Chapter E-12.001" (2016), http://www .ces.gouv.qc.ca/documents/publications/anglais.pdf; Egill Bjarnason and Christine Hauser, "Iceland Makes Companies Prove They're Not Paying Women Less," *New York Times*, January 20, 2018; Neomi Rao, memo to Victoria Lipnic, regarding "EEO-1 Form; Review and Stay," Office of Information and Regulatory Affairs, August 29, 2017, https://www .reginfo.gov/public/jsp/Utilities/Review_and_Stay_Memo_for_EEOC.pdf.

47. "Salary History Bans: A Running List of States and Localities That Have Outlawed Pay History Questions," *HR Dive*, December 19, 2018, https://www.hrdive.com/news/salary -history-ban-states-list/516662/.

48. Michael Barr, "Minority and Women Entrepreneurs: Building Capital, Networks, and Skills," Hamilton Project Discussion Paper, Brookings Institution, March 10, 2015, https://www.brookings.edu/research/minority-and-women-entrepreneurs-building-capital -networks-and-skills/; Ellen Seidman, "Capital Access Programs: CDFI Case Study on the California Capital Access Program," Urban Institute, Washington, DC, April 2018, https://www.urban.org/sites/default/files/publication/98051/capital_access_programs_cdfi _case_study_on_the_california_capital_access_programs_0.pdf.

49. Didem Tüzemen and Thealexa Becker, "Does Health-Care Reform Support Self-Employment?," Economic Review, Federal Reserve Bank of Kansas City, Third Quarter 2014, https://www.kansascityfed.org/publicat/econrev/pdf/14q3Tuzemen-Becker.pdf.

50. "Who We Are," Opportunity@Work, n.d., accessed April 4, 2018, http://www .opportunityatwork.org/about-us/.

51. Ben Casselman, "As Labor Pool Shrinks, Prison Time Is Less of a Hiring Hurdle," *New York Times*, January 13, 2018; Dean Baker and Jared Bernstein, *Getting Back to Full Employment: A Better Bargain for Working People* (Washington: Center for Economic and Policy Research, 2013).

52. Cowen, "My Conversation with Raj Chetty."

## II. How Inequality Subverts

1. Jeffrey A. Winters, *Oligarchy* (Cambridge: Cambridge University Press, 2011).

## 3. Public Spending

1. Individual income tax receipts were reduced by about $250 million in 2013, by $730 million in 2014, by $890 million in 2015, by $850 million in 2016, and by $920 million in 2017. When much of Brownback's tax cuts were reversed, individual income tax receipts increased by $1 billion from 2017 to 2018. "Kansas Tax Facts: 2018 Supplement to the Eighth Edition," Kansas Legislative Research Department, December 2018, http://www .kslegresearch.org/KLRD-web/Publications/TaxFacts/2018TaxFactsSupp.pdf. On the effects of the cuts, see Michael Leachman and Chris Mai, "Lessons for Other States from Kansas' Massive Tax Cuts," Center on Budget and Policy Priorities, Washington, DC, March 26, 2014, https://www.cbpp.org/research/lessons-for-other-states-from-kansas-massive-tax-cuts; Michael Mazerov, "Kansas Provides Compelling Evidence of Failure of 'Supply-Side' Tax Cuts," Center on Budget and Policy Priorities, January 19, 2018, https://www.cbpp.org /research/state-budget-and-tax/kansas-provides-compelling-evidence-of-failure-of-supply -side-tax-cuts; and Amanda Holpuch, "Kansas School Funding Cuts Mean Summer Comes Uncomfortably Early," *Guardian*, May 5, 2015.

2. Julie Bosman, Mitch Smith, and Monica Davey, "Brownback Tax Cuts Set Off a Revolt by Kansas Republicans," *New York Times*, June 7, 2017.

3. On the poll numbers, see Jonathan Shorman, "Poll: Majority of Kansans 'Very Dissatisfied' with Sam Brownback's Job Performance," *Topeka Capital*, February 26, 2016, http://www.cjonline.com/article/20160226/NEWS/302269683; Cameron Easley, "Most Popular Governors in America 2017," *Morning Consult* (blog), April 11, 2017, https:// morningconsult.com/governor-rankings-april-2017/.

4. Indeed, Brownback held fast to it long after most in his state saw that the theory was failing in practice. In December 2017, he told Paul Solman of *PBS NewsHour*, "Growing the economy will create jobs. And more jobs mean more Kansans working, and more Kansans working produces more revenue for the state to fund our important services that we have." "Do Tax Cuts Spur Growth? What We Can Learn from the Kansas Budget Crisis," *PBS NewsHour*, December 7, 2017, https://www.pbs.org/newshour/show/do-tax -cuts-spur-growth-what-we-can-learn-from-the-kansas-budget-crisis. On the Laffer Curve, see Binyamin Appelbaum, "This Is Not Arthur Laffer's Famous Napkin," *New York Times*, October 13, 2017; Austan Goolsbee, "Evidence on the High-Income Laffer Curve from Six Decades of Tax Reform," Brookings Papers on Economic Activity, no. 2, 1999), https://www .brookings.edu/wp-content/uploads/1999/06/1999b_bpea_goolsbee.pdf, Goolsbee pp. 1–47; commentary follows.

5. Stephen S. Lim, Rachel L Updike, Alexander S. Kaldjian, Ryan M Barber, and Krycia Cowling, "Measuring Human Capital: A Systematic Analysis of 195 Countries and Territories, 1990–2016," *Lancet* 392, no. 10154 (2018), 1217–1234, DOI: 10.1016/ S0140-6736(18)31941-X.

6. On teacher walkouts, see Cory Turner, Clare Lombardo, and Erin B. Logan, "Teacher Walkouts: A State by State Guide," *NPREd.Org* (blog), April 25, 2018, https://www.npr.org /sections/ed/2018/04/25/602859780/teacher-walkouts-a-state-by-state-guide. On paid leave, see National Partnership for Women and Families, "Voters' Views on Paid Family + Medical Leave: Findings from a National Survey," National Partnership for Women and Families, October 2018; Emily Ekins, "Poll: 74% of Americans Support Federal Paid Leave Program When Costs Not Mentioned—60% Oppose If They Got Smaller Pay Raises in the Future,"

*Cato Institute* (blog), December 11, 2018, https://www.cato.org/survey-reports/cato
-institute-2018-paid-leave-survey.

7. Matthew Yglesias, "New Poll Shows What Americans Really Think about Taxes: The Rich Should Pay More," *Vox*, April 14, 2017, https://www.vox.com/2017/4/14/15297488
/tax-poll-rich-pay-more. On the effects of inequality on political outcomes, see for example Benjamin I. Page and Martin Gilens, *Democracy in America? What Has Gone Wrong and What We Can Do About It* (Chicago: University of Chicago Press, 2017), http://www.press
.uchicago.edu/ucp/books/book/chicago/D/bo27316263.html; Larry M. Bartels, *Unequal Democracy: The Political Economy of the New Gilded Age* (New York: Russell Sage Foundation, 2008).

8. Thomas Piketty, Emmanuel Saez, and Stefanie Stantcheva, "Optimal Taxation of Top Labor Incomes: A Tale of Three Elasticities," *American Economic Journal: Economic Policy* 6, no. 1 (2014), 230–271, DOI: 10.1257/pol.6.1.230; Heather Boushey, "In Conversation: Emmanuel Saez," February 25, 2019, https://equitablegrowth.org/in-conversation-with
-emmanuel-saez/.

9. Bruce Bartlett, "House Democratic Forum on Tax Reform," testimony before the Democrats of the House Ways and Means Committee, September 27, 2017, https://www.c
-span.org/video/?434723-1/house-democrats-hold-forum-tax-reform. See also Bruce R. Bartlett, *Reaganomics: Supply Side Economics in Action* (Westport, CT: Arlington House, 1981).

10. American Economic Association, "Emmanuel Saez, Clark Medalist 2009," https://www.aeaweb.org/about-aea/honors-awards/bates-clark/emmanuel-saez. See also B. Douglas Bernheim, "Emmanuel Saez: 2009 John Bates Clark Medalist," *Journal of Economic Perspectives* 24, no. 3 (2010), 183–206, DOI: 10.1257/jep.24.3.183; Thomas Piketty and Emmanuel Saez, "Income Inequality in the United States, 1913–1998," *Quarterly Journal of Economics* 118, no. 1 (2003), 1–39. Piketty and Saez regularly update their data at https://eml.berkeley.edu/~saez/.

11. "Historical Highest Marginal Income Tax Rates," Tax Policy Center, Urban Institute and Brookings Institution, March 22, 2017, http://www.taxpolicycenter.org/statistics
/historical-highest-marginal-income-tax-rates.

12. Lawrence Kudlow, "Cut Taxes, Starve the Beast," *Wall Street Journal*, September 30, 1996; "About the Taxpayer Protection Pledge," Americans for Tax Reform, Washington, DC, n.d., accessed July 9, 2018, https://www.atr.org/about-the-pledge.

13. See, for example: Aviva Aron-Dine and Richard Kogan, "Claim That Tax Cuts 'Pay for Themselves' Is Too Good to Be True," Center on Budget and Policy Priorities, Wash-ington, DC, November 17, 2008, https://www.cbpp.org/research/claim-that-tax-cuts-pay-for
-themselves-is-too-good-to-be-true. On deficit projections, see "The Budget and Economic Outlook: 2019 to 2029," Congressional Budget Office, January 2019, https://www.cbo.gov
/publication/54918.

14. Peter Diamond and Emmanuel Saez, "The Case for a Progressive Tax: From Basic Research to Policy Recommendations," *Journal of Economic Perspectives* 25, no. 4 (2011): 165–190, 172, DOI: 10.1257/jep.25.4.165.

15. Jon Bakija, Adam Cole, and Bradley T. Heim, "Jobs and Income Growth of Top Earners and the Causes of Changing Income Inequality: Evidence from US Tax Returns Data" unpublished manuscript, April 2012, https://web.williams.edu/Economics/wp/Bakija
ColeHeimJobsIncomeGrowthTopEarners.pdf; Kevin F. Hallock, "Reciprocally Interlocking Boards of Directors and Executive Compensation," *Journal of Financial and Quantitative Analysis* 32, no. 3 (1997), 331–344, DOI: 10.2307/2331203.

16. Phil Abraham, "Out of Town," *Mad Men* (AMC, n.d.), https://www.imdb.com/title
/tt1439792/; Ginia Bellafante, "Not-So-'Mad' Ideas About Taxes," *New York Times*, March 24, 2012.

17. Boushey, "In Conversation: Emmanuel Saez."

18. Jason Matthew DeBacker, Bradley Heim, Shanthi Ramnath, and Justin M. Ross, "The Impact of State Taxes on Pass-Through Businesses: Evidence from the 2012 Kansas Income Tax Reform," *SSRN Electronic Journal*, September 2017, DOI: 10.2139/ssrn.2958353.

19. Paul Krugman, "For Richer," *New York Times*, October 20, 2002; See also David Card and John DiNardo, "Skill-Biased Technological Change and Rising Wage Inequality: Some Problems and Puzzles," *Journal of Labor Economics* 20, no. 4 (2002), 733–783.

20. This is covered in Chapter 4. See also David Weil, *The Fissured Workplace: Why Work Became So Bad for So Many and What Can Be Done to Improve It* (Cambridge, MA: Harvard University Press, 2014).

Over the late twentieth century, economists developed three productivity-focused hypotheses to explain rising income inequality: globalization, technological change, and superstars. See, for example Chinhui Juhn, Kevin M. Murphy, and Brooks Pierce, "Wage Inequality and the Rise in Returns to Skill," *Journal of Political Economy* 101, no. 3 (1993), 410–442; Sherwin Rosen, "The Economics of Superstars," *American Economic Review* 71, no. 5 (1981), 845–858.

Another issue is that, at that time, the available data was from surveys that didn't capture income in the top 1 percent or higher very well. In no small part because of the evidence available, analysis focused instead on the growing gap between college-educated workers and others.

21. Piketty, Saez, and Stantcheva, "Optimal Taxation of Top Labor Incomes."

22. Claudia Goldin, author interview, December 2013, Cambridge, MA.

23. J. Bradford DeLong, Claudia Goldin, and Lawrence Katz, "Sustaining US Economic Growth," in *Agenda for the Nation*, ed. Henry J. Aaron, James M. Lindsay, and Pietro S. Nivola (Washington, DC: Brookings Institution, 2003), 47–48.

24. On Jim Crow and the GI Bill, see Ira Katznelson, *When Affirmative Action Was White: An Untold History of Racial Inequality in Twentieth-Century America* (New York: W. W. Norton, 2005). More generally on the GI bill, see Harold Hyman, *American Singularity: The 1787 Northwest Ordinance, the 1862 Homestead and Morrill Acts, and the 1944 G.I. Bill* (Athens, GA: University of Georgia Press, 2008); Edward Humes, *Over Here: How the G.I. Bill Transformed the American Dream* (Orlando: Harcourt, 2006). On California's trends, see Michael Beeli, "UC Tuition Delay Does Not Solve California's Higher Ed Crisis," *Highlander*, May 8, 2018, https://www.highlandernews.org/33039/uc-tuition-delay-not-solve-californias-higher-ed-crisis/; John Aubrey Douglass and Zachary Bleemer, "Approaching a Tipping Point? A History and Prospectus of Funding for the University of California," Center for Studies in Higher Education, UC Berkeley, August 2018, https://cshe.berkeley.edu/publications/approaching-tipping-point-history-and-prospectus-funding-university-california-john.

25. Steven R. Weisman, Reuven S. Avi-Yonah, Bruce E. Cain, and William Hogeland, "Tax Revolts: Some Succeed, Most Don't," *New York Times*, blog, April 15, 2009.

26. "Disaster Day by Day: A Detailed Flint Crisis Timeline," Bridge, MI, February 4, 2016, http://www.bridgemi.com/truth-squad-companion/disaster-day-day-detailed-flint-crisis-timeline; Siddhartha Roy, "MDEQ Mistakes and Deception Created the Flint Water Crisis," *Flint Water Study Updates* (blog), September 30, 2015, http://flintwaterstudy.org/2015/09/commentary-mdeq-mistakes-deception-flint-water-crisis/; Paul Duggan, Lori Aratani, and Robert McCartney, "Metro Will Shut Down Sections of Lines for Year-Long Subway Repair Work," *Washington Post*, May 6, 2016; "Collapse of I-35W Highway Bridge Minneapolis, Minnesota August 1, 2007," Accident Report, NTSB HAR-08/03, National Transportation Safety Board, November 14, 2008, https://www.ntsb.gov/investigations/AccidentReports/Reports/HAR0803.pdf.

27. See Michael Della Rocca, Tyler Duvall, and Rob Palter, "The Road to Renewal: How to Rebuild America's Infrastructure" McKinsey and Company, March 2017, https://www .mckinsey.com/industries/capital-projects-and-infrastructure/our-insights/the-road-to -renewal-how-to-rebuild-americas-infrastructure; National Academies of Sciences, Engineering, and Medicine, *Renewing the National Commitment to the Interstate Highway System: A Foundation for the Future* (Washington: National Academies Press, 2019); Adie Shivaram, Elizabeth Kneebone, and Ranjitha Shivaram, "Signs of Digital Distress: Mapping Broadband Availability and Subscription in American Neighborhoods," Brookings Institution, Washington, DC, September 12, 2017, https://www.brookings.edu/research/signs -of-digital-distress-mapping-broadband-availability/.

28. Mariana Mazzucato, *The Entrepreneurial State: Debunking Public vs. Private Sector Myths* (London: Anthem Press, 2013); Leslie Berlin, *Troublemakers: Silicon Valley's Coming of Age* (New York: Simon and Schuster, 2017).

29. Boushey, "In Conversation: Emmanuel Saez."

30. Douglas Clement, "Interview with Claudia Goldin," *The Region: Federal Reserve Bank of Minneapolis*, September 2004, https://www.minneapolisfed.org/publications/the -region/issues/9-2004.

31. Tom Jensen, "Overwhelming Majority of Americans Support More Federal Funding for Roads and Bridges; Voters See Crumbling Infrastructure as Threat" Public Policy Polling, Raleigh, NC, September 26, 2016, https://www.publicpolicypolling.com/polls /overwhelming-majority-of-americans-support-more-federal-funding-for-roads-and-bridges -voters-see-crumbling-infrastructure-as-threat/; Jonathan Easley, "Poll Finds Overwhelming Support for Tax Reform and Infrastructure Spending," *The Hill*, September 22, 2017, http://thehill.com/homenews/administration/351984-poll-finds-overwhelming-support-for -tax-reform-and-infrastructure.

In February 2018, YouGov polled citizens on their support of increased federal spending for roads, bridges, mass transit, and other infrastructure, and found that 71 percent were in favor either "strongly" or "somewhat." Kathy Frankovic, "Spending on Infrastructure Is Popular, but There's No Easy Way to Pay for It," YouGov, February 1, 2018, https://today .yougov.com/news/2018/02/01/spending-infrastructure-popular-theres-no-easy-way/.

32. Williamson found that 96 percent of respondents agree that "it is every American's civic duty to pay their fair share of taxes." Vanessa Williamson, *Read My Lips Why Americans Are Proud to Pay Taxes* (Princeton: Princeton University Press, 2017).

33. "Taxes," Gallup, n.d., accessed August 22, 2017, http://www.gallup.com/poll/1714 /Taxes.aspx. Indeed, in 2018, only 45 percent said they considered the federal tax they had to pay too high—the lowest percentage in Gallup's more than sixty years of asking the question.

34. Cait Lamberton, Jan-Emmanuel De Neve, and Michael Norton, "Can Giving Taxpayers a Voice Increase Tax Compliance?," *VoxEU.Org* (blog), May 30, 2014, https://voxeu.org/article/tax-compliance-and-taxpayers-voice.

35. "Voters' Views on Paid Family + Medical Leave: Findings from a National Survey," National Partnership for Women and Families, Washington, DC, October 2018, http://www .nationalpartnership.org/our-work/resources/workplace/paid-leave/voters-views-on-paid -family-medical-leave-survey-findings-august-2018.pdf; Emily Ekins, "Poll: 74% of Americans Support Federal Paid Leave Program When Costs Not Mentioned—60% Oppose If They Got Smaller Pay Raises in the Future," *Cato Institute* (blog).

36. Benjamin I. Page and Lawrence R. Jacobs, *Class War? What Americans Really Think about Economic Inequality* (Chicago: University of Chicago Press, 2009); Vanessa Williamson, "What Makes Taxes Seem Fair?" Tax Policy Center, Urban Institute and Brookings Institution, March 29, 2017, http://www.taxpolicycenter.org/publications/what -makes-taxes-seem-fair/full; Vanessa Williamson, "Tax Me. Please," *New York Times*, October 8, 2016.

Stantcheva, Alesina and Teso's finding was more likely among those with more left-wing politics. Importantly, though, the exposure of these respondents to information around intergenerational mobility drove opinion polarization. See Alberto Alesina, Stefanie Stantcheva, and Edoardo Teso, "Intergenerational Mobility and Support for Redistribution," *American Economic Review* 108, no. 2 (2018), 521–554.

Even so, Kuziemko, Saez, Stantcheva, and Norton conducted a survey of four thousand people in 2013 and found that, while those who were provided additional information about economic inequality in the United States were much more likely to say that inequality was a problem and to be in favor of an estate tax, the increase in preferences for redistribution was quite small. Ilyana Kuziemko, Michael I. Norton, Emmanuel Saez, and Stefanie Stantcheva, "How Elastic Are Preferences for Redistribution? Evidence from Randomized Survey Experiments," NBER Working Paper No. 18865, National Bureau of Economic Research, Cambridge, MA, March 2013, rev. December 2014, https://www.nber .org/papers/w18865.

37. Chris Matthews, "Here's How Much Tax Cheats Cost the US Government a Year," *Fortune*, April 29, 2016, http://fortune.com/2016/04/29/tax-evasion-cost/. A recent estimate for a national paid family and medical leave program puts it at around $33 billion annually, and puts addressing childcare for young children at around $140 billion annually. "Esti-mating Usage and Costs of Alternative Policies to Provide Paid Family and Medical Leave in the United States," Issue Brief, IMPAQ International and Institute for Women's Policy Research, January 2017, https://www.dol.gov/asp/evaluation/completed-studies/IMPAQ -Family-Leave-Insurance.pdf; Engineering National Academies of Sciences, *Transforming the Financing of Early Care and Education* (Washington: National Academies Press, 2018), DOI: 10.17226/24984; Gabriel Zucman, "How Corporations and the Wealthy Avoid Taxes (and How to Stop Them)," *New York Times*, November 10, 2017; Annette Alstadsæter, Niels Johannesen, and Gabriel Zucman, "Tax Evasion and Inequality," unpublished manuscript, October 23, 2018, http://gabriel-zucman.eu/files/AJZ2017.pdf.

38. Ruth Simon and Richard Rubin, "Crack and Pack: How Companies Are Mastering the New Tax Code," *Wall Street Journal*, April 3, 2018.

39. See Alexia Fernández Campbell, "The 4 Companies That Lobbied Most on Tax Overhaul—and What They Got for It," *Vox* (blog), December 7, 2017, https://www.vox .com/policy-and-politics/2017/12/7/16709586/republican-tax-bills-lobbying; Richard Lardner, "Money Spent on Lobbying Skyrocketed during Tax Overhaul," *AP News*, February 12, 2018, https://apnews.com/bd8a878c5fe84ea48ffbcf05b4edba0e; Lisa Gilbert, "Swamped: More Than Half the Members of Washington's Lobbying Corps Have Plunged Into the Tax Debate," Public Citizen, Washington, DC, December 1, 2017, https://www .citizen.org/sites/default/files/swamped-tax-lobbying-report.pdf; Harry Enten, "Will Passing the Tax Bill Help the GOP In 2018? Probably Not," *FiveThirtyEight* (blog), December 18, 2017, https://fivethirtyeight.com/features/will-passing-the-tax-bill-help-the-gop-in-2018 -probably-not/.

40. "Chambers for US Infrastructure Investment," Association of Chamber of Commerce Executives, March 3, 2015, https://columbus.org/2015/03/chambers-for-u-s-infrastructure -investment/; Anny Sivilay, "Highlights from the First of Three Rowlett Chamber of Commerce Candidates Forum," *Rowlett Lakeshore Times*, August 11, 2017, http:// starlocalmedia.com/rowlettlakeshoretimes/highlights-from-the-first-of-three-rowlett -chamber-of-commerce/article_e9aa66b6-7dfb-11e7-8650-7b234ccb5da8.html; Carrie Brooks, "Standing Firm on Infrastructure," US Chamber of Commerce, August 2, 2017, https://www.uschamber.com/above-the-fold/standing-firm-infrastructure; "US Chamber of Commerce Transportation Infrastructure Polling," Morning Consult, May 2017, https:// morningconsult.com/wp-content/uploads/2017/05/170504-USCC-Transport-1-1.pdf; US Chamber of Commerce and Institute for a Competitive Workforce, "Why Business Should

Support Early Childhood Education," September 8, 2010, http://www.uschamberfoundation
.org/publication/ready-set-go-why-business-should-support-early-childhood-education.

41. Martin Gilens and Benjamin I. Page, "Testing Theories of American Politics: Elites, Interest Groups, and Average Citizens," *Perspectives on Politics* 12, no. 3 (2014), 564–581; See also Martin Gilens, "Preference Gaps and Inequality in Representation," *PS: Political Science and Politics* 42, no. 2 (2009), 335–341; Larry M. Bartels, *Unequal Democracy: The Political Economy of the New Gilded Age* (New York: Russell Sage Foundation, 2008).

42. Jacob S. Hacker and Paul Pierson, *Winner-Take-All Politics: How Washington Made the Rich Richer-and Turned Its Back on the Middle Class* (New York: Simon and Schuster, 2010); Jacob Hacker and Paul Pierson, "On Winner Take All Politics," interview by Bill Moyers, January 13, 2012, quote at 23:15, https://vimeo.com/35036408; Benjamin I. Page, Larry M. Bartels, and Jason Seawright, "Democracy and the Policy Preferences of Wealthy Americans," *Perspectives on Politics* 11, no. 1 (2013), 51–73, DOI: 10.1017/S153759271200360X.

43. *Citizens United v. Federal Election Commission*, 558 US 310 (2010).

44. Nicholas Confessore, Sarah Cohen, and Karen Yourish, "The Families Funding the 2016 Presidential Election," *New York Times*, October 10, 2015.

45. Center for Responsive Politics, "Cost of 2018 Election to Surpass $5 Billion, CRP Projects," *OpenSecrets*, October 17, 2018, https://www.opensecrets.org/news/2018/10/cost -of-2018-election/; Victor Reklaitis and Katie Marriner, "How America's Top CEOs Are Spending Their Own Money on the Midterm Elections," *MarketWatch*, October 22, 2018, https://www.marketwatch.com/story/ceos-are-spending-their-own-money-on-the-midterm -elections-heres-how-2018-10-18.

46. Benjamin I. Page and Martin Gilens, *Democracy in America? What Has Gone Wrong and What We Can Do About It* (Chicago: University of Chicago Press, 2017), http://www.press.uchicago.edu/ucp/books/book/chicago/D/bo27316263.html.

47. See Robert Alan Dahl, *Who Governs? Democracy and Power in an American City*, 2nd ed. (New Haven: Yale University Press, 2005).

48. See John Voorheis, Nolan McCarty, and Boris Shor, "Unequal Incomes, Ideology and Gridlock: How Rising Inequality Increases Political Polarization," unpublished manuscript, August 23, 2015, https://papers.ssrn.com/sol3/papers.cfm?abstract_id=2649215; Nolan M. McCarty, Keith T. Poole, and Howard Rosenthal, "Political Polarization and Income Inequality," *SSRN Electronic Journal*, January 2003, DOI: 10.2139/ssrn.1154098; Nolan M. McCarty, Keith T. Poole, and Howard Rosenthal, *Income Redistribution and the Realignment of American Politics*, AEI Studies on Understanding Economic Inequality (Washington: AEI Press, 1997).

49. Diamond and Saez, "Case for a Progressive Tax," 167.

50. For more on these ideas, see David Kamin, "Taxing Capital: Paths to a Fairer and Broader US Tax System," Washington Center for Equitable Growth, August 2016, https:// equitablegrowth.org/wp-content/uploads/2016/08/081016-kamin-taxing-capital.pdf.

51. "History of the Alaska Permanent Fund," Alaska Permanent Fund Corporation, n.d., accessed May 12, 2018, https://apfc.org/who-we-are/history-of-the-alaska-permanent-fund/.

52. National Academies of Sciences, Engineering, and Medicine, *Valuing Climate Damages: Updating Estimation of the Social Cost of Carbon Dioxide* (Washington: National Academies Press, 2017), DOI: 10.17226/24651.

53. Bureau of Labor Statistics, "Table 3. Union Affiliation of Employed Wage and Salary Workers by Occupation and Industry," US Department of Labor, January 19, 2018, http://www.bls.gov/news.release/union2.t03.htm; Henry S. Farber, Daniel Herbst, Ilyana Kuziemko, and Suresh Naidu, "Unions and Inequality Over the Twentieth Century: New Evidence from Survey Data," NBER Working Paper No. 24587, National Bureau of Economic Research, Cambridge, MA, May 2018, https://www.nber.org/papers/w24587;

Daniel DiSalvo, "Janus Decision Reins in Unions' Political Power," *New York Times*, June 28, 2018.

54. Todd Tucker, "Seven Strategies to Rebuild Worker Power for the 21st Century Global Economy: A Comparative and Historical Framework for Policy Action," Report, Roosevelt Institute, New York, September 2018, http://rooseveltinstitute.org/wp-content /uploads/2018/09/Seven-Strategies-to-Rebuild-Worker-Power-final.pdf.

55. Annie Lo, "Current Citizen Efforts to Reform Redistricting," Brennen Center for Justice blog, November 7, 2018, https://www.brennancenter.org/analysis/current-citizen -efforts-reform-redistricting; Kurt Erickson, "Despite Election Night Victory, Fight over Ethics Overhaul in Missouri May Not Be Over," *St. Louis Post-Dispatch*, November 11, 2018, https://www.stltoday.com/news/local/govt-and-politics/despite-election-night-victory -fight-over-ethics-overhaul-in-missouri/article_420965d6-af95-5529-9673-7d0f7cc8f0b3 .html.

56. Alex Tausanovitch and James Lagasse, "The Small-Donor Antidote to Big-Donor Politics" Center for American Progress, June 11, 2018, https://www.americanprogress.org /issues/democracy/reports/2018/06/11/451787/small-donor-antidote-big-donor-politics/; Jennifer Heerwig and Brian J. McCabe, "Democracy Vouchers Broadened Seattle's 2017 Donor Base" Brennan Center for Justice blog, May 29, 2018, https://www.brennancenter .org/blog/democracy-vouchers-broadened-seattles-2017-donor-base.

57. Bartlett, testimony; James Surowiecki, "Tax Evasion," *New Yorker*, October 29, 2007.

## 4. Market Structure

1. "Historical US Brewery Count," Brewers Association, Boulder, CO, n.d., accessed July 1, 2018, https://www.brewersassociation.org/statistics/number-of-breweries/; "National Beer Sales & Production Data," Brewers Association, Boulder, CO, n.d., accessed July 1, 2018, https://www.brewersassociation.org/statistics/national-beer-sales-production-data/.

2. Molson Coors is incorporated in the United States but is a multinational company like Anheuser-Busch InBev. Jim Koch, "Is It Last Call for Craft Beer?," *New York Times*, April 7, 2017; "Major Suppliers," *Beer Marketer's Insights*, accessed April 17, 2019, https://www.beerinsights.com/index.php?option=com_k2&view=item&id=19559:major -supplier-shipments-and-share-2017-vs-2016; Jeff Spross, "What Beer Reveals about Monopoly Power," *The Week*, November 9, 2017, http://theweek.com/articles/736059/what -beer-reveals-about-monopoly-power; Leah Douglas, "ABI's Venture Capital Fund Quietly Expanding the Mega-Brewer's Reach," *Food & Power*, November 2, 2017, http://www .foodandpower.net/2017/11/02/abis-venture-capital-fund-quietly-expanding-the-mega -brewers-reach/.

3. There is no academic study proving causality, however, local journalists reported this: "The cuts did not come because of business struggles at Anheuser-Busch. Shortly before the takeover, A-B posted the best quarterly results in recent memory. The company said it is 'pleased' with its US beer sales and will 'continue to invest in growing our brands.'" Jeremiah McWilliams, Tim Bryant, and Tim Logan, "1,400 Jobs to Be Cut by Buyer of Anheuser-Busch Brewery," *St. Louis Post-Dispatch*, December 8, 2008, https://www .pantagraph.com/business/jobs-to-be-cut-by-buyer-of-anheuser-busch-brewery/article _9fb91d96-6630-5c8c-83f2-035d766b218c.html; "AB InBev Unveils US Job Cuts in Savings Drive," Reuters, December 8, 2008, https://www.reuters.com/article/us-abinbev/ab-inbev -unveils-u-s-job-cuts-in-savings-drive-idUSTRE4B75Z020081208; Tripp Mickle and Laurence Norman, "AB InBev Warns of Thousands of Merger-Related Job Losses," *Wall Street Journal*, August 26, 2016.

4. See, for example, "Benefits of Competition and Indicators of Market Power," Council of Economic Advisers, April 2016, Obama White House Archives, https://obamawhitehouse.archives.gov/sites/default/files/page/files/20160414_cea_competition_issue_brief.pdf.

5. For a nice review of this history, see Lina Khan and Sandeep Vaheesan, "Market Power and Inequality: The Antitrust Counterrevolution and Its Discontents," *Harvard Law and Policy Review* 11, no. 1 (2017), 235–337.

6. The health care industry, which includes retailer CVS Health, pharmaceutical distributor McKesson, and health insurer UnitedHealth Group, employs about sixteen million people in the United States. See Kimberly Leonard, "US Sees Historic Jump in Health Care's Share of the Economy," *US News & World Report*, December 2, 2016; Derek Thompson, "Health Care Just Became the US's Largest Employer," *Atlantic*, January 9, 2018, https://www.theatlantic.com/business/archive/2018/01/health-care-america-jobs/550079/; "Consumer Expenditures in 2016," BLS Reports, no. 1073, US Bureau of Labor Statistics, April 2018, https://www.bls.gov/opub/reports/consumer-expenditures/2016/home.htm; and John Dunham and Associates, "A Study of the US Beer Industry's Economic Contribution in 2016," May 2017, http://www.beerinstitute.org/wp-content/uploads/2017/06/2017-Beer-Serves-America-Report.pdf. On the technological advances in healthcare, see "10 Biggest Technological Advancements for Healthcare in the Last Decade," Becker's Health IT and CIO Report, January 28, 2014, https://www.beckershospitalreview.com/healthcare-information-technology/10-biggest-technological-advancements-for-healthcare-in-the-last-decade.html and Laura Landro, "How Apps Can Help Manage Chronic Diseases," *Wall Street Journal*, June 25, 2017.

7. Leemore Dafny, "Rules of Business: The Health Care Profit Cycle," presentation at "New Risk, New Business Models," NEJM Catalyst Event, Boston, October 6, 2016, https://catalyst.nejm.org/videos/profit-cycle-business-rules-health-care/.

8. Of course, the United States is the outlier in this view and most of our economic competitors do not see health care as something that society should rely on the private market to provide. See Organisation for Economic Co-operation and Development, *Health at a Glance 2017: OECD Indicators* (Paris: OECD Publishing, 2017), http://www.oecd.org/health/health-systems/health-at-a-glance-19991312.htm; and Edward R. Berchick, Emily Hood, and Jessica C Barnett, "Health Insurance Coverage in the United States: 2017," US Census Bureau, September 12, 2018, https://www.census.gov/library/publications/2018/demo/p60-264.html. On Dafny's role in this debate, see Jeanna Smialek, "Obamacare Competition Has Roots in Economist's Passion," *Bloomberg News*, May 30, 2013.

9. Justin Giovannelli and Emily Curran, "How Did State-Run Health Insurance Marketplaces Fare in 2017?" Commonwealth Fund, New York, March 21, 2018, https://www.commonwealthfund.org/publications/issue-briefs/2018/mar/how-did-state-run-health-insurance-marketplaces-fare-2017; Some states offer their own small business (SHOP) exchanges as well. See Emily Curran, Sabrina Corlette, and Kevin Lucia, "State-Run SHOPs: An Update Three Years Post ACA Implementation," The Commonwealth Fund, July 29, 2016, http://www.commonwealthfund.org/publications/blog/2016/jul/state-run-shops.

10. Heather Boushey, "In Conversation: Leemore Dafny," June 21, 2018, https://equitablegrowth.org/in-conversation-with-karen-dynan/.

11. Leemore S. Dafny, "Are Health Insurance Markets Competitive?," *American Economic Review* 100, no. 4 (2010): 1399–1431, 1400, DOI: 10.1257/aer.100.4.1399.

12. Leemore Dafny, Mark Duggan, and Subramaniam Ramanarayanan, "Paying a Premium on Your Premium? Consolidation in the US Health Insurance Industry," *American Economic Review* 102, no. 2 (2012): 1161–85, DOI: 10.1257/aer.102.2.1161. On the merger, see Milt Freudenheim, "Aetna to Buy Prudential's Health Care Business for $1 Billion," *New York Times*, December 11, 1998; Jesse Migneault, "Top 5 Largest Health

Insurance Payers in the United States," HealthPayerIntelligence, April 13, 2017, https://
healthpayerintelligence.com/news/top-5-largest-health-insurance-payers-in-the-united-states;
Aetna Inc, "Aetna Facts—About Us," accessed October 16, 2018, https://www.aetna.com
/about-us/aetna-facts-and-subsidiaries/aetna-facts.html.

13. Cynthia Cox and Ashley Semanskee, "Analysis of UnitedHealth Group's Premiums
and Participation in ACA Marketplaces," *Henry J. Kaiser Family Foundation* (blog),
April 18, 2016, https://www.kff.org/health-reform/issue-brief/analysis-of-unitedhealth
-groups-premiums-and-participation-in-aca-marketplaces/.

14. Hemsley stepped down as CEO in September 2017 and took on a newly created role
of executive chairman of UnitedHealth Group. Christopher Snowbeck, "UnitedHealthcare
Will Stay on Just Three Exchanges," *Star Tribune* [Minneapolis], June 1, 2018.

The research by Dafny and her colleagues only applies to affected markets. Leemore
Dafny, Jonathan Gruber, and Christopher Ody, "More Insurers Lowers Premiums: Evidence
from Initial Pricing in the Health Insurance Marketplaces," *American Journal of Health
Economics* 1, no. 1 (2015): 53–81, DOI: 10.1162/AJHE_a_00003.

15. Boushey, "In Conversation: Leemore Dafny."

16. Leemore Dafny, Kate Ho, and Robin Lee, "The Price Effects of Cross-Market
Hospital Mergers," NBER Working Paper No. 22106, National Bureau of Economic
Research, Cambridge, MA, March 2016, rev. October 2018, http://www.nber.org/papers
/w22106.pdf.

A large body of literature shows consolidation between competitors increases prices for
hospital services. For a summary of the literature, see Martin Gaynor, "Examining the
Impact of Health Care Consolidation: Statement before the Committee on Energy and
Commerce Oversight and Investigations Subcommittee," February 14, 2018, 7–9, https://
docs.house.gov/meetings/IF/IF02/20180214/106855/HHRG-115-IF02-Wstate-GaynorM
-20180214.pdf; see also Leemore S. Dafny, "Estimation and Identification of Merger
Effects: An Application to Hospital Mergers," *Journal of Law and Economics* 52, no. 3
(2009): 523–550, https://www.hbs.edu/faculty/Pages/item.aspx?num=51474.

17. "Pay-for-Delay: How Drug Company Pay-Offs Cost Consumers Billions," US
Federal Trade Commission, January 2010, https://www.ftc.gov/sites/default/files/documents
/reports/pay-delay-how-drug-company-pay-offs-cost-consumers-billions-federal-trade
-commission-staff-study/100112payfordelayrpt.pdf. *Federal Trade Commission v. Actavis,
Inc., et al.,* No. 12–416 (Supreme Court of the United States June 17, 2013); Robin
Feldman, Evan Frondorf, Andrew K. Cordova, and Connie Wang, "Empirical Evidence of
Drug Pricing Games—A Citizen's Pathway Gone Astray," *Stanford Technology Law Review*
20, no. 1 (2017): 39–91.

Monopolies based on intellectual property rights allow profits to accrue in firms that
have a lower propensity to invest and shift profits to reduce their taxes–more easily than the
industrial giants of the 1960s. Firms with valuable intellectual property rights are also able
to outsource physical capital and nonessential labor, leaving them with a small and highly
paid workforce, further concentrating wage income. Herman Mark Schwartz, "Wealth and
Secular Stagnation: The Role of Industrial Organization and Intellectual Property Rights,"
*Russell Sage Foundation Journal of the Social Sciences* 2, no. 6 (2016): 226–249, DOI:
10.7758/rsf.2016.2.6.11.

18. Recent summaries of this include William Galston and Clara Hendrickson, "A Policy
at Peace with Itself: Antitrust Remedies for Our Concentrated, Uncompetitive Economy,"
Brookings Institution, Washington, DC, January 5, 2018, https://www.brookings.edu
/research/a-policy-at-peace-with-itself-antitrust-remedies-for-our-concentrated
-uncompetitive-economy/; "Benefits of Competition and Indicators of Market Power,"
Council of Economic Advisers; Jason Furman and Peter Orszag, "A Firm-Level Perspective
on the Role of Rents in the Rise in Inequality," presentation at "A Just Society" Centennial
Event in Honor of Joseph Stiglitz, Columbia University, October 16, 2015.

The Herfindahl-Hirschman Index is defined as the sum of the squares of the market share of firms within the unit of analysis, such as industry or sector, ranging from 0 to 1.0, with 1 being an industry or sector with one monopolist firm with a market share of 100 percent. It is also sometimes expressed in terms of "points" ranging from 0 to 10,000, where an HHI of 0.25 is the same as 2,500 points. The Department of Justice and Federal Trade Commission says that a market is highly concentrated when this index is above 2,500. According to the American Hospital Association, in 1987, mean hospital market concentration was 2,340 points; this rose to 2,440 in 1992 and 3,261 in 2006. Mark V. Pauly, Thomas G. McGuire, and Pedro Pita Barros, eds., *Handbook of Health Economics* (Amsterdam: North Holland, 2012); See also "Herfindahl-Hirschman Index," Department of Justice, https://www.justice.gov/atr/herfindahl-hirschman-index.

19. Gene Kimmelman and Mark Cooper, "A Communications Oligopoly on Steroids," Washington Center for Equitable Growth, July 18, 2017, http://equitablegrowth.org/report /a-communications-oligopoly-on-steroids/; Cecilia Kang, Edmund Lee, and Emily Cochrane, "AT&T Wins Approval for $85.4 Billion Time Warner Deal in Defeat for Justice Dept.," *New York Times*, June 12, 2018.

20. Kenneth Arrow, "Economic Welfare and the Allocation of Resources for Invention," in *The Rate and Direction of Inventive Activity: Economic and Social Factors,* A Report of the National Bureau of Economic Research, 609–626 (Princeton: Princeton University Press, 1962), 620, quoted in Carl Shapiro, "Competition and Innovation: Did Arrow Hit the Bull's Eye?" in *The Rate and Direction of Inventive Activity Revisited,* eds. Joshua Lerner and Scott Stern, 361–404 (Chicago: University of Chicago Press, 2012).

Arrow predicted that big and small firms would play different roles in innovation and this may be contingent on the institutions prevailing at the time. In 1993, he wrote: "It is concluded that there is likely to be tendency toward specialization, less costly and more original innovations will come from small firms, and those involving higher development costs but less radical departures in principle will come from larger firms. This specialization creates opportunities for trade, as all specialization does; in this case, the trade will frequently be in firms as such; that is, takeovers and mergers." This presages exactly what we've seen happen in the beer and health care industries. Kenneth Arrow, "Innovation in Large and Small Firms," *Journal of Entrepreneurial Finance* 2, no. 2 (1993): 111–124, 113, https://digitalcommons.pepperdine.edu/jef/vol2/iss2/2.

21. Joseph Schumpeter, *Capitalism, Socialism and Democracy* (New York: Harper Perennial, 1962), 83.

22. For more on the Arrow / Schumpeter debate, see Douglas Clement, "Creative Disruption: Economic Theory Has Been Unable to Explain the Bond between Competition and Innovation. Until Now," *The Region: Federal Reserve Bank of Minneapolis,* September 2008, https://minneapolisfed.org/publications/the-region/creative-disruption.

23. James Estrin, "Kodak's First Digital Moment," *New York Times,* Lens blog, August 12, 2015, https://lens.blogs.nytimes.com/2015/08/12/kodaks-first-digital-moment/. More recent results show that 6.4 percent of pharmaceutical mergers and acquisitions are intended to block promising but competing innovation. Colleen Cunningham, Florian Ederer, and Song Ma, "Killer Acquisitions," Washington Center for Equitable Growth, April 16, 2019, https://equitablegrowth.org/working-papers/killer-acquisitions.

24. Thomas J. Holmes, David K. Levine, and James A. Schmitz, "Monopoly and the Incentive to Innovate When Adoption Involves Switchover Disruptions," *American Economic Journal: Microeconomics* 4, no. 3 (2012): 1, DOI: 10.1257/mic.4.3.1.

25. The researchers do find, however, that vertical mergers—between companies at different stages of the production process—can increase productivity. Bruce A. Blonigen and Justin R. Pierce, "Evidence for the Effects of Mergers on Market Power and Efficiency," NBER Working Paper No. 22750, National Bureau of Economic Research, Cambridge, MA, October 2016, http://www.nber.org/papers/w22750.

26. James Tobin, "A General Equilibrium Approach to Monetary Theory," *Journal of Money, Credit and Banking* 1, no. 1 (1969): 15–29, DOI: 10.2307/1991374; Germán Gutiérrez and Thomas Philippon, "Investment-Less Growth: An Empirical Investigation," *Brookings Papers on Economic Activity,* Fall 2017): 89–169, https://www.brookings.edu /bpea-articles/investment-less-growth-an-empirical-investigation/.

27. Gauti Eggertsson, Jacob A. Robbins, and Ella Getz Wold, "Kaldor and Piketty's Facts: The Rise of Monopoly Power in the United States," Working Paper Series, Washington Center for Equitable Growth, Washington, DC, February 2018, http:// equitablegrowth.org/working-papers/kaldor-piketty-monopoly-power/.

28. Jonathan Baker and Fiona Scott Morton, "Antitrust Enforcement against Platform MFNs," *Yale Law Journal* 127, no. 7 (2018), 2176–2202.

29. Jay Shambaugh, Ryan Nunn, Audrey Breitwieser, and Patrick Liu, "The State of Competition and Dynamism: Facts about Concentration, Start-Ups, and Related Policies," Hamilton Project, Brookings Institution, Washington, DC, June 13, 2018, 21, http://www .hamiltonproject.org/assets/files/CompetitionFacts_20180611.pdf.

30. Shambaugh et al., "The State of Competition and Dynamism"; Ian Hathaway and Robert E. Litan, "Declining Business Dynamism in the United States: A Look at States and Metros," Report, Brookings Institution, May 5, 2014, https://www.brookings.edu/research /declining-business-dynamism-in-the-united-states-a-look-at-states-and-metros/.

31. Titan Alon, David Berger, Robert Dent, and Benjamin Pugsley, "Older and Slower: The Startup Deficit's Lasting Effects on Aggregate Productivity Growth," *Journal of Monetary Economics* 93 (2018): 68–85, DOI: 10.1016/j.jmoneco.2017.10.004.

It's also increasingly the case that large capital funds hold majority stakes in the few actors in a market, bringing to the fore the question of whether this makes those markets a monopoly in practice. In a *New York Times* op-ed, Fiona Scott Morton, along with Eric Posner and Glen Weyl, lay out the rapid concentration of ownership. "In 1950," they report, "institutional investors owned about 7 percent of the United States stock market; today they own almost 70 percent. If you count them as a single investor, BlackRock, Vanguard and State Street are the largest owner of 88 percent of the companies in the Standard & Poor's 500." They go on to say that these investors often are the largest stakeholders in the largest companies within an industry. Vanguard, for example, owns the largest or second-largest stake in "JPMorgan Chase, Bank of America, Citigroup, Wells Fargo, US Bancorp and PNC Bank," giving them enormous say over leadership in the banking industry. The jury is still out on what this means especially since index funds are one of the only ways for small investors, including workers with 401(k) plans, to diversify their savings. Eric Posner, Fiona Scott Morton, and Glen Weyl, "Monopoly Donald Trump Can Pop," *New York Times*, December 7, 2016.

32. Loukas Karabarbounis and Brent Neiman, "The Global Decline of the Labor Share," *The Quarterly Journal of Economics* 129, no. 1 (2014): 61–103, DOI: 10.1093/qje/qjt032; Nicholas Kaldor, "A Model of Economic Growth," *Economic Journal* 67, no. 268 (1957): 591–624.

There is still debate over the role of the relative price of investment goods that Karabarbounis and Neiman emphasize. Gonzalez and Trivín, for example, argue that "the decline in the labour income share is not the irreversible consequence of technological or structural factors . . . but the result of a change in the functioning of financial markets and its relation with corporate investment decisions." Ignacio Gonzalez and Pedro Trivín, "Finance and the Global Decline of the Labour Share," unpublished manuscript, September 15, 2016, https://editorialexpress.com/cgi-bin/conference/download.cgi?db_name=SAEe2016&paper _id=468.

33. Jan De Loecker and Jan Eeckhout, "The Rise of Market Power and the Macroeconomic Implications," NBER Working Paper No. 23687, National Bureau of Economic Research, August 2017, https://www.nber.org/papers/w23687.

34. "Benefits of Competition and Indicators of Market Power," Council of Economic Advisers; Kimmelman and Cooper, "A Communications Oligopoly on Steroids."

35. Edward Wolff, "Household Wealth Trends in the United States, 1962 to 2016: Has Middle Class Wealth Recovered?," NBER Working Paper No. 24085, National Bureau of Economic Research, Cambridge, MA, November 2017, https://www.nber.org/papers /w24085; Danielle Kurtzleben, "While Trump Touts Stock Market, Many Americans Are Left Out of the Conversation," NPR, March 1, 2017, https://www.npr.org/2017/03/01 /517975766/while-trump-touts-stock-market-many-americans-left-out-of-the-conversation; Germán Gutiérrez and Thomas Philippon, "Investment-Less Growth."

36. Researchers have used data from Compustat to determine CEO and other executive pay going back to the 1950s. It wasn't until Dodd-Frank that companies were required to publish the ratio of CEO to worker pay. Industry pressure has delayed implementation of this rule, but in September 2017 the SEC approved guidance for companies to begin complying in early 2018. See Lawrence Mishel and Jessica Schieder, "CEO Pay Remains High Relative to the Pay of Typical Workers and High-Wage Earners" Report, Economic Policy Institute, July 20, 2017, https://www.epi.org/files/pdf/130354.pdf; Dean Baker, *Rigged: How Globalization and the Rules of the Modern Economy Were Structured to Make the Rich Richer* (Washington, DC: Center for Economic and Policy Research, 2016); Jon Bakija, Adam Cole, and Bradley T. Heim, "Jobs and Income Growth of Top Earners and the Causes of Changing Income Inequality: Evidence from US Tax Returns Data," unpublished manuscript, April 2012, https://web.williams.edu/Economics/wp/BakijaColeHeimJobs IncomeGrowthTopEarners.pdf.

37. Thomas Piketty, *Capital in the Twenty-First Century*, trans. Arthur Goldhammer (Cambridge, MA: Belknap Press of Harvard University Press, 2014), chap. 8.; There are certainly many scholars focused on reasons for why income inequality has been increasing other than productivity, including bargaining power. See, for example, Lawrence Mishel, Heidi Shierholz, and John Schmitt, "Don't Blame the Robots: Assessing the Job Polarization Explanation of Growing Wage Inequality," EPI-CEPR Working Paper, Economic Policy Institute and Center for Economic and Policy Research, November 19, 2013, http://s3.epi .org/files/2013/technology-inequality-dont-blame-the-robots.pdf.

38. Alan Krueger, "Reflections on Dwindling Worker Bargaining Power and Monetary Policy," Luncheon Address at the Jackson Hole Economic Symposium, August 24, 2018, https://www.kansascityfed.org/~/media/files/publicat/sympos/2018/papersandhandouts /824180824kruegerremarks.pdf?la=en.

39. Anna Sokolova and Todd Sorensen, "Monopsony in Labor Markets: A Meta-Analysis," IZA Discussion Paper No. 11966, IZA Institute of Labor Economics, Bonn, November 2018, https://www.iza.org/publications/dp/11966/monopsony-in-labor-markets-a -meta-analysis; Jamie Ducharme, "Why Are Boston's Nurses So Damn Angry?," *Boston Magazine*, October 1, 2017, https://www.bostonmagazine.com/health/2017/10/01/boston -nurses-strikes/.

40. Nathan Wilmers, "Wage Stagnation and Buyer Power: How Buyer-Supplier Relations Affect US Workers' Wages, 1978 to 2014," *American Sociological Review* 83, no. 2 (April 1, 2018): 213–242, DOI: 10.1177/0003122418762441; Efraim Benmelech, Nittai Bergman, and Hyunseob Kim, "Strong Employers and Weak Employees: How Does Employer Concentration Affect Wages?" NBER Working Paper No. 24307, National Bureau of Economic Research, Cambridge, MA, February 2018, https://www.nber.org /papers/w24307; Barry C. Lynn, *Cornered: The New Monopoly Capitalism and the Economics of Destruction* (Hoboken: John Wiley, 2010).

41. The researchers used data from CareerBuilder.com for over eight thousand geographic-occupational labor markets. José Azar, Ioana Marinescu, and Marshall I. Steinbaum, "Labor Market Concentration," NBER Working Paper No. 24147, National Bureau of Economic Research, Cambridge, MA, December 2017, https://www.nber.org

/papers/w24147. Larry Mishel critiques this by noting the finding may be an artifact of rural versus urban data. See Josh Bivens, Lawrence Mishel, and John Schmitt, "It's Not Just Monopoly and Monopsony: How Market Power Has Affected American Wages," Report 145564, Economic Policy Institute, April 25, 2018, https://www.epi.org/files/pdf/145564.pdf.

42. Jordan D. Matsudaira, "Monopsony in the Low-Wage Labor Market? Evidence from Minimum Nurse Staffing Regulations," *Review of Economics and Statistics* 96, no. 1 (2014): 92–102, http://dx.doi.org/10.1162/REST_a_00361.

43. Douglas A. Webber, "Firm Market Power and the Earnings Distribution," *Labour Economics* 35 (2015): 123–134, DOI: 10.1016/j.labeco.2015.05.003; See also Samuel Muehlemann, Paul Ryan, and Stefan C. Wolter, "Monopsony Power, Pay Structure, and Training," *Industrial and Labor Relations Review* 66, no. 5 (2013): 1097–1114, DOI: 10.1177/001979391306600504.

44. David Weil, *The Fissured Workplace: Why Work Became So Bad for So Many and What Can Be Done to Improve It* (Cambridge, MA: Harvard University Press, 2014).

45. Elizabeth Weber Handwerker, "Increased Concentration of Occupations, Outsourcing, and Growing Wage Inequality in the United States," unpublished manuscript, April 2017, http://www.sole-jole.org/17733.pdf.

46. Complaint, *United States v. Aetna and The Prudential Insurance Company*, No. 3-99 CV 398-H (United States District Court for the Northern District of Texas June 21, 1999).

47. Dafny, Duggan, and Ramanarayanan, "Paying a Premium on Your Premium?"

48. Dafny, Duggan, and Ramanarayanan, "Paying a Premium on Your Premium?"

49. Jon Leibowitz, interview with author, June 2018, Washington, DC.

50. Woodrow Wilson, *The New Freedom: A Call For the Emancipation of the Generous Energies of a People* (New York: Doubleday, Page, 1913), cited in Daron Acemoglu and James Robinson, *Why Nations Fail: The Origins of Power, Prosperity, and Poverty* (New York: Crown, 2012), 323.

51. Matthew Goldstein, "As CEO Pay Packages Grow, Top Executives Have the President's Ear," *New York Times*, May 26, 2017.

52. Robert H. Bork, *The Antitrust Paradox: A Policy at War with Itself* (New York: Basic Books, 1978).

53. "Equitable Growth Comments to the Federal Trade Commission on the Agency's Proposed Competition Hearings," Washington Center for Equitable Growth, August 20, 2018, https://equitablegrowth.org/equitable-growth-comments-to-the-federal-trade-commission-on-the-agencys-proposed-competition-hearings/; Liz Crampton, "Klobuchar Antitrust Legislation Nods to Progressives," *Bloomberg Law*, News. September 22, 2017, https://www.bna.com/klobuchar-antitrust-legislation-n73014464374/.

54. Ioana Marinescu and Herbert Hovenkamp, "Anticompetitive Mergers in Labor Markets," Working Paper Series, Washington Center for Equitable Growth, June 2018, 5, https://equitablegrowth.org/working-papers/anticompetitive-mergers/. Similar issues are taken up in Brian Callaci, "Franchising as Power-Biased Organizational Change," Working Paper Series, Washington Center for Equitable Growth, December 2018, https://equitablegrowth.org/working-papers/franchising-as-power-biased-organizational-change/; Office of Congresswoman Linda Sanchez, "House Democrats Unveil Legislation to Protect American Workers against Anti-Competitive Employment Practices," press release, April 26, 2018, https://lindasanchez.house.gov/media-center/press-releases/house-democrats-unveil-legislation-protect-american-workers-against-anti.

At a 2018 Congressional hearing, FTC Chairman Joseph Simons announced that FTC staff had been instructed to "look for potential effects on the labor market with every merger they review." US Congress, "Oversight of the Enforcement of the Antitrust Laws,"

Senate Judiciary Committee, 2018, https://www.judiciary.senate.gov/meetings/10/03/2018/oversight-of-the-enforcement-of-the-antitrust-laws.

55. Suresh Naidu, Eric A. Posner, and Glen Weyl, "Antitrust Remedies for Labor Market Power," *Harvard Law Review* 132, no. 2 (2018): 536–601.

56. Bruce Western and Jake Rosenfeld, "Unions, Norms, and the Rise in US Wage Inequality," *American Sociological Review* 76, no. 4 (2011): 513–537, DOI: 10.1177/0003122411414817; Richard B Freeman and James L. Medoff, *What Do Unions Do?* (New York: Basic Books, 1984); David Card, "The Effect of Unions on Wage Inequality in the US Labor Market," *Industrial and Labor Relations Review* 54, no. 2 (2001): 296–315, DOI: 10.1177/001979390105400206.

57. Michael Kades, "Merger Enforcement Statistics," Washington Center for Equitable Growth, presentation to Congressional Antitrust Caucus, January 19, 2018, https://live-equitablegrowth.pantheonsite.io/wp-content/uploads/2018/03/merger_stats-1.pdf; John Kwoka, "US Antitrust and Competition Policy Amid the New Merger Wave," research report, Washington Center for Equitable Growth, July 27, 2017, http://equitablegrowth.org/report/u-s-merger-policy-amid-the-new-merger-wave/.

58. Jonathan D. Salant and Lizzie O'Leary, "Six Lobbyists per Lawmaker Work on Health Overhaul," *Bloomberg*, August 14, 2009.

59. Jay Hancock, "The Stealth Campaign to Kill Off Obamacare," *New York Times*, August 1, 2018; Kimmelman and Cooper, "A Communications Oligopoly on Steroids."

60. Marianne Bertrand, Matilde Bombardini, Raymond Fisman, Bradley Hackinen, and Francesco Trebbi, "Hall of Mirrors: Corporate Philanthropy and Strategic Advocacy," NBER Working Paper No. 25329, National Bureau of Economic Research, Cambridge, MA, December 2018, https://www.nber.org/papers/w25329.

## III. How Inequality Distorts

1. Jean-Baptiste Say, *A Treatise on Political Economy; or the Production, Distribution, and Consumption of Wealth*, trans. C.R. Prinsep, New America Edition (Philadelphia: Lippincott, Grambo, 1855), 57.

2. Heesun Wee, "Don't Tax the Job Creators: Romney," CNBC, July 23, 2012, https://www.cnbc.com/id/48290347; David Sherfinski, "Growth from Corporate Tax Cut Will Offset Initial Cost, Trump Economic Adviser Says," *Washington Times*, November 21, 2017.

## 5. The Economic Cycle

1. "Here Is the Full Inequality Speech and Slideshow that Was Too Hot for TED," from Nick Hanauer, *Atlantic*, *National Journal*, May 17, 2012, https://www.theatlantic.com/business/archive/2012/05/here-is-the-full-inequality-speech-and-slideshow-that-was-too-hot-for-ted/257323/. Ironically, Hanauer's example is a good that today is mostly imported. Bernard A. Gelb, "Textile and Apparel Trade Issues," Congressional Research Service, January 5, 2007, http://nationalaglawcenter.org/wp-content/uploads/assets/crs/RL31723.pdf.

2. Karen E. Dynan, Jonathan Skinner, and Stephen P. Zeldes, "Do the Rich Save More?," *Journal of Political Economy* 112, no. 2 (2004): 397–444, 416–417, DOI: 10.1086/381475.

3. Matthew D. Shapiro and Joel Slemrod, "Consumer Response to Tax Rebates," *American Economic Review* 93, no. 1 (2003): 381–396, DOI: 10.1257/000282803321455368; Matthew D. Shapiro and Joel Slemrod, "Did the 2008 Tax

Rebates Stimulate Spending?," *American Economic Review* 99, no. 2 (2009): 374–79, DOI: 10.1257/aer.99.2.374.

4. Jacob S. Hacker and Elisabeth Jacobs, "The Rising Instability of American Family Income, 1969–2004: Evidence from the Panel Study of Income Dynamics," EPI Briefing Paper No. 213, Economic Policy Institute, Washington, DC, May 29, 2008, https://www.epi .org/files/page/-/old/briefingpapers/213/bp213.pdf; James Ziliak, Bradley Hardy, and Christopher Bollinger, "Earnings and Income Volatility in America: Evidence from Matched CPS," Discussion Paper 2010-05, University of Kentucky Center for Poverty Research, 2010, https://uknowledge.uky.edu/cgi/viewcontent.cgi?referer=https://www.google.com /&httpsredir=1&article=1051&context=ukcpr_papers.

5. "Karen Dynan, Bio," Department of Economics, Harvard University, n.d., accessed March 29, 2019, https://scholar.harvard.edu/kdynan/bio.

6. Alan Krueger, conversation with author, Washington, DC.

7. Alan Krueger, "The Rise and Consequences of Inequality," remarks prepared for delivery at the Center for American Progress, Washington, DC, January 12, 2012, https://cdn.americanprogress.org/wp-content/uploads/events/2012/01/pdf/krueger.pdf, 7–8. This math assumes that every dollar that went toward higher inequality would otherwise have been spent on consumption, not on investment. Had the counterfactual been the actual, the US would have seen growth rates over the past four decades akin to China's, which is probably too high given that China is still catching up developmentally. See also Nathan Serota, "Krueger Appointed to Head Obama's CEA," Princeton University Press Club, Faculty section, September 3, 2011, http://www.universitypressclub.com/archive/2011 /09/krueger-appointed-to-head-obamas-cea/.

8. John Maynard Keynes, *The General Theory of Employment, Interest, and Money* (New York: Harcourt Brace Jovanovich, 1953). He discusses involuntary unemployment on p. 8.

9. Keynes, *General Theory of Employment*, 97 (italics in original).

10. Keynes, *General Theory of Employment*, chap. 10.

11. Keynes, *General Theory of Employment*, 46.

12. Royal Swedish Academy of Sciences, "The Prize in Economics 1976," press release, October 14, 1976, https://www.nobelprize.org/nobel_prizes/economic-sciences/laureates /1976/press.html.

13. Milton Friedman, *A Theory of the Consumption Function* (Princeton: Princeton University Press, 1957), 28.

14. Keynes, General Theory of Employment, 97.

15. Heather Boushey, "In Conversation: Karen Dynan," April 19, 2018, https:// equitablegrowth.org/in-conversation-with-karen-dynan/.

16. This isn't to say there weren't empirical investigations. Friedman's work generated a bevy of research, mostly in the 1950s and 1960s. The last major research push on this question was in the early 1970s when Thomas Mayer looked at the available studies. His review of the literature concluded that the evidence was mixed, finding evidence that people did save more in years when they temporarily had a higher income, but the evidence didn't support the idea people know their lifetime—permanent—income. In his words: "However, [the evidence] does not support the claims of the new theories that consumption is proportional to permanent income and that it is independent of transitory income. Nor does it accept the very long lag in the consumption function which supporters of the new theories think they have found." Thomas Mayer, *Permanent Income, Wealth, and Consumption: A Critique of the Permanent Income Theory, the Life-Cycle Hypothesis, and Related Theories* (Berkeley: University of California Press, 1972), 5.

17. Dynan, Skinner, and Zeldes, "Do the Rich Save More?," 399.

18. For example, Thomas Mayer found that the change in consumption with respect to permanent income is not much different from the change in consumption based on one year of income. Mayer, *Permanent Income*.

19. Dynan, Skinner, and Zeldes, "Do the Rich Save More?"

20. See Christopher Carroll, Jiri Slacalek, Kiichi Tokuoka, and Matthew N. White, "The Distribution of Wealth and the Marginal Propensity to Consume," *Quantitative Economics* 8, no. 3 (November 2017): 977–1020, DOI: 10.3982/QE694; Jonathan Fisher, David Johnson, Jonathan Latner, Timothy Smeeding, and Jeffrey Thompson, "Estimating the Marginal Propensity to Consume Using the Distributions of Income, Consumption, and Wealth," Working Paper Series, Washington Center for Equitable Growth, April 2018, https://equitablegrowth.org/working-papers/marginal-propensity-consume/.

21. Atif Mian, Kamalesh Rao, and Amir Sufi, "Household Balance Sheets, Consumption, and the Economic Slump," *Quarterly Journal of Economics* 128, no. 4 (November 2013): 1687–1726, DOI: 10.1093/qje/qjt020.

22. Greg Kaplan, Kurt Mitman, and Giovanni L. Violante, "Non-Durable Consumption and Housing Net Worth in the Great Recession: Evidence from Easily Accessible Data," NBER Working Paper No. 22232, National Bureau of Economic Research, Cambridge, MA, May 2016, http://www.nber.org/papers/w22232; Greg Kaplan, Giovanni Violante, and Justin Weidner, "The Wealthy Hand-to-Mouth," Discussion Paper, Brookings Institution, Washington, DC, Spring 2014, http://www.brookings.edu/~/media/projects/bpea/spring -2014/2014a_kaplan.pdf. For an accessible explanation of this research, see Greg Kaplan and Giovanni Violante, "Wealthy 'Hand-to-Mouth' Households: Key to Understanding the Impacts of Fiscal Stimulus," *Microeconomic Insights* (blog), February 8, 2016, http:// microeconomicinsights.org/wealthy-hand-to-mouth-households-key-to-understanding-the -impacts-of-fiscal-stimulus/.

23. Karen Dynan, Douglas Elmendorf, and Daniel Sichel, "The Evolution of Household Income Volatility," *B.E. Journal of Economic Analysis & Policy* 12, no. 2 (2012), DOI: 10.1515/1935-1682.3347; Tullio Jappelli, "Who Is Credit Constrained in the US Economy?," *Quarterly Journal of Economics* 105, no. 1 (1990): 219–234, DOI: 10.2307/2937826; Christian E. Weller, *Retirement on the Rocks: Why Americans Can't Get Ahead and How New Savings Policies Can Help* (New York: Palgrave Macmillan, 2016); Reda Cherif and Fuad Hasanov, "The Volatility Trap: Precautionary Saving, Investment, and Aggregate Risk," IMF Working Paper No. 12/134, International Monetary Fund, May 2012, 21, https://www.imf.org/en/Publications/WP/Issues/2016/12/31/The-Volatility -Trap-Precautionary-Saving-Investment-and-Aggregate-Risk-25943.

24. On the trends, see Matthew Michaels, "Jeff Bezos Made an Average of $107 Million per Day Last Year—Here's How Much the Richest People in the World Earned Every 24 Hours," *Business Insider* (blog), March 21, 2018, https://www.businessinsider.com/how -much-jeff-bezos-richest-billionaires-make-every-day-2018-3; Thomas Piketty, Emmanuel Saez, and Gabriel Zucman, "Distributional National Accounts: Methods and Estimates for the United States," *Quarterly Journal of Economics* 133, no. 2 (2018): Appendix tables II: distributional series, available at http://gabriel-zucman.eu/usdina/ (last accessed April 2019).

25. Suzette Parmley, "Traditional Mall Anchors Are Fading Away," *Philly.Com* (blog), January 3, 2016, http://www.philly.com/philly/business/20160103_Traditional_mall _anchors_are_fading_away.html; Lauren Thomas, "Here Are the Stores Macy's Is Closing Next," CNBC, January 4, 2018, https://www.cnbc.com/2018/01/04/here-are-the-stores -macys-is-closing-next.html; Michael Corkery, "Sears, the Original Everything Store, Files for Bankruptcy," *New York Times*, October 16, 2018; Chris Isidore, "Will JCPenney Be Able to Avoid Sears' Fate?," *CNN Business*, November 14, 2018, https://www.cnn.com /2018/11/14/business/jcpenney-future/index.html; Lauren Thomas, "JC Penney to Close 8 Stores in 2018. Here's Where They Are," CNBC, February 15, 2018, https://www.cnbc.com /2018/02/15/jc-penney-to-close-8-stores-in-2018-heres-where-they-are.html; Shelly Banjo and Rani Molla, "Not All Malls Are Dying," *Bloomberg Gadfly* (blog), December 23, 2015, https://www.bloomberg.com/gadfly/articles/2015-12-23/high-end-malls-defy-death.

26. Mya Frazier, "Dollar General Hits a Gold Mine in Rural America," *Bloomberg* (blog), October 11, 2017, https://www.bloomberg.com/news/features/2017-10-11/dollar -general-hits-a-gold-mine-in-rural-america.

27. Xavier Jaravel, "The Unequal Gains from Product Innovations: Evidence from the US Retail Sector," *Quarterly Journal of Economics* 134, no. 2 (2019): 715–783, DOI: 10.1093/qje/qjy031.

28. Jared Bernstein, "The Impact of Inequality on Growth," Center for American Progress, Washington, DC, December 2013, https://www.americanprogress.org/wp-content /uploads/2013/12/BerensteinInequality.pdf; Atif Mian and Amir Sufi, *House of Debt: How They (and You) Caused the Great Recession, and How We Can Prevent It from Happening Again* (Chicago: University Of Chicago Press, 2014).

29. "Quarterly Report on Household Debt and Credit 2018: Q4," Federal Reserve Bank of New York, February 2019, https://www.newyorkfed.org/medialibrary/interactives /householdcredit/data/pdf/HHDC_2018Q4.pdf; Michael Ahn, Mike Batty, and Ralf R. Meisenzahl, "Household Debt-to-Income Ratios in the Enhanced Financial Accounts," FEDS Note, Board of Governors of the Federal Reserve System, January 11, 2018, https://www.federalreserve.gov/econres/notes/feds-notes/household-debt-to-income-ratios-in -the-enhanced-financial-accounts-20180109.htm; Christian Weller and Jessica Lynch, "Household Wealth in Freefall: Americans' Private Safety Net in Tatters," Center for American Progress, Washington, DC, April 23, 2009; J. W. Mason, "Income Distribution, Household Debt, and Aggregate Demand: A Critical Assessment," unpublished manuscript, 2017, https://www.stlouisfed.org/~/media/Files/PDFs/HFS/assets/2017/JW_Mason.pdf?la =en; Matthew Klein, "America's Household Debt Binge *Was* About Income Inequality," *Financial Times*, March 1, 2017; Mian and Sufi, *House of Debt*.

30. "Mortgage Debt Outstanding, All Holders," FRED, Federal Reserve Bank of St. Louis, May 11, 2018, https://fred.stlouisfed.org/series/MDOAH.

31. "S&P/Case-Shiller US National Home Price Index," FRED Federal Reserve Bank of St. Louis, February 27, 2018, https://fred.stlouisfed.org/series/CSUSHPISA.

32. "S&P/Case-Shiller US National Home Price Index"; annual average cash-out refinances from "Loan Purposes by Quarter," House Price Index Datasets, Federal Housing Finance Agency, n.d., http://www.fhfa.gov/DataTools/Downloads/Pages/House-Price-Index -Datasets.aspx; Christina Rexrode, "Tapping Your Home Equity for Cash Is Big Again," *Wall Street Journal*, August 27, 2017; Mian and Sufi, *House of Debt*.

Economist J.W. Mason argues that since household debt today is more concentrated at the top of the income and wealth distributions—and was during the run-up of the housing bubble also—this trend ignores rising inequality in consumption. This trend may be explained by homeowners near the top of the income ladder "trying to keep up with the Joneses," but whatever the case, Mason argues that policymakers' failure to lower interest rates in response to signs that nominal incomes were stagnating or falling over the course of the twenty-first century helped create the housing crisis in the first place. Mason, "Income Distribution."

33. "Consumer Credit–G.19," Board of Governors of the Federal Reserve System, accessed March 7, 2018, https://www.federalreserve.gov/releases/g19/current/default.htm.

34. Jeffrey Thompson, "Do Rising Top Incomes Lead to Increased Borrowing in the Rest of the Distribution?," *Economic Inquiry* 56, no. 2 (2018): 686–708, DOI: 10.1111/ ecin.12520.

It's important to note that, when inequality increased sharply in the 1980s, debt did not rise that much—at least not in the aggregate—but women's labor force participation continued its upward climb. During the 1990s, when inequality did not grow that much, debt grew sharply and, at the end of the decade, increases in women's labor-force participation stalled. While it is a compelling story to say that people borrowed more to make up for the lack of income growth, the data only really supports this claim for the period from 2000 to 2007. There is not a substantial consumer debt bubble in early 2019, but the 2000 to 2007 years could easily repeat themselves.

35. Adam Seth Levine, Robert H. Frank, and Oege Dijk, "Expenditure Cascades," unpublished manuscript, September 13, 2010, http://papers.ssrn.com/abstract=1690612; Marianne Bertrand and Adair Morse, "Trickle-Down Consumption," *Review of Economics and Statistics* 98, no. 5 (2016): 863–879, DOI: 10.1162/REST_a_00613.

36. "Employed Full Time: Median Usual Weekly Real Earnings: Wage and Salary Workers: 16 Years and Over: Men," Weekly and Hourly Earnings from the Current Population Survey, US Bureau of Labor Statistics, January 17, 2018, https://fred.stlouisfed .org/series/LES1252881900Q; US Bureau of Labor Statistics, "Civilian Labor Force Participation Rate: Women," US Bureau of Labor Statistics, March 9, 2018, https://fred .stlouisfed.org/series/LNS11300002; "Median Family Income in the United States," Income and Poverty in the United States, US Bureau of the Census, September 13, 2017, https://fred .stlouisfed.org/series/MEFAINUSA646N; "Economy: Historical Trends," Gallup, accessed October 1, 2018, https://news.gallup.com/poll/1609/Consumer-Views-Economy.aspx; "Current Economic Conditions Index," Survey of Consumers, University of Michigan, 2018, http://www.sca.isr.umich.edu/files/chicch.pdf.

37. The trends of the past few decades are not a uniquely American story. Looking around the world, it's common to see debt rise in times of growing inequality. In fact, out of thirty-four member countries of the Organisation for Economic Co-operation and Development, only two have seen a reduction in household debt as a percentage of net disposable income since 1995: Germany and Japan. Organisation for Economic Co-operation and Development *National Accounts at a Glance 2015,* rev. version (Paris: OECD Publishing, 2016), Table 20.1, "Household Debt," 55, http://www.oecd.org/sdd/na /national-accounts-at-a-glance-22200444.htm; "Effective Federal Funds Rate," FRED, Federal Reserve Bank of St. Louis, accessed June 26, 2018, https://fred.stlouisfed.org/series /FEDFUNDS.

38. "All Employees: Total Nonfarm Payrolls," FRED, Federal Reserve Bank of St. Louis, March 9, 2018, https://fred.stlouisfed.org/series/PAYEMS; "H.R.1–11th Congress (2009–2010): American Recovery and Reinvestment Act of 2009," February 17, 2009, https://www .congress.gov/bill/111th-congress/house-bill/1; Congressional Budget Office, "Estimated Impact of the American Recovery and Reinvestment Act on Employment and Economic Output in 2014," February 2015, https://www.cbo.gov/publication/49958.

39. Boushey, "In Conversation: Karen Dynan."

40. Mark Zandi and Alan Blinder, "The Financial Crisis: Lessons for the Next One," Center on Budget and Policy Priorities, Washington, DC, October 5, 2015, https://www .cbpp.org/research/economy/the-financial-crisis-lessons-for-the-next-one.

In 2001 and again in 2008, as the economy was sliding into recession, the US Congress passed legislation and President George W. Bush signed into law two quick, one-time injections of cash to families. Having studied both experiments, economists now conclude that getting cash into the hands of people with low incomes and those who are cash-constrained is one of the most effective ways to support economic growth. The first study is by David S. Johnson, Jonathan A. Parker, and Nicholas S. Souleles. They use the random variation in the timing of the 2001 tax rebates to separate the effect of a change in income from other factors that affect spending decisions. They find that households spent on average 20 percent to 40 percent of their 2001 tax rebate on nondurable goods within the first three months after they received their checks. Yet low-income households and households with few liquid assets spent a significantly greater share of their rebates than the typical household. This suggests that these households either expected to have a higher income in the near future, which is unlikely, or that they have a high propensity to consume from one-time or highly liquid funds. Similarly, the same authors with an additional coauthor, Robert McClelland, find similar results in an analysis of the 2008 tax rebates. These findings, however, are not statistically significant for those who were liquidity constrained. This may mean that in the depths of the Great Recession, those families not at financial breaking point were able to cut back on previously debt-driven spending to help make ends meet when they received the 2008 tax rebates. David S. Johnson, Jonathan A. Parker, and Nicholas S. Souleles, "Household Expenditure and the Income Tax Rebates of 2001," *American Economic Review* 96, no. 5 (2006): 1589–1610, DOI: 10.1257/ aer.96.5.1589; Jonathan A Parker, Nicholas S. Souleles, David S. Johnson, and Robert McClelland, "Consumer Spending and the Economic Stimulus Payments of 2008," *American Economic Review* 103, no. 6 (October 2013): 2530–2553, DOI: 10.1257/ aer.103.6.2530.

41. Katelin P. Isaacs and Julie M Whittaker, "Emergency Unemployment Compensation (EUC08): Status of Benefits Prior to Expiration," Congressional Research Service, August 11, 2014, https://fas.org/sgp/crs/misc/R42444.pdf.

42. Wayne Vroman and Jacob Benus, "The Role of Unemployment Insurance as an Automatic Stabilizer During a Recession," IMPAQ International and Urban Institute, July 2010, 66, https://wdr.doleta.gov/research/FullText_Documents/ETAOP2010-10.pdf.

Ganong and Noel found that, between the first and second monthly receipt of unemployment insurance, spending in high-benefit states fell by only 4.6 percent as compared to 7.3 percent in low-benefit states. They calculated that the marginal propensity to consume overall rose by 38 cents for every dollar's worth of unemployment benefits—and when benefits expire, spending drops by 13 percent. Peter Ganong and Pascal J. Noel, "Consumer Spending During Unemployment: Positive and Normative Implications," NBER Working Paper No. 25417, National Bureau of Economic Research, Cambridge, MA, January 2019, https://www.nber.org/papers/w25417.

43. Olivier Coibion, Yuriy Gorodnichenko, and Mauricio Ulate, "Real-Time Estimates of Potential GDP: Should the Fed Really Be Hitting the Brakes?" Center on Budget and Policy Priorities, Washington, DC, January 31, 2018, https://www.cbpp.org/research/full -employment/real-time-estimates-of-potential-gdp-should-the-fed-really-be-hitting-the.

44. Paul Krugman, "How Did We Know The Stimulus Was Too Small?," *The Conscience of a Liberal* (blog), July 28, 2010, https://krugman.blogs.nytimes.com/2010/07/28/how-did -we-know-the-stimulus-was-too-small/; Gerald A. Carlino, "Did the Fiscal Stimulus Work?"; Robert Greenstein, Richard Kogan, and Roderick Taylor, "Program Spending Outside Social Security and Medicare Historically Low as a Percent of GDP and Projected to Fall Further," Center on Budget and Policy Priorities, Washington, DC, June 26, 2018, https://www.cbpp.org/research/federal-budget/program-spending-outside-social-security-and -medicare-historically-low-as-a; Kim S. Rueben and Megan Randall, "Balanced Budget Requirements: How States Limit Deficit Spending," Urban Institute, Washington, DC, November 22, 2017, https://www.urban.org/research/publication/balanced-budget -requirements; Tracy Gordon, "State and Local Budgets and the Great Recession," Brookings Institution, December 31, 2012, https://www.brookings.edu/articles/state-and -local-budgets-and-the-great-recession/.

45. Other significant portions were devoted to infrastructure spending (6 percent) and tax breaks for households and businesses (51 percent). Author's calculations are based on data from Alan S. Blinder and Mark Zandi, "How the Great Recession Was Brought to an End," July 27, 2010, http://www.economy.com/mark-zandi/documents/End-of-Great -Recession.pdf; Gerald A. Carlino, "Did the Fiscal Stimulus Work?," Federal Reserve Bank of Philadelphia, First Quarter 2017, https://www.philadelphiafed.org/-/media/research-and -data/publications/economic-insights/2017/q1/eiq117_did-the-fiscal-stimulus-work.pdf?la =en; Shoshana Lew and John Porcari, "Eight Years Later: What the Recovery Act Taught Us

about Investing in Transportation," Brookings Institution blog, February 22, 2017, https://www.brookings.edu/blog/the-avenue/2017/02/22/eight-years-later-what-the-recovery-act-taught-us/; "US Senate Roll Call Votes 111th Congress–1st Session (Motion to Waive Sec. 201 of S. Con. Res. 21, 110th Congress Re: Amdt. No. 570)," February 10, 2009, https://www.senate.gov/legislative/LIS/roll_call_lists/roll_call_vote_cfm.cfm?congress=111&session=1&vote=00060; Adam Tooze, *Crashed: How a Decade of Financial Crises Changed the World* (New York: Viking, 2018).

46. In a paper on stabilization policy, Olivier Blanchard and Larry Summers note that the policy thinking about optimal automatic stabilizers has not been fully fleshed out and there's much work to do. Olivier Blanchard and Lawrence Summers, "Rethinking Stabilization Policy: Back to the Future," Conference Paper, Peterson Institute for International Economics, October 8, 2017, https://piie.com/system/files/documents/blanchard-summers20171012paper.pdf. On automatic stabilizers, see Heather Boushey, Ryan Nunn, and Jay Shambaugh, "Recession Ready: Fiscal Policies to Stabilize the American Economy," Hamilton Project and the Washington Center on Equitable Growth, Washington, DC, May 2019, https://equitablegrowth.org/wp-content/uploads/2019/05/AutomaticStabilizers_FullBook_web_20190513.pdf.

47. Margot L Crandall-Hollick, "The Earned Income Tax Credit (EITC): A Brief Legislative History," CRS Report R44825, Congressional Research Service, March 20, 2018, https://fas.org/sgp/crs/misc/R44825.pdf.

48. Annie Lowrey, *Give People Money: How a Universal Basic Income Would End Poverty, Revolutionize Work, and Remake the World* (New York: Crown, 2018); Chris Hughes, *Fair Shot: Rethinking Inequality and How We Earn* (New York: St. Martin's Press, 2018).

49. As of the second quarter of 2018, outstanding student debt was $1.5 trillion, more than double the $0.6 trillion just a decade earlier. Board of Governors of the Federal Reserve System, "G.19 Consumer Credit," accessed October 4, 2018, https://www.federalreserve.gov/releases/g19/; David M. Herszenhorn and Tamar Lewin, "Student Loan Overhaul Approved by Congress," *New York Times*, March 25, 2010.

50. Mark Zandi, "What Does Rising Inequality Mean for the Macroeconomy?," in *After Piketty: The Agenda for Economics and Inequality*, ed. Heather Boushey, J. Bradford DeLong, and Marshall Steinbaum (Cambridge, MA: Harvard University Press, 2017); Gabriel Zucman, "Simplified Distributional National Accounts" (Annual Economic Association Annual Meeting, Atlanta, GA, 2019).

51. Andy Haldane and Arthur Turrell, "An Interdisciplinary Model for Macroeconomics," Working Paper, Bank of England, November 24, 2017, http://www.bankofengland.co.uk/working-paper/2017/an-interdisciplinary-model-for-macroeconomics; Rafa Baptista et al., "Macroprudential Policy in an Agent-Based Model of the UK Housing Market," Working Paper, Bank of England, October 7, 2016, http://www.bankofengland.co.uk/working-paper/2016/macroprudential-policy-in-an-agent-based-model-of-the-uk-housing-market; Jonathan D. Ostry, Andrew Berg, and Charalambos G. Tsangarides, "Redistribution, Inequality, and Growth," IMF Staff Discussion Note 14/02, International Monetary Fund, February 2014, http://www.imf.org/external/pubs/ft/sdn/2014/sdn1402.pdf.

## 6. Investment

1. "Off With the Red Tape," Policy Brief, Illinois Policy Institute, February 7, 2011, https://www.scribd.com/document/48354354/Repealer2-7; Kansas Office of the Governor, "Executive Order 11-01," January 21, 2011, https://kslib.info/DocumentCenter/View/3182/EO-11-01?bidId=; 13 News, "Office of the Repealer to Tour Kansas," WIBW 13,

September 30, 2011, http://www.wibw.com/home/headlines/Office_Of_The_Repealer_To
_Tour_Kansas_130857783.html.

2. Nancy L. Rose, ed., *Economic Regulation and Its Reform: What Have We Learned?*,
National Bureau of Economic Research Conference Report (Chicago: University of Chicago
Press, 2014). During the signing of the Gramm-Leach-Bliley Financial Services Modernization Act, President Clinton stated that "Removal of barriers to competition will enhance the
stability of our financial services system. Financial services firms will be able to diversify
their product offerings and thus their sources of revenue. They will also be better equipped
to compete in global financial markets." Bill Clinton, "Statement on Signing the Gramm-
Leach-Bliley Act," November 12, 1999, http://www.presidency.ucsb.edu/ws/?pid=56922.

3. Kenneth Jones and Tim Critchfield, "Consolidation in the US Banking Industry: Is the
'Long, Strange Trip' About to End?," *FDIC Banking Review* 17, no. 4 (2005), https://papers
.ssrn.com/sol3/papers.cfm?abstract_id=882094.

4. Heather Boushey, "In Conversation: Atif Mian," June 21, 2018, https://
equitablegrowth.org/in-conversation-with-atif-mian/.

5. To understand how financial deregulation affects investment, Mian, Sufi, and Verner
took advantage of the fact that states deregulated at different times, comparing the
experiences of those that deregulated earlier to those that did so later. They found that
states that deregulated earlier saw much larger increases in household debt than states that
deregulated later. Households used those loans to purchase more expensive homes and
other goods and services that economists refer to as "non-tradables"—think retail stores or
construction. This higher demand led to rising home prices and more inflation, alongside
increases in employment and wages in these non-tradable sectors. In the short run, that
boosted growth because it boosted consumption. When the downturn came, the non-
tradable sectors' higher prices meant that those states' local economies were less competitive; their higher wages meant more layoffs. On the other hand, tradable sectors of the
economy—think manufacturing—did not see as sharp a rise in employment or wages and
did not suffer as badly in the ensuing downturn. Atif R. Mian, Amir Sufi, and Emil Verner,
"How Do Credit Supply Shocks Affect the Real Economy? Evidence from the United States
in the 1980s," Working Paper, Washington Center for Equitable Growth, July 11, 2017,
https://equitablegrowth.org/working-papers/how-credit-supply-shocks-affect-the-economy/.

6. John Maynard Keynes, *The General Theory of Employment, Interest, and Money*
(New York: Harcourt Brace Jovanovich, 1953), 28.

7. Boushey, "In Conversation: Atif Mian."

8. Amir Sufi, "Academic Research," http://faculty.chicagobooth.edu/amir.sufi/chronology
.html; FT Interactive Graphics, "Best Business Books," FT Business book of the year award,
accessed December 1, 2018, https://ig.ft.com/sites/business-book-award/; "IMF Lists 25
Brightest Young Economists," *International Business Times* UK, August 27, 2014,
https://www.ibtimes.co.uk/imf-lists-25-brightest-young-economists-1462827; "Fischer Black
Prize - American Finance Association," https://www.afajof.org/page/FischerBlackPrize; "40
under 40: Amir Sufi," *Crain's Chicago Business*, 2015, http://www.chicagobusiness.com
/section/40-under-40-2015?recipient=Sufi.

9. Atif Mian and Amir Sufi, *House of Debt: How They (and You) Caused the Great
Recession, and How We Can Prevent It from Happening Again* (Chicago: University Of
Chicago Press, 2014), 18; The fall in employment is measured from the height of employ-
ment in January 2008 through February 2010, when employment fell to its then post–Great
Recession low. "All Employees: Total Nonfarm Payrolls," FRED, Federal Reserve Bank of
St. Louis, March 9, 2018, https://fred.stlouisfed.org/series/PAYEMS; "Real Median Family
Income in the United States," FRED, Federal Reserve Bank of St. Louis, September 13,
2017, https://fred.stlouisfed.org/series/MEFAINUSA672N; "Households and Nonprofit
Organizations; Net Worth, Level," FRED, Federal Reserve Bank of St. Louis, December 16,

2018, https://fred.stlouisfed.org/series/TNWBSHNO; Emmanuel Saez and Gabriel Zucman, "Wealth Inequality in the United States since 1913: Evidence from Capitalized Income Tax Data," *Quarterly Journal of Economics* 131, no. 2 (2016): 519–578, DOI: 10.1093/qje/qjw004.

10. Mian and Sufi, *House of Debt.*

11. Mian and Sufi, *House of Debt*, 74–77.

12. Yuliya Demyanyk and Otto Van Hemert, "Understanding the Subprime Mortgage Crisis," *Review of Financial Studies* 24, no. 6 (2011): 1848–1880, 1849, DOI: 10.1093/rfs/hhp033.

13. Michael Lewis, *The Big Short: Inside the Doomsday Machine* (New York: W.W. Norton, 2011).

14. Mian and Sufi, *House of Debt*, 45; 36–37.

15. Mian and Sufi, *House of Debt*, chap. 3.

16. Atif Mian and Amir Sufi, "House Prices, Home Equity-Based Borrowing, and the US Household Leverage Crisis," *American Economic Review* 101, no. 5 (2011): 2132–2156, DOI: 10.1257/aer.101.5.2132; Freddie Mac, "Freddie Mac Quarterly Refinance Statistics Archive," Freddie Mac, 2017, fig. Annual Cash-Out Volume for All Prime Conventional Loans, http://www.freddiemac.com/research/datasets/refinance-stats/archive.html.

17. Mian and Sufi, "House Prices, Home Equity-Based Borrowing"; Mian and Sufi, *House of Debt*; "9.3 Percent of US Properties Seriously Underwater in Q2 2018," *ATTOM Data Solutions* (blog), August 8, 2018, https://www.attomdata.com/news/market-trends/home-equity-underwater-report-q2-2018/.

18. Mian and Sufi, *House of Debt*, 3. At a recent conference, Sufi noted two papers that are emblematic of this approach: Gabriel Chodorow-Reich, John Coglianese, and Loukas Karabarbounis, "The Macro Effects of Unemployment Benefit Extensions: A Measurement Error Approach," *Quarterly Journal of Economics* 134, no. 1 (2019): 227–279, DOI: 10.1093/qje/qjy018; and Emi Nakamura and Jón Steinsson, "Identification in Macroeconomics," *Journal of Economic Perspectives* 32, no. 3 (2018): 59–86, DOI: 10.1257/jep.32.3.59.

19. Boushey, "In Conversation: Atif Mian." See also Atif Mian and Amir Sufi, "Why the Income Distribution Matters for Macroeconomics," *House of Debt* (blog), March 24, 2014, http://houseofdebt.org/2014/03/27/why-income-distribution-matters-for-macroeconomics.html.

20. Saez and Zucman, "Wealth Inequality in the United States since 1913," 563.

Rachel and Smith find that, in the United States between 1980 and 2013, the richest fifth of the population saw their share of national income rise by about seven percentage points. The top fifth saves about a third of new income, which translates into a three-percentage point rise in desired savings. However, the fall in the income share of the bottom four-fifths reduces the demand for savings, so the net rise in desired savings is about two percentage points. Lukasz Rachel and Thomas D Smith, "Secular Drivers of the Global Real Interest Rate," Working Paper No. 571, Bank of England, December 2015, https://www.bankofengland.co.uk/working-paper/2015/secular-drivers-of-the-global-real-interest-rate; "Gross Domestic Product 2016," World Development Indicators database, April 17, 2018, https://datacatalog.worldbank.org/dataset/world-development-indicators.

21. "Median Age of the US Population 1960–2017," Statista, accessed May 18, 2018, https://www.statista.com/statistics/241494/median-age-of-the-us-population/; Ben S. Bernanke, "The Global Saving Glut and the US Current Account Deficit," Sandridge Lecture, Virginia Association of Economists, Richmond, VA, March 10, 2005, https://www.federalreserve.gov/boarddocs/speeches/2005/200503102/; Ben S. Bernanke, "Global Imbalances: Recent Developments and Prospects," Bundesbank Lecture, Berlin, September 11, 2007, https://www.federalreserve.gov/newsevents/speech/bernanke20070911a

.htm; US Department of the Treasury. Fiscal Service, "Federal Debt Held by Foreign and International Investors," FRED, Federal Reserve Bank of St. Louis, https://fred.stlouisfed.org /series/FDHBFIN.; "Major Foreign Holders of Treasury Securities," US Department of the Treasury, accessed June 18, 2018, http://ticdata.treasury.gov/Publish/mfh.txt.

22. Author's calculation based on US Bureau of Economic Analysis, "Corporate Profits After Tax with Inventory Valuation Adjustment (IVA) and Capital Consumption Adjustment (CCAdj)," FRED, Federal Reserve Bank of St. Louis, June 7, 2018, https://fred .stlouisfed.org/series/CPATAX; Thomas Piketty, Emmanuel Saez, and Gabriel Zucman, "Distributional National Accounts: Methods and Estimates for the United States," *Quarterly Journal of Economics* 133, no. 2 (2018): 553–609, DOI: 10.1093/qje/qjx043; William Lazonick, "Profits without Prosperity," *Harvard Business Review*, September 2014, https://hbr.org/2014/09/profits-without-prosperity; William Lazonick, "The Financialization of the US Corporation: What Has Been Lost, and How It Can Be Regained," *Seattle University Law Review* 36, no. 2 (2013): 857–909, https://digitalcommons.law.seattleu.edu /sulr/vol36/iss2/17.

23. "Private Residential Fixed Investment," FRED, Federal Reserve Bank of St. Louis, accessed March 29, 2018, https://fred.stlouisfed.org/series/PRFI; US Bureau of Economic Analysis, "Gross Private Domestic Investment: Fixed Investment: Nonresidential: Equipment," FRED, Federal Reserve Bank of St. Louis, https://fred.stlouisfed.org/series /Y033RC1Q027SBEA.

24. Thomas Philippon, *The Great Reversal: How America's Markets Lost Their Competitive Edge* (Cambridge, MA: Harvard University Press, forthcoming); Germán Gutiérrez and Thomas Philippon, "Investment-Less Growth: An Empirical Investigation," *Brookings Papers on Economic Activity* Vol. 48:2 (2017): 89–190; Juan M. Sanchez and Emircan Yurdagul, "Why Are Corporations Holding So Much Cash?," Regional Economist, Federal Reserve Bank of St. Louis, January 2013, https://www.stlouisfed.org/publications /regional-economist/january-2013/why-are-corporations-holding-so-much-cash.

25. Some call this "shareholder capitalism." Loizos Heracleous and Luh Luh Lan, "The Myth of Shareholder Capitalism," *Harvard Business Review*, April 2010, https://hbr.org /2010/04/the-myth-of-shareholder-capitalism; John Asker, Joan Farre-Mensa, and Alexander Ljungqvist, "Corporate Investment and Stock Market Listing: A Puzzle?," *Review of Financial Studies* 28, no. 2 (2015): 342–390, DOI: 10.1093/rfs/hhu077; Nick Bunker, "Are Low-Interest Rates Contributing to Low Business Investment?," Washington Center for Equitable Growth, June 7, 2016, http://equitablegrowth.org/equitablog/are-low-interest -rates-contributing-to-low-business-investment/; See also Philippon, *Great Reversal*.

26. Heather Boushey, "In Conversation: Larry Summers," February 11, 2016, http:// equitablegrowth.org/equitable-growth-in-conversation-an-interview-with-lawrence-summers/.

27. Paul Krugman, "Secular Stagnation: The Book," *Paul Krugman* (blog), August 15, 2014, https://krugman.blogs.nytimes.com/2014/08/15/secular-stagnation-the-book/.

28. The term secular stagnation was introduced by the late Harvard economist Alvin Hansen in a speech entitled, "Economic Progress and Declining Population Growth," which he gave at the American Economic Association meeting in 1938. He argued at the time that slower population growth—necessarily a long-term phenomenon—created a lack of demand that hampered economic growth. Summers updated the idea by asking whether "the economy re-equilibrates." Alvin Hansen, "Economic Progress and Declining Population Growth," *American Economic Review* 29, no. 1 (1939): 1–15; Lawrence H Summers, "US Economic Prospects: Secular Stagnation, Hysteresis, and the Zero Lower Bound," *Business Economics* 49, no. 2 (2014): 65–73, DOI: 10.1057/be.2014.13; Keynes, *General Theory of Employment,* 28; Adrien Auclert and Matthew Rognlie, "Aggregate Demand and the Top 1%," *American Economic Review* 107, no. 5 (2017): 588–592, DOI: 10.1257/aer. p20171004.

29. Robert J. Gordon, "Secular Stagnation: A Supply-Side View," *American Economic Review* 105, no. 5 (2015): 54–59, DOI: 10.1257/aer.p20151102; Robert J. Gordon, "The Demise of US Economic Growth: Restatement, Rebuttal, and Reflections," NBER Working Paper No. 19895, National Bureau of Economic Research, Cambridge, MA, February 2014, http://www.nber.org/papers/w19895.

30. Part of the challenge that Summers and other economists see is that in an economy, overall savings must equal investment. Any excess savings or lack of investment opportunities create downward pressure on interest rates; this means that it's cheap to borrow, which should then encourage more investment and move the economy back to full employment. There are perverse implications, however, when what's driving the rate of interest down is an excess of savings looking for a place to park. Furthermore, excessive savings means a shortfall in demand, which slows growth and lowers inflation. Gauti Eggertsson, Neil Mehrotra, and Jacob Robbins have formalized this model and found that "The key for successful fiscal policy is that it must reduce the oversupply of savings and raise the natural rate of interest." Gauti B. Eggertsson, Neil R. Mehrotra, and Jacob A. Robbins, "A Model of Secular Stagnation: Theory and Quantitative Evaluation," NBER Working Paper No. 23093, National Bureau of Economic Research, Cambridge, MA, January 2017, 2–3, https://www.nber.org/papers/w23093; Summers, "US Economic Prospects"; Ben S. Bernanke, "Why Are Interest Rates So Low?," March 30, 2015, blog post, Brookings Institution, Washington, DC, https://www.brookings.edu/blog/ben-bernanke/2015/03/30/why-are-interest-rates-so-low/; Ben S. Bernanke, "Why Are Interest Rates So Low, Part 2: Secular Stagnation," blog post, Brookings Institution, Washington, DC, March 31, 2015, https://www.brookings.edu/blog/ben-bernanke/2015/03/31/why-are-interest-rates-so-low-part-2-secular-stagnation/.

31. "Effective Federal Funds Rate," FRED, Federal Reserve Bank of St. Louis, accessed June 26, 2018, https://fred.stlouisfed.org/series/FEDFUNDS.

32. Bernanke, "Why Are Interest Rates So Low, Part 2; Ben S. Bernanke, "Why Are Interest Rates so Low, Part 3: The Global Savings Glut," blog post, Brookings Institution, Washington, DC, April 1, 2015, https://www.brookings.edu/blog/ben-bernanke/2015/04/01/why-are-interest-rates-so-low-part-3-the-global-savings-glut/.

33. To be sure, the savings and loan crisis in the 1990s was also caused by a lack of regulatory oversight. Prior to that, the last major financial crisis was the Great Depression, also the result of too-limited financial regulation. Eugene Nelson White, Kenneth A. Snowden, and Price Van Meter Fishback, eds., *Housing and Mortgage Markets in Historical Perspective*, National Bureau of Economic Research Conference Report (Chicago: University of Chicago Press, 2014).

34. See, for example, James K. Galbraith, *Inequality and Instability: A Study of the World Economy Just before the Great Crisis* (New York: Oxford University Press, 2012); Gerald A. Epstein, ed., *Financialization and the World Economy* (Cheltenham: Elgar, 2005); Matthew Sherman, "A Short History of Financial Deregulation in the United States," Center for Economic and Policy Research, Washington, DC, July 2009, 5, http://cepr.net/documents/publications/dereg-timeline-2009-07.pdf.

35. Thorsten Beck, Ross Levine, and Alexey Levkov, "Big Bad Banks? The Winners and Losers from Bank Deregulation in the United States," *Journal of Finance* 65, no. 5 (2010): 1637–1667, DOI: 10.1111/j.1540-6261.2010.01589.x; Alan Greenspan, "Testimony before the Committee on Banking, Housing and Urban Affairs, United States Senate," July 12, 1990, https://fraser.stlouisfed.org/content/?item_id=8436&filepath=/files/docs/historical/greenspan/Greenspan_19900712.pdf; See also John Cassidy, "Where Larry Summers Went Wrong," *New Yorker*, July 30, 2013.

36. Robert Rubin, "Testimony before the Subcommittee on Finance and Hazardous Materials House Committee on Commerce," May 5, 1999, https://www.treasury.gov/press-center/press-releases/Pages/rr3131.aspx.

The debate was quite robust. One of the signature achievements of Lawrence Summers, Treasury Secretary for eighteen months at the end of the Clinton Adminstration, was the bipartisan passage of the Gramm-Leach-Bliley Act. In 1998 testimony before a Senate committee, Summers said: "The parties to these kinds of contract are largely sophisticated financial institutions that would appear to be eminently capable of protecting themselves from fraud and counterparty insolvencies and most of which are already subject to basic safety and soundness regulation under existing banking and securities laws." Lawrence H. Summers, "Testimony before the Senate Committee on Agriculture, Nutrition, and Forestry on the CFTC Concept Release," July 30, 1998, https://www.treasury.gov/press-center/press-releases/Pages/rr2616.aspx. See also Michael Kirk, "Brooksley Born, The Warning," *Frontline*, PBS, October 20, 2009, https://www.pbs.org/wgbh/pages/frontline/warning/interviews/born.html; "Joint Statement by Treasury Secretary Robert E. Rubin, Federal Reserve Board Chairman Alan Greenspan and Securities and Exchange Commission Chairman Arthur Levitt," press release, US Department of the Treasury, May 7, 1998, https://www.treasury.gov/press-center/press-releases/Pages/rr2426.aspx; Raffaele Scalcione, *The Derivatives Revolution: A Trapped Innovation and a Blueprint for Regulatory Reform*, Frederick, MD: Kluwer Law International, 2011, 169.

37. Kenneth R. Harney, "Appraisers under Pressure to Inflate Values," *Washington Post*, February 3, 2007.

38. David Dayen, *Chain of Title: How Three Ordinary Americans Uncovered Wall Street's Great Foreclosure Fraud* (New York: New Press, 2016).

39. Tobias Adrian and Hyun Song Shin, "The Changing Nature of Financial Intermediation and the Financial Crisis of 2007–2009," *Annual Review of Economics* 2, no. 1 (2010): 603–618, 610, DOI: 10.1146/annurev.economics.102308.124420.

40. William Black, "How to Rob a Bank (From the Inside, That Is)," TEDxUMKC speech, September 2013, https://www.ted.com/talks/william_black_how_to_rob_a_bank_from_the_inside_that_is; William K. Black, interview by Bill Moyers, "Bill Moyers Journal," PBS, April 3, 2009, https://www.pbs.org/moyers/journal/04032009/watch.html; Ivy L. Zelman, Dennis McGill, Justin Speer, and Alan Ratner, "Mortgage Liquidity Du Jour: Underestimated No More," Equity Research, Credit Suisse Sector Review, March 12, 2007; Atif R. Mian and Amir Sufi, "Fraudulent Income Overstatement on Mortgage Applications During the Credit Expansion of 2002 to 2005," *Review of Financial Studies* 30, no. 6 (2017): 1831–1864, https://papers.ssrn.com/sol3/papers.cfm?abstract_id=2561366; Mian and Sufi, *House of Debt*, chap. 7; October Research Cooperation, "Executive Overview," National Appraisal Survey 2007," vol. 1, Appraisal Business Practices, December 2006, https://fcic-static.law.stanford.edu/cdn_media/fcic-docs/2007-00-00%20October%20Research%202007%20Nationa%20Appraisal%20Survey.pdf.

41. Thomas Philippon, "Has the Finance Industry Become Less Efficient? Or, Where Is Wal-Mart When We Need It?," *VoxEU.Org* (blog), December 2, 2011, http://voxeu.org/article/where-wal-mart-when-we-need-it; Author's calculations based on "Table 6.16D. Corporate Profits by Industry," National Income and Product Accounts, Bureau of Economic Analysis, Washington, DC, March 28, 2018, https://www.bea.gov; Shawn Donnan, "Financial Sector in Advanced Economies Is Too Big, Says IMF," *Financial Times*, May 12, 2015; See also Ratna Sahay et al., "Rethinking Financial Deepening: Stability and Growth in Emerging Markets," IMF Staff Discussion Note SDN/15/08, International Monetary Fund, May 2015, http://elibrary.imf.org/view/IMF006/22501-9781498312615/22501-9781498312615/22501-9781498312615.xml.

42. Noah Smith, "Too Many of America's Smartest Waste Their Talents," *Bloomberg*, June 19, 2018; Thomas Philippon and Ariell Reshef, "Wages and Human Capital in the US Finance Industry: 1909–2006," *Quarterly Journal of Economics* 127, no. 4 (2012): 1551–1609, DOI: 10.1093/qje/qjs030.

43. Atif Mian, Amir Sufi, and Francesco Trebbi, "The Political Economy of the US Mortgage Default Crisis," *American Economic Review* 100, no. 5 (2010): 1967–1988, 1990–1991, DOI: 10.1257/aer.100.5.1967.

44. Simon Johnson and James Kwak, *13 Bankers: The Wall Street Takeover and the Next Financial Meltdown* (New York: Pantheon, 2010).

45. Atif Mian and Amir Sufi, "Secular Stagnation and Wealth Inequality," *Economist's View* (blog), March 23, 2014, https://economistsview.typepad.com/economistsview/2014/03/secular-stagnation-and-wealth-inequality.html.

46. The toxic effects of too much debt on macroeconomic outcomes can be seen time and time again. This pattern is familiar to anyone paying attention to the state of the European economy in the twenty-first century. The introduction of the euro in 1999 increased credit flows to countries such as Greece and Spain, acting in a similar way to the increase in credit from deregulation in the United States in that earlier period. The result, at least in Spain, was a large boost to household debt and the construction industry, followed by a housing bust, recession, and a grindingly slow economic recovery. Ireland found itself in a similar situation. Its banks were deeply involved in the intricate web of highly volatile and risky mortgage-backed assets and derivatives that fueled the bubble in the United States. Facing a banking crisis, the Irish state stepped in, as did the European Union and the International Monetary Fund, and both guaranteed the losses of the banks and bought their toxic assets. This fueled a massive increase in their public debt, with debt-to-gross domestic product climbing over thirty percentage points, to 120 percent, from 2010 to 2012. "Ireland: 2017 Article IV Consultation," press release and IMF Country Report No. 17/171. International Monetary Fund, Washington, DC, June 2017, http://elibrary.imf.org/view/IMF002/24385-9781484305539/24385-9781484305539/24385-9781484305539.xml; "Irish PM Confirms EU Rescue Deal," *BBC News*, November 22, 2010, http://www.bbc.com/news/business-11807730; "Report of the Joint Committee of Inquiry into the Banking Crisis," Houses of the Oireachtas, Dublin, January 2016, https://inquiries.oireachtas.ie/banking/wp-content/uploads/2016/01/02106-HOI-BE-Report-Volume1.pdf.

47. "About TARP," US Department of the Treasury, November 15, 2016, https://www.treasury.gov/initiatives/financial-stability/about-tarp/Pages/default.aspx. The Home Affordable Modification Program, which was started in 2009, placed an inefficient emphasis on reducing borrowers' total mortgage debt, instead of focusing on lowering monthly payments and boosting the cash they had to meet everyday needs. Peter Ganong and Pascal Noel, "Liquidity vs. Wealth in Household Debt Obligations: Evidence from Housing Policy in the Great Recession," NBER Working Paper No. 24694, National Bureau of Economic Research, Cambridge, MA, August 2018, https://www.nber.org/papers/w24964.

48. Boushey, "In Conversation: Atif Mian."

49. Baird Webel, "The Dodd-Frank Wall Street Reform and Consumer Protection Act: Background and Summary," Congressional Research Service, April 2017, https://fas.org/sgp/crs/misc/R41350.pdf.

50. Alan Rappeport, "Bill to Erase Some Dodd-Frank Banking Rules Passes in House," *New York Times*, December 22, 2017; Diana Olick, "Subprime Mortgages Morph into 'Non-Prime' Loans—and Demand Soars," CNBC, April 12, 2018, https://www.cnbc.com/2018/04/12/subprime-mortgages-morph-into-non-prime-loans-and-demand-soars.html; "Quarterly Report on Household Debt and Credit 2018:Q1," Federal Reserve Bank of New York, May 2018, https://www.newyorkfed.org/medialibrary/interactives/householdcredit/data/pdf/HHDC_2018Q1.pdf.

51. In 2018, the national conversation turned to considering the idea of a Green New Deal as laid out in House Resolution 109, "Recognizing the duty of the Federal Govern-

ment to create a Green New Deal," 116th Congress, https://www.congress.gov/bill/116th
-congress/house-resolution/109/text. See also Josh Bivens and Hunter Blair, "A Public
Investment Agenda That Delivers the Goods for American Workers Needs to Be Long-
Lived, Broad, and Subject to Democratic Oversight," Report 117041, Economic Policy
Institute, Washington, DC, December 8, 2016, https://www.epi.org/publication/a-public
-investment-agenda-that-delivers-the-goods-for-american-workers-needs-to-be-long-lived
-broad-and-subject-to-democratic-oversight/; Roger Altman, Aaron Klein, and Alan Krueger,
"Financing US Transportation Infrastructure in the 21st Century," Hamilton Project,
Brookings Institution, Washington, DC, May 2015, http://www.hamiltonproject.org/papers
/financing_us_transportation_infrastructure; "The Ways and Means to Unlock Private
Finance for Green Growth," Green Investment Report, World Economic Forum, Geneva,
2013, http://wef.ch/GJqoAC; Institute for Health Metrics and Evaluation, "Unprecedented
Study Finds US Ranks 27th among Nations Investing in Education, Health Care," *Eu-
rekAlert!,* AAAS, September 24, 2018, https://www.eurekalert.org/pub_releases/2018-09
/ifhm-usf092018.php.
        52. "Declining Natural Rate of Interest," paper session, Heather Boushey, Chair,
American Economic Association Annual Meeting, Philadelphia, January 7, 2018.

## Conclusion

        1. Joseph Fishkin and William E. Forbath, "Wealth, Commonwealth, and the Constitu-
tion of Opportunity," in *Wealth,* ed. Jack Knight and Melissa Schwartzberg (New York:
NYU Press, 2017).
        2. Bureau of Economic Analysis, US Department of Commerce, "Table 1.1.5. Gross
Domestic Product," National Income and Product Accounts, https://www.bea.gov/iTable
/iTable.cfm?reqid=19&step=2#reqid=19&step=3&isuri=1&1921=survey&1903=2.
        3. According to the Bureau of Economic Analysis, the "US national income and product
statistics were first presented as part of a complete and consistent accounting system in the
July 1947 supplement to the Survey of Current Business." *National Income and Product
Accounts of the United States, 1929–97,* 2 vols. (Washington DC: US Department of
Commerce, Bureau of Economic Analysis, 2001), https://fraser.stlouisfed.org/title/181/item
/5416; Genevieve Podleski, "Dismal Facts: Measuring the Economy Before GDP," Federal
Reserve Bank of St. Louis, *Inside FRASER* (blog), October 3, 2017, https://insidefraser
.stlouisfed.org/2017/10/measuring-the-economy-before-gdp/; Simon Kuznets, "National
Income, 1929–1932," Letter from the Acting Secretary of Commerce transmitting in
response to Senate Resolution No. 220, 1934, https://fraser.stlouisfed.org/title/971; Diane
Coyle, *GDP: A Brief but Affectionate History* (Princeton: Princeton University Press, 2014),
16, https://press.princeton.edu/titles/10183.html.
        4. As British economist Geoff Tily writes, in early years, "the value of GDP . . . was of
only slight interest." Geoff Tily, "The National Accounts, GDP and the 'Growthmen,'"
review of Coyle, *GDP,* Policy Research in Macroeconomics (Prime), London, January 2015,
https://static1.squarespace.com/static/541ff5f5e4b02b7c37f31ed6/t
/54b3afeae4b0d2480d43d760/1421062122575/CoyleReview_Tily.pdf, 10. See also
Matthias Schmelzer, *The Hegemony of Growth: The OECD and the Making of the
Economic Growth Paradigm* (Cambridge: Cambridge University Press, 2017).
        5. Jason Furman, "Should Policymakers Care Whether Inequality Is Helpful or Harmful
For Growth?" (draft of presentation for Rethinking Macroeconomic Policy Conference,
Washington, DC, October 2017, https://piie.com/system/files/documents
/furman20171012paper.pdf.

A variety of measures that are alternatives to GDP are briefly summarized in Catherine Rampell, "Alternatives to the G.D.P.," *Economix Blog* (blog), October 30, 2008, https://economix.blogs.nytimes.com/2008/10/30/alternatives-to-the-gdp/.

6. National Income is GDP with depreciation taken out and income from abroad added in. Income from abroad captures income from investments Americans have in foreign countries. Depreciation is excluded because it is not income in any traditional sense and would inflate the income of capital owners unrealistically.

One of the more challenging aspects is that traditional sources of measures of inequality, such as the Current Population Survey (conducted by the US Census Bureau and the US Department of Labor's Bureau of Labor Statistics) or the Survey of Consumer Finances (conducted by the Federal Reserve Board), and even administrative tax records maintained by the IRS, don't add up to the National Accounts data. This makes the project that Zucman and his coauthors developed so important: we are learning more and more about where income is generated and where it goes. See Thomas Piketty, Emmanuel Saez, and Gabriel Zucman, "Distributional National Accounts: Methods and Estimates for the United States," *Quarterly Journal of Economics* 133, no. 2 (2018): 553–609, DOI: 10.1093/qje/qjx043.

7. Heather Boushey, "In Conversation: Gabriel Zucman," April 3, 2018, https://equitablegrowth.org/in-conversation-with-gabriel-zucman/.

8. Boushey, "In Conversation: Gabriel Zucman."

9. As Kuznets put it: "For some of the constituent parts of the total . . . the available data are abundant and reliable; for others both direct and indirect information is quite scanty and the resulting estimate is subject to a wide margin of error. . . . The national income total is thus an amalgam of accurate and approximate estimates rather than a unique, highly precise measurement." Kuznets, *National Income, 1929–1932*.

10. A high-profile attempt to address this came when French president Nicolas Sarkozy commissioned economists Joseph Stiglitz, Amartya Sen, and Jean-Paul Fitoussi to suggest how GDP could be rethought to more accurately measure economic and social progress. The commission's 2009 report contains a long list of suggested improvements that address inequality as well as thoughts on how environmental quality and life satisfaction could be better accounted for in national economic statistics. Using GDP as the main metric of success, it claims, distorts policymaking by focusing policymakers' attention on a metric that neglects the costs of environmental degradation and doesn't tell us anything specifically about human well-being. Joseph Stiglitz, Amartya Sen, and Jean-Paul Fitoussi, "Report by the Commission on the Measurement of Economic Performance and Social Progress," September 2009, https://ec.europa.eu/eurostat/documents/118025/118123/Fitoussi+Commission+report; Matthew Fright, "The King Was in His Counting House Counting All His Money," Goldsmiths University of London, Institute of Management Seminar, November 15, 2017.

11. Adam Smith, *The Essential Adam Smith*, ed. Robert L. Heilbroner, with the assistance of Laurence J. Malone (New York: W. W. Norton, 1987), 258.

12. Quoted in Janet Nguyen and David Brancaccio, "For Many Millennials, Socialism Isn't the 'Dirty Word' It Once Was," *Marketplace*, Minnesota Public Radio, May 17, 2018, http://www.marketplace.org/2018/05/17/economy/millennials-socialism-isnt-dirty-word-it-was-other-generations.

13. Darren Walker, "What's Next for the Ford Foundation?," Ford Foundation blog, June 11, 2015, https://www.fordfoundation.org/ideas/equals-change-blog/posts/whats-next-for-the-ford-foundation; Larry Kramer, "Beyond Neoliberalism: Rethinking Political Economy," Hewlett Foundation blog, April 26, 2018, https://hewlett.org/library/beyond-neoliberalism-rethinking-political-economy/.

14. Andrea Grisold and Hendrik Theine, "How Come We Know? The Media Coverage of Economic Inequality," *International Journal of Communication* 11 (2017): 4265–4284, http://ijoc.org/index.php/ijoc/article/view/6669.

15. The first group includes businesses, financial institutions, and organizations representing business interests, such as job-listing platforms and research consultancy firms. The second group consists of policymakers, academic economists, and workers; Amanda Bayer and Cecilia Elena Rouse, "Diversity in the Economics Profession: A New Attack on an Old Problem," *Journal of Economic Perspectives* 30, no. 4 (2016): 221–242, DOI: 10.1257/jep.30.4.221.

16. Suresh Naidu, Dani Rodrik, and Gabriel Zucman, "Economics After Neoliberalism," *Boston Review*, February 27, 2019, https://bostonreview.net/forum/suresh-naidu-dani-rodrik-gabriel-zucman-economics-after-neoliberalism.

# Acknowledgments

When I began my studies in economics at the Graduate Faculty at New School for Social Research, I was looking for a deeper understanding of how the economy worked and what policymakers could do to improve the lives of working families like mine. The New School has a long history of exploring the intersection between social and political institutions and underlying economic dynamics. The ideas laid out in this book are deeply influenced by my time there and the perspectives of the scholars I studied with, especially David M. Gordon's research on social structures of accumulation and Anwar Shaikh's work on the theory of competition. I continue to be inspired by New School scholars who continue in that tradition, bringing to the fore important, real-world questions with rigorous analysis of how the economy works.

In the spring of 2013, John Podesta gave me the opportunity to put economic ideas into action when he came to my office and asked, "Hey, do you want to go start up a new think tank?" I gladly said yes and we got to work. It's been a privilege to lead the Washington Center for Equitable Growth for the past six years and a source of joy to have a job where I get to spend every day focused on elevating new and important ideas and policies that are grounded in evidence.

This book was possible because of the incredibly talented and dedicated people who have joined our project at Equitable Growth. I will start by thanking our steering committee members. They have guided our work and shaped our understanding of the latest economic evidence. Those who helped us launch were Melody Barnes, Alan Blinder, Raj Chetty, Emmanuel Saez, Bob

Solow, and Laura Tyson. They were joined later by Janet Currie, Karen Dynan, Jason Furman, and Janet Yellen. I cannot thank them enough; a number of them—Raj, Emmanuel, Janet C., and Karen—agreed to be interviewed for this book. Alongside them, our board—Steve Daetz, Byron Auguste, and Ira Fishman, who also provided comments on the whole manuscript—have supported me and the development of our organization every step of the way. Of course, I also thank our blogger Brad DeLong, who's been a treat to work with and always interesting to read, and who helped me think through these ideas early on.

I'm also very grateful for the time with the many other economists whose work is held up in the preceding pages, including Leemore Dafny, Hilary Hoynes, Atif Mian, Diane Whitmore Schanzenbach, and Gabriel Zucman. They all gave generously of their time to talk to me about their research. A special thanks goes to Alan Krueger; he was a mentor to me and to our team and he's left a great hole in our hearts.

At Equitable Growth, I am fortunate to work with a wonderful group of people, each of whom contributed to my thinking about how the economy works, even though some have now moved on to other places. Our first employee was Sarah Miller, who is now helping lead another new think tank, Open Markets. She, along with the estimable Eryn Sepp, set up Equitable Growth and led the march to the launch. Nick Bunker worked with me at the Center for American Progress and when he heard about this project, he immediately asked to be hired. He joined the team in the summer of 2013 and swiftly became an integral part of our organization. He was soon joined by Kate Crawford, who set up our grants program for our first year. By the time we launched on November 16, 2014, we already had a terrific team—also consisting of Carter Price, Pedro Spivakovsky-Gonzalez, and Bridget Ansel. Olenka Mitukiewicz was my research assistant at the Center for American Progress and gamely joined our venture.

These veterans of our launch were soon joined by many others, among them Elisabeth Jacobs, Marshall Steinbaum, Robert Lynch, Ben Zipperer, Enjoli Timmons, Korin Davis, Kavya Vaghul, Jessica Fulton, John Schmitt, Kate Wagenblass, Sherice Nelson, David Johnson, Katie Banks, Carmen Ye, Rose Batt, Nisha Chikhale, Dionna Cheatham, Gabe Matthews, Daniel Estes, Daria Stepanova, Aidan Orsino, Nicole Townsend, Barry Toiv, Diane Wren, Dinetta Parrott, Delaney Crampton, Raksha Kopparam, Will McGrew, Corey Husak, Farmata Fall, Maria Monroe, Alix Gould-Werth, Tyjen Conley, and Bonnie Kavoussi. Over the past five years, in ways large and small, they all helped enliven and communicate the importance of academic research in the policy-making process.

Throughout the writing of this book, I relied heavily on a number of individual Equitable Growth staff for good ideas, invaluable feedback, and moral support. A number of them commented on the manuscript; I'm grateful for feedback from Greg Leiserson, Nick Bunker, Austin Clemens, Kate Bahn, Bridget Ansel, Liz Hipple, and Michael Kades. Ed Paisley helps me become a better writer with unfailing good cheer and swift editorial guidance. Dave Evans offered his artistic eye and skills on the graphics and especially the great illustrations. Casey Schoeneberger and Alyssa Fisher help me figure out how to talk about these ideas. Erica Handloff, Christian Edlagan, Corey Husak, and David Mitchell are all helping to make sure the book reaches its audience.

Throughout this process, I have been aided by two fantastic research assistants, Matt Markezich and Somin Park. They, more than anyone, know how much I relied on their hard work. I hope they also know how much I appreciate their help. From finding the right fact or graphic to making sure that we always speak from the evidence, they have helped me put this book together, and have markedly improved it.

A long list of people gave feedback on the manuscript and helped me think through these ideas. In particular, Kim Clausing and Suresh Naidu did me the service of reading the whole book and provided valuable insights and comments. I thank Christian Weller, Mike Pyle, Michael Linden, and Sam Bell for their help as I worked through the ideas.

It's been—as always—a delight to be able to work with Ian Malcolm and the team at Harvard University Press. This is the third book I've had the opportunity to work on with them, and each one has been more fun than the one before. In particular, I thank Julia Kirby, Olivia Woods, Keith Kuhn, and Rebekah White at the Press for applying their skills in editing, project management, design, and publicity.

Of course, any and all errors remaining in the text are entirely my own.

■ ■ ■

The most important thank you goes to Todd Tucker. He put up with me (and the absence of me) as we sought to find hope during the year of 2017 and I decided to take on the challenge of writing this book. His feedback on the ideas, our long conversations, the walks with our pup, Tanya, and many wonderful dinners all made it possible. His support allowed me to find the time and energy to do this work and for that—and everything else—I'm deeply grateful.

# Index